S0-BRM-378

Poem,
Revised

Poem,
Revised

54 Poems,
Revisions,
Discussions

Edited by Robert Hartwell Fiske
and Laura Cherry

Marion Street Press, Inc.
www.marionstreetpress.com
Oak Park, Illinois

To all who write and revise poems

Cover illustration by Judy Benson

Copyright © 2008 by Marion Street Press, Inc.
Copyrights of individual poems belong to the poets.

All Rights Reserved

ISBN 1-933338-25-3
ISBN 13: 978-1-933338-25-5

Printed in U.S.A.
Printing 10 9 8 7 6 5 4 3 2 1

Marion Street Press, Inc.
PO Box 2249
Oak Park, IL 60303
708-488-8820
www.marionstreetpress.com

4

About the Editors

Robert Hartwell Fiske is the author of *The Dictionary of Concise Writing*, *The Dimwit's Dictionary*, and *The Dictionary of Disagreeable English Deluxe Edition*. He is the editor of *Vocabula Bound 1: Outbursts, Insights, Explanations, and Oddities*, and *Vocabula Bound 2: Our Wresting, Writhing Tongue*. He is also the editor and publisher of *The Vocabula Review*, a monthly online journal about the English language.

Laura Cherry's chapbook, *What We Planted*, was awarded the 2002 Philbrick Poetry Award by the Providence Athenaeum. Her work has been published in journals, including *Asphodel*, *Argestes*, *Forklift: Ohio*, *Agenda*, and *The Vocabula Review*. It has also appeared in the anthologies *Present Tense: Writing and Art by Young Women* (Calyx Press), *Vocabula Bound 1* (Vocabula Books), and *Letters to the World* (Red Hen Press).

Contents

12. Susan Rich: Reclamation

20. Kathrine Varnes: The Apprentice Siren

30. Jehanne Dubrow: Souvenir

35. Francis Blessington: The Winter Moths

41. Shoshauna Shy: Jeans, Size Zero

46. Mark Vinz: The Penitent

51. Annie Finch: Revelry

59. Leslie Shinn: Three

65. Anne Harding Woodworth: Quiet Air

69. Lyn Lifshin: Rose Devorah

76. Susanna Rich: The Buck

85. Juleigh Howard-Hobson: Memorial Day Storm

90. Elizabeth Farrell: Birthday Tulips

94. Tracy Koretsky: *La Poir Hautaine*

98. Rhoda Greenstone: A Letter from L.A.

107. Diane Halsted: Singing On

111. Janis Butler Holm: A Magazine of Bare, Naked Ladies

126. Brian Gilmore: o. j. simpson in the ford bronco on the los angeles freeway (on NBC Television, June 17, 1994)

134. Derek Sheffield: Ornithology 101

140. Peter Schmitt: Sleeping Through the Fire

147. Phil Hey: Apology to a neighbor who lost his place

152. Ernie Wormwood: Shampoo

156. Janet McCann: Life List

159. Jay Rubin: Exodus

167. David Radavich: Writing Eye

173. Winifred Hughes: Depth of Field

181. Jannett Highfill: Last In

187. Ken Cockburn: On the fly-leaf of Goethe's *Venetian Epigrams*

192. Beverley Bie Brahic: Summer Dresses

195. Ellen Peckham: Confessional Self-Portrait: Liar

200. Ernest Hilbert: Magnificent Frigatebird

210. Roy Jacobstein: HIV Needs Assessment

215. Patty Seyburn: Anatomy of Disorder

221. Scott Wiggerman: Ants

225. Martin Walls: A God not of *forces*, but *things*

231. Deena Linett: Above the River

243. Jeanne M. Lesinski: Through the Plots

246. Gary J. Whitehead: Monument

254. Kathleen Kirk: Middletown

264. Catherine Wiley: Skating on Lake Monona

271. Phebus Etienne: Meditation on My Name

279. Nate Pritts: Brown Tree, Yellow Bird

283. Rasma Haidri: Lottery

298. Kathleen Flenniken: A Bedroom Community

303. Judith Strasser: On Reading *Descartes' Error*

309. Sarah Pemberton Strong: Given

314. Robin E. Sampson: Lacuna

318. Mary-Sherman Willis: Habit

323. Lucy Anderton: Leaving Eden

329. Holly Clark: My Mother Keeps Dying in the Bed by My Cradle

337. Judith H. Montgomery: Shiver-Man

351. Jenifer Browne Lawrence: It Was Snowing and It Was Going to Snow

357. Laura Cherry: Jack in Love

361. Brian Taylor: In the First Place

INTRODUCTION

When we were assembling the manuscript for this anthology, we looked for essays with depth and enlivening detail; essays with quirky or upright character, well-defined points of view, and occasional humor; and essays that viscerally brought the reader into the act of writing a poem, turning the process inside out. Most of all, we sought essays from which we could learn something, enjoying ourselves along the way. We're delighted with the result: fifty-four pieces that together show a representative range of poetic styles, tones, and "schools," from experienced poets who can express concretely how they go about capturing the ethereal. Accompanying these excellent prose pieces are fifty-four poems that stand – whether comfortably or impressively or starkly – on their own, many of which have appeared previously in journals, poetry collections, and other anthologies.

Though the poems' subject matter was not a criterion for selection, it has been instructive for us to see their sources, reflecting the concerns of the moment or of the age. Erotic poems and elegies are mainstays. Birds are a surprisingly popular theme, offering their fresh and flighty symbolism. Inspiration may come through art or through news articles; the weightiest subjects may be given the lightest touch. Brian Gilmore's poem, "o.j. simpson in the ford bronco on the los angeles freeway" is a provocative and challenging piece on racial stereotyping and the media circus. Jehanne Dubrow illuminates Polish anti-Semitism through the figures of souvenirs sold to tourists. There are lyrical meditations on names (Lyn Lifshin and Phebus Etienne), on the politics of torture (David Radavich), and on the international health crisis (Roy Jacobstein). Some poems came with complementary graphics: Jannett Highfill's ingenious table demonstrating the impact of repositioning lines; in several cases, a scanned-in draft from a journal or even a napkin, capturing an early, significant scrawl; perhaps most strikingly, Ernest Hilbert's visual source of inspiration, Audubon's "Magnificent Frigatebird."

Poetry isn't written in a vacuum. Many of the poets here indicate that an important step in their revision process is consulting with readers, who may be workshop peers, sweethearts, or respected mentors. These poets are also guided by the prose of other poets. Most often, they reference Richard Hugo's wonderful book on craft, *The Triggering Town*, though other insights derive from Jim Harrison, Donald Hall, Joan Didion, J.D. Mc-Clatchy, Wallace Stevens, Gertrude Stein, Sharon Olds, Philip Levine, Elizabeth Bishop, William Stafford, Valéry, Baudelaire, Robert Creeley, Goethe, Ezra Pound, W.B. Yeats, William Carlos Williams, William Wordsworth, and Juan Ramon Jimenez. Clearly, this is a well-read crew.

The essays and especially the drafts in *Poem, Revised* demonstrate the potential for transforming what might seem the most unpromising beginning – sometimes just through tightening and tweaking, sometimes through wholesale rewriting. Now and then you can *feel* the rightness of the changes as they evolve, literally evoking a satisfied "ahhh." Occasionally, you might even disagree with a poet's choices for revision, making it clear that a poem isn't truly a puzzle, with a single way of fitting the picture-postcard pieces together; it's a series of intuitive decisions without a fixed stopping point. As Jay Rubin says, paraphrasing Valéry's bon mot, "Eventually… a poem is simply abandoned, released to the world – warts and all."

In bringing to life the compelling but quiet drama of revision, these poets describe the large and small lessons they've learned (sometimes half-consciously), frequently in contradiction with each other:

"I always write the first draft longhand and uncritically." (Francis Blessington)

"Even before a poem is committed handwritten to a page, a good deal of it will probably have been composed in my head – as many lines as possible until some threaten to spill from memory. So by the time the first words touch my lined yellow pad, they've typically been revised already a few times, though I wouldn't say polished." (Peter Schmitt)

"I started by annotating it, as if it weren't my poem at all, writing notes in the margins to clarify what I thought 'the poet' meant, or wanted to mean." (Kathrine Varnes)

"Composing a poem is a premeditated activity for me, an intense, disciplined process that is only briefly caressed by romantic inspiration. In plain words, crafting a poem is hard work." (Rhoda Greenstone)

"I like to take my poems for walks…. An old man smiles at me and I realize the ending that's eluded me is in the color of his worn sports coat." (Susan Rich)

"I'm on automatic pilot, trying to get all the way to the end of my thought before the inner censor kicks in." (Beverly Bie Brahic)

"I make changes as I sit there working through my thoughts whether on the bus, at work, in meetings, at home, anywhere really." (Brian Gilmore)

"After I baked my first draft, I let it sit on the windowsill to cool a while." (Ernest Hilbert)

For most poems, the path from initial idea to finished version requires lengthy and attentive detail work; along with providing a context for this work, these essays examine the work itself. Every smallest word, every last article, can be crucial to a poem's intention; Diane Halsted notes, "Removing the word *the* from a poem is one of the first things I do when I start revising." Finding her way into a poem, Leslie Shinn creates "a useful, springboard-like conglomeration" of words that may not be included in the final version, but allow her to take the next step. Phil Hey posits a series of rules to keep poems on track, beginning with "Rule 1: Finish what you start."

For a poet or student of poetry, there are certainly techniques to be learned here, tricks to try, mechanics to tinker with. You might take on Lyn Lifshin's name exercise. Or, after reading Phil Hey's piece, build a villanelle brick by brick, with a long pause after each to set the mortar. If a draft seems floppy, you might follow the examples of Scott Wiggerman and Ernest Hilbert and revise from free verse into form. Or you might let the essays work a deeper magic, sparking connections to follow up without examining them too closely, at least at first. Tweak your revision process gently or overhaul it radically. Be patient and tireless, hungry and hopeful. In Rasma Haidri's words, "Perhaps *everything is still possible*."

Laura Cherry and Robert Hartwell Fiske
January 2007

RECLAMATION

SUSAN RICH

"Art and virtue are measured in tiny grains. Only when revisions are precise may the building stand square and plumb," wrote the Chinese poet, Lu Chi, seventeen hundred years ago. Some things never change, it seems. Revision is still at the heart of poetic practice. At least for this poet. I tell my students if it weren't for learning the fine art of revision, I would never have become a published poet. I suspect this is true for most writers. But does what one writer learns about revision have any bearing on what works for another?

Recently, at a conference in Vancouver, a woman approached me. She explained that she'd attended a workshop that I gave on revision three years ago in Los Angeles and that she still kept the handouts and notes from the class to refer to when she's writing. It struck me as odd that showing her and the other participants the messy, muddled, often embarrassing worksheets for my own poetry could be useful in their own poetic practice. However, here was a former student telling me it was so. This chance meeting in Vancouver convinced me that there's something useful to be gleaned by looking deeply into another writer's practice, even if it is only the pleasure of literary voyeurism.

First some confessions. I am a slow writer. It is not unusual for a poem to take me at least a year to get right. Many pieces lie in old computer files for a decade until I figure out what to do with them. And when I am working on a poem, my methods can be unconventional. For example, I like to take my poems for walks. Perhaps I'll spend the morning working on a piece and after a few hours get to the point where I've changed the word *remodel* back to *reclamation* four or five times. That's when I know it's time for a change of scene. I grab my clipboard, the poem, a pen, and throw on a warm jacket.

As I walk, something relaxes in my body, the rhythm of putting one foot in front of the other in quick succession gives me something other than words to focus on. I'm freed from the judging eye of my computer screen; the day seems full of possibilities. I feel foolishly happy. I am a writer in the world. I think of myself as following the fine tradition of Wallace Stevens, who, it was rumored, wrote all of his poems in his head as he walked an

Reclaimation

~~Remodel~~

Marks I'd put on a student's paper of a colleague

6-8 syllable line

I've never had it before —
a place to rip up the floorboards.
chip away at cabinets, disappear
an interior wall all the way
to where it meets the basement
stairwell. How naked this seems —

exposed beams and dark cool air
yielding old baseboards. the irresistible allure
of behind-the-scenes

molding carpet, years
of silence and hurt. Tomorrow
the carpenter will come with ~~pinhnin~~
and ~~unfinished~~ fir; he'll create a frame,
~~inlay~~ a bookcase into this waiting space,
this theater that's been masked

and unmasked through ~~fifty~~ some years
of inhabitants. This space

that's ~~ever changing~~ the
ever moving forward to its next
demolition of desire.
and

exhume
excavate
reclaimation
cloistered

molding carpet
and mice
leavings.

Scavenged

3

more food poem
— Stanbery

hour each morning to his office where he sold insurance.

So where does the revision come in? As I roam my neighborhood, clipboard in hand, I glance down at the black squiggles on the page. I read them aloud to the seagulls and pretend I'm learning lines for a play. I'm an actress or maybe a singer. And here's the secret: I lull myself into believing that the poem on the clipboard was written by someone else. Now I can see those same words I struggled with for hours with fresh, playful eyes. I can see more clearly what is working and what needs to disappear. The image I've been looking for might appear as I see cyclists, dogs, and silver scooters flying by. An old man smiles at me and I realize the ending that's eluded me is in the color of his worn sports coat.

In any case, the trick is to figure out how you can work on your poem until it, figuratively speaking, sings. The French poet, Paul Valéry, claimed poems are never finished, only abandoned, but I don't think that's true. A poem is born, moves into adolescence, and eventually reaches the prime of its life. The skill of the writer is to recognize that stage of life and to let the poem be before it transitions into the twilight of old age.

Perhaps the best way to illustrate this is to show you a poem of mine from inception to publication. This poem, now called "Reclamation," began as an exercise that I gave my students during a one-night workshop at Highline Community College in Des Moines, Washington, as part of the Jumpstart Series. The prompt was simple: write about a place, past or present, you consider your home. We closed our eyes and imagined that mysterious place where we felt most comfortable in the world. I told them to remember a best friend's kitchen or the cottage they visited one August years ago, whatever came to mind. However, when I closed my eyes, all I could see was the dark hole that the carpenter had just created in my living room. This was my first year living in the first house that was all mine. At the time of the workshop, I was immersed in a remodeling job: one ugly pair of cabinets taken out and replaced by a small built-in bookcase.

I wrote the lines of "Poetic Remodeling" down in ten minutes. Here it is typed so you can read it:

Draft 1

Poetic Remodeling

I've never had it before —

a place to rip up floorboards
and cabinets, strip down
the interior wall all the way down
to the downstairs stairwell.
How naked it seems — exposed beams
and dark cool air escaping
years of being hidden and hurt.

Tomorrow the carpenter comes back
with walnut and fir, he'll create a frame inlay
the five tiered bookcase into this empty space,
this theater that's been masked and unmasked,
this space that's ever changing — ever moving
forward to its next demolition and desire.

What struck me at the time and made me star this "start" as something to come back to was that I liked both the opening and closing lines. I had my poetry bookends even if the hardbound volumes themselves had yet to appear. The first line "I've never had it before a place to rip up floorboards," seemed emblematic to me of more than just installing a new bookcase. And the last line, "This space that's ever-changing, ever-moving forward to its next demolition and desire," also hinted at something about home and place that I had yet to figure out. The fact that my own poem seemed mysterious to me seemed an excellent starting point.

By Draft 3, "Remodel" had found its form and I had my line length of seven to eight syllables, further refined into couplets. There is a note to myself on the worksheet to "figure out what I'm doing." About halfway down the page a line about years "of silence and hurt" hiding in that empty space is circled. I recognize it as a place-marker for some emotional state. The language is abstract, weak, but what hides behind it is important to discover. As always, my mind wanders while I write, and there is another note to myself, "more food poems? Strawberry?" at the bottom of the page.

Finally, by Draft 9, the poem, "Reclamation," is beginning to emerge. *What is it we're seeking?* is the hinge that opens the poem for me. I've allowed myself the freedom within the poem to figure out what it is I'm writing about, to enlarge the poem from something about a specific construction project (green carpet, mouse leavings) and to risk sentimentality with a move into "gardening, fires, flood — / aren't we put on this

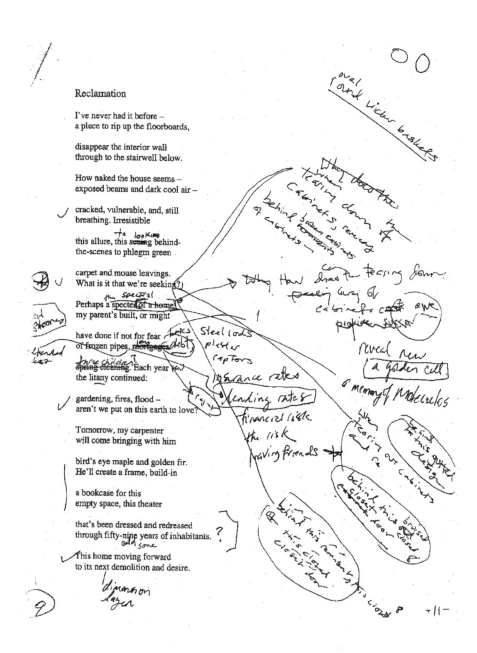

Reclamation

I've never had it before –
a place to rip up the floorboards,

disappear the interior wall
through to the stairwell below.

How naked the house seems –
exposed beams and dark cool air –

cracked, vulnerable, and, still
breathing. Irresistible

this allure, this seeing behind-
the-scenes to phlegm green

carpet and mouse leavings.
What is it that we're seeking?

Perhaps a specter of a home
my parent's built, or might

have done if not for fear
of frozen pipes, mortgages,

spring cleaning. Each year
the litany continued:

gardening, fires, flood –
aren't we put on this earth to love?

Tomorrow, my carpenter
will come bringing with him

bird's eye maple and golden fir.
He'll create a frame, build-in

a bookcase for this
empty space, this theater

that's been dressed and redressed
through fifty-nine years of inhabitants.

This home moving forward
to its next demolition and desire.

16

earth to love?" What compels me toward, or holds me back from, creating this illusive place we crave? Home. It seems natural at this point to return to childhood and the home my parents had or didn't have, how their fears kept them from buying the house they dreamed of.

It's Draft 9 that teaches me the most. The worksheet shows my notes about syllable count, word choice (a memory vault or a memory in molecules? fear of frozen pipes or financial risk?), and everything except the middle of the poem is pretty much fixed. I can look back on this paper and see that the form and the content are emerging together. As Robert Creeley said in an interview a year before his recent death, "Content is never more than an extension of form and form is never more than an extension of content. They sort of go together is the absolute point. It's really hard to think of one without the other; in fact, I don't think it's possible."

By the time "Reclamation" is finished, Draft 36, the poem seems complete. How can I tell? Because I sense an effortlessness to its movement, because the couplets on the page look good together, because I can read the poem aloud from start to finish without hesitation or correction. One of the reasons I choose to write in couplets is that they keep me honest. The weak lines have nowhere to hide. All that white space around the words calls attention to every consonant and vowel on the page.

Draft 36

Reclamation

I've never had it before —
a place to rip up the floorboards,

disappear the interior wall
through to the stairwell below.

How naked the house seems —
exposed beams and dark cool air —

cracked, vulnerable, and, still
breathing. Irresistible

this allure, to look behind-the-scenes to phlegm green

carpet and mouse leavings.
What is it that I'm seeking

behind this ex-closet door?
A memory vault of what

my parents might have built
if not for fear of bursting

pipes, falling trees, their children?
Each year the litany began:

gardening, fires, flood —
aren't we put on this earth to love?

Tomorrow, my carpenter
will come bringing with him

bird's eye maple and golden fir.
He'll create a frame, build in

a bookcase for this empty space,
this theater that's been dressed

and redressed for some fifty years.
This home moving forward —

along with the inhabitants —
to its next demolition or desire.

When "Reclamation" found its home in the *Seattle Review*, the editor chose it for a themed issue on the nature of, what else, home. And even though the poem went through more than thirty drafts, it now looks to me like the poem that was meant to be. Begun in the deep of winter and completed seven months later in late August, the poem emerged as I studied every draft. I wanted to see what I could learn about revision by paying close attention to my process.

Here's what I wrote in my journal that summer:

> Know that everything you've written begins with one word haltingly followed by another ~ a profoundly pathetic lack of rhythm. Often, not even one image stays intact. And you call yourself a writer? ~ But let it live there awhile, even a couple of years, if that's what's needed, and the dusty fragment of an idea will take shape, the ineffable ring ~ What made you willing to scribble down the code with no way to decipher it, until something else comes along.

Perhaps that woman in Vancouver just wanted to know that no one gets it right the first time. Perhaps she needed permission to dust her house as she revised, as Marianne Moore used to do, or to work on a poem for sixteen years, as Elizabeth Bishop did with "The Moose." I could write another essay tomorrow on the revision process I followed for another poem, and it would certainly look very different from the process followed for "Reclamation." The point is this: revision is the difference between the adequate poem and the excellent one. It is the magic of a word positioned just right in a harmonious line of sound; it is the title changed and re-changed again. It is believing in your own poem.

Susan Rich is the author of two collections of poetry, *Cures Include Travel* and *The Cartographer's Tongue Poems of the World,* which won the PEN USA Award for Poetry and the Peace Corps Writers Award for Best Poetry Book. She has been the recipient of an Artist Trust Award and a Fulbright Fellowship. Her poems have appeared in the *Alaska Quarterly Review, Green Mountains Review, Poetry International,* and *Quarterly West.*

The Apprentice Siren

KATHRINE VARNES

Revising can feel pleasant, familiar like cleaning or chopping vegetables. *Well*, I might say to myself, *that's better! That's finished!* Sometimes, I know that's true; I revise with an ease born of clarity, when I know just what to fix to make the poem work. But I don't remember those revisions. No, the ones I recall are more torturous. Such as the time I spent four hours revising a poem, having wrenched myself into a tight little knot, every ligament straining at this word choice, that line break, the cascading rhythm of that penultimate line and then: *poof!* The power went out for no good reason (just a furious storm I failed to notice taking shape outside), and no, I never did hit that Save button. Yes, I remember the frustrating ones.

The poem that I came to call "The Apprentice Siren" took shape through many, many drafts and about ten years of intermittent attention. I made some radical cuts and changes over that time, but the kernel of the poem stayed. From the start, I wanted to work out the way a love relationship can dive into degeneration, which can get associated with certain objects, and, having recently read some Dante, I thought terza rima would be the right form for this descent into lover's hell. Besides, I'd not worked much with terza rima, and I wanted to see what a good chunk of it could do for me. Early on, too, a figure of a contemporary apprentice siren presented herself, someone who didn't fully understand her powers, someone lost. And I could identity with that state of things, too. In my mind, that way of thinking about the speaker in the poem became central, but it took several years to set her free. The first draft, which I showed no one (until now!), went like this:

Things Lost

Ten years ago I bought a microphone
to lift my voice into the smoky bars:
I kept the customers from going home

and eased their drinking. You couldn't say that stars
were in my eyes — not any more than usual —

but when I saw them stumbling to their cars,

my head was full of music, my ears dull
to their cat calls and slurred compliments,
my eyes on the equipment and getting it all

locked safely in the car. And if I leant
a mic stand up against my bumper, I
held my knee right there. I never bent

or broke or lost a stand or cord or mic
in those three years of moving music from place
to place, no matter how late in the night

or how near sleep my limbs. Then it was your face
that I played all my quiet music to,
and on that day I wrapped myself in lace,

my heart thought it would always sing for you.
I lost sight of the details, let lipstick stale
on the foam rubber windscreen, the silver blue

mic case gather dust, the electric tail
grow sticky from spilt beer. Our words grew vague.
It was then my voice began to trail

off, and you began to come home late.
I got good at making soups — since soup
would keep well on the stove. I'd read and wait

for you to finish writing up your scoop
at the paper. I'd make light pencil marks
in the margins and turn the silence into food.

Sometimes I'd eat in anger, and hear you park
the car from inside my dreams. I'd stay asleep
and barely hear you undressing in the dark;

as deft as any burglar, you would creep
under the covers, and a comfort in the sound
of familiar breath would let my dreams fall deep.

Some weekends we would sing together — loud
enough for neighbors to compliment the song —
but sometimes, the guitar and mics would crowd

into your car and go somewhere else for a long
time. Somehow it became yours. Equipment my
money bought before we met was gone.

(Now you say, over the phone, that you're *thinking*
but you can't say what happened to that mic —
and I know why, for two years, I stopped singing.)

I critiqued the piece myself a few days later as too rambling and too
blaming. No one wants to read that. It didn't have enough polish either, in
my view. The *stars* rhyme seemed gratuitous and forced. (It's a wonder I revised the thing at all. I've piles of drafts like this that never get a second
chance.) But I couldn't let it lie. First I just added another stanza.

My voice sank under a roaring quiet,
and I couldn't keep you home or ease your drinking:
I couldn't find a reason left to fight.

Then I revised the annoying start, pushing a little harder on the
metaphor of song:

Ten years ago I bought a microphone
to lift my voice into the smoky bars:
I kept the customers from going home

and eased their drinking. Their lungs took in tar,
their blood took up the song of alcohol;

I also added a middle stanza (that later got the ax for being off topic):

They lined up, showed their I.D.s, paid the cover:
Now I know some came each night to this place,
the band obligatory as the rubber

and as rarely used. Then it was your face

Well, that fixed the smaller problems (or some of it did), but not the larger ones. But I was at a loss at how to tackle them. I think it was at this point that I got some advice from a few fellow poets — Anne Colwell, James Keegan, and Devon Miller-Duggan helped out quite a bit. I was lucky to know W.D. Snodgrass and see him frequently in those days. My Delaware readers didn't let much past them; I wanted to see if they could direct me through the problems of the poem. They were generous, liking the poem in general. The sticky tail in particular drew admiring comments, and they could see what I was up against in terms of form. But they remained unconvinced by a few vague areas in the narrative and what really amounted to ramblings. Then I got serious, hacking the poem up and putting it back together again. I put brackets around areas that didn't seem clear or weren't driving the poem forward. The transitions in the narrative just took too much time — my readers were right — and I felt constrained with the length. I wanted a new structure, but I didn't want to let go of the rhymes either. This called for a new title, too. Perhaps that would focus the poem as well. I renamed the poem, going for something more specific (as I thought), suggesting in my mind that the relationship almost failed on technicalities rather than big issues. (This was, incidentally, wholly misguided, as later became apparent, but at least I got away from the lame passive of "Things Lost.") I also tried numbered sections:

Technicalities

1.
Ten years ago I bought a microphone
to lift my voice into the smoky bars:
I kept the customers from going home

and eased their drinking. Their lungs took in tar,
their blood took up the song of alcohol;
but when I saw them stumbling to their cars,

my head was full of music, my ears dull
to their cat calls and slurred compliments,
my hands on the equipment. I'd lock it all

safe in the car. An apprentice siren's sense
for melody, I had no notion of
the lure of rocks, the ocean's violence.

2.
One thing is, you had such a sober face
and we sang okay together, so I knew
on that day I wrapped myself in lace,

that all the parts fit right: I was safe with you.
I lost sight of the details, let lipstick stale
on the foam rubber windscreen, the silver blue

mic case gather dust, the electric tail
grow sticky from spilt beer. Incorporated,
I didn't worry when my voice began to trail

off, and you began to come home late.
Some weekends, we would mouth the lyrics to songs
we didn't know. Then our own words got vague.

3.
Some nights I'd eat alone, and hear you park
the car from inside my dreams. I'd stay asleep,
to keep my breathing quiet in the dark.

As deft as any burglar, you would creep
under the covers, and a comfort in the sound
of familiar breath would let my dreams fall deep.

Those nights when the guitar and mics would crowd
into your car and leave me to the waves
inside my ears, I worried that you'd found

a place to go. But you heard no escape.
My voice tucked in your pocket like a signal
to find home by, it tricked us as it saved

what we called marriage. Always kind and civil,
we spoke of love like diplomats — no bark
of passion, our constitutions mutual.

4.
Or so we thought. The sirens know or ought
to know that their songs are accompaniment
to hunger. Those good promises we fought

to keep became the rocks we broke against.
So many melodies that we forgot
to sing for courage against the elements.

That seemed okay, or at least not embarrassing. The numbered sections let the poem breathe, and I was able to have little rests before tackling another idea. It had shape, the argument of the poem had turns, where the speaker could shift positions and dictions ("One thing is, you had such a sober face"). I was able to work in this idea of the husband being attractive for what he was not, not a barfly or drunk, rather than what he was. I'd been at work on the poem for a couple months, felt rather taxed by the beast, but I felt a little proud, too. I'd gotten some clarity. When I went back to my readers, they liked the changes but remained unconvinced at a few places where I'd truly hoped the dazzle of metaphor would pull the poem through. And they couldn't trace out what happened in the end, not exactly. Or rather, they didn't buy it.

Rats.

I was discouraged. I put the damn thing in a file. Time passed. A few years even. I couldn't believe I'd let it sit untended for so long when I rediscovered it. Surely, I could try again; I could make it work.

In order to get back into the poem, I started by annotating it, as if it weren't my poem at all, writing notes in the margins to clarify what I thought "the poet" meant, or wanted to mean. That turned into a useful exercise that I still use sometimes, especially with longer poems. I tried some tinkering, coming up with variations like

> Weekends, we'd go through fake books, choosing songs
> to get by heart, then put them off for later.

Is that better? I wasn't sure. I changed "one thing is" to "the thing is," which seemed more conversational and more of a shift from the formality of section one. I tinkered and fiddled and got it closer, inch by inch. I knew expanding that last stanza had to happen but just couldn't find the words. Argh. I put it aside for a couple of years more.

Then, seven years after the first draft, I needed poems for a manuscript. I read through it and tackled it again, this time with a clearer sense of the poem's charms. Why not call it "The Apprentice Siren"? It's really about her, that state of mind, after all. Then I realized that "ten years ago" to start the poem makes the poem about "now" in the speaker's world, too, since we must think "Ten years from when?" So I revised to "At twenty years" to put the focus squarely on that apprentice siren in the past, wherever she may be now. And why not clarify the tenses and heighten the nautical language as I revise? I also fine-tuned some lines, making the lines carry as much information and image as they can pack, turning, for instance,

> my head was full of music, my ears dull

to the more specific

> my ears ring with temperate music. Dull

and sharpening

> on that day I wrapped myself in lace,

to

> that summer day I wrap myself in lace,

Then I expanded that last stanza, getting the husband back in with "old sailor" and putting more blame on the speaker's shoulders:

> Those good promises we fought

to keep became the rocks we broke against,
old sailor. I forgave your perfect ear
as we pitched against the elements,
and I bent quarter tones too far, too far
cascading down the cliffs until I forgot —
in the greedy winds — all my repertoire.

I called it finished. Finally! And that indeed was the version circulating, until a real old sailor, Robert Ward, accepted it for publication in *The Susquehanna Quarterly* and made some further suggestions to help emphasize the nautical aspect, some of which I greedily took, some tweaked. He advised further tense changes and even pointed out a misplaced modifier in my first section. This spurred me on to yet more changes, expanding on an old bit of marginalia about the other sirens who were instructing the apprentice. Ten years after the first impulse, then, I had this:

The Apprentice Siren

1.
At twenty years, I bought a microphone
to lift my voice into the smoky bars:
I kept the customers from going home

and eased their drinking. Their lungs took in tar;
their blood took up the song of alcohol,
but when I saw them stumbling to their cars,

my ears rang with a temperate music. Dull
to whistled catcalls and slurred compliments,
I ferried out equipment, locked it all

safe in the trunk. An apprentice siren's sense
for melody — and yet no notion of
the lure of rocks, the ocean's violence.

2.
The thing is, he had such a sober face

and we sang okay together, so I was sure,
that summer day I wrapped myself in lace,

that all the parts fit right; our motives were pure.
Then I lost sight of details, let lipstick stale
on the foam rubber windscreen, the blue silver

mic case gather dust, the electric tail
grow sticky from spilt beer. My good teachers
watched their words unravel, a vapor trail

of lessons fading with my voice, clean shores
where my first wrecks washed up. Incorporated,
I schooled myself in blend, domestics, creature

comforts. Then he began to come home late.
Weekends, we went through fake books, choosing songs
to get by heart, then put them off for later.

3.
These nights I eat alone. I hear him park
from deep within my dreams. I surface, keep
my body silent near his rustling dark.

As deft as any burglar, he will creep
under the covers, and comfort in the sound
of his familiar breath will ease my sleep.

Then: 4-track, stands, guitar, and mics crowded
into his backseat, he leaves me to the waves
inside my ears. I worry that he's found

a place to go. But he hears no escape.
My voice, tucked in his pocket like a signal
to find home by, tricks us as it saves

what we call marriage. Always kind and civil,
we speak of love like diplomats — no bark
of passion. But no perfidious storm. No ripple.

4.

Or so we thought. The sirens know or ought
to know that their songs are accompaniment
to hunger. Those good promises we fought

to keep became the rocks we broke against,
old sailor. I forgave your perfect ear
as we pitched against the elements,

and I bent quarter tones too far, too far.
Fetching against the cliffs, lost, I forgot —
in the greedy winds — all my repertoire.

Kathrine Varnes was born near Köln, Germany, on the day after John F. Kennedy was shot. From the age of four, she grew up in Los Angeles, learning to keep her cool around famous people. Some of her odd jobs have included filing engine gaskets, painting the names on boats, and singing in bars. Kathrine is author of *The Paragon* (Word Tech Editions, 2005), co-editor with Annie Finch of *An Exaltation of Forms* (University of Michigan Press, 2002), and a coordinator of collaborative sonnet crowns. She has an MA in Creative Writing from San Francisco State and a PhD in English from The University of Delaware.

Souvenir

Jehanne Dubrow

In the summer of 2004, I lived and worked in the Polish town of Oświęcim, or Auschwitz, as it is known to the outside world. Although I had spent seven years of my childhood in Poland, my upbringing was a sheltered one, the glittering world of embassies and cocktail parties. Returning to Poland after many years away allowed me to experience the country the way a stranger would. As I walked through Kazimierz, the old Jewish section of Kraków, I observed the carved figurines of Hasidim, which tourists could purchase on any street corner. With their hooked noses and greedy, grasping hands, these awful collectibles gave a face to anti-Semitism.

From the moment I decided to write about the wooden Jews, I knew the subject matter demanded a sonnet. Within the sonnet's compressed space, I could explore fully the influence of tiny objects. The formal constraints of the sonnet would also serve as a counterbalance to the anger I felt when I stared at those carved Jews, my kin.

> In Kraków's Market Square, the vendors sell
> small ~~wooden~~ men at thirty złotys each:
> the Jew ~~holding~~ a ~~siddur~~ in his hands,
> a beggar Jew, the money-counting Jew,
> the bobble-headed Jew who sways and nods
> with every gust of air, the foolish Jew…

Because I tend to revise while I'm in the process of writing a first draft, it was the end of this sixth line and my inadvertent repetition of the word *Jew* at the end of the line that suddenly triggered a thought: What if I rhymed "Jew" with "Jew" throughout the sonnet? The idea struck me as right, both in terms of form and content. I liked the challenge of using the "Jew," hammering that single syllable into a reader's ear, while still allowing the word's use as end rhyme to remain almost invisible. And, after having spent the summer in Poland, I understood the power of anti-Semitism lies is its ability to flourish, pervasive even in places where no Jews exist. As I began to visualize the full shape of the sonnet, I saw that the repeated figure of the wooden Jew — as the embodiment of antisemitic iconography — would allow a reader to see the innocuous shape anti-Semitism can take.

> In Kraków's ~~Market Square~~, the ~~vendors sell~~
> small men at thirty złotys each: the Jew
> who grips the Torah in his wooden hands,

In the second line, I changed "small wooden men" to "small men" because I needed space to move the word *Jew* from the beginning of the third line to the end of the second. Still, "wooden" seemed like a crucial detail. Readers needed concrete detail in order to imagine the figurines. I wrote of the Jew's hands as gripping instead of merely holding. I replaced the siddur, a prayer book, with the more distinctive shape of the Torah scroll. And "hands" became "wooden hands."

It occurred to me that I needed to consider the lines that would not rhyme with "Jew." Looking at the third line, which ended with "hands," I thought that a mix of slant and masculine rhyme would offset the heavy sound of the repeated "Jew." I revised the first line to read "the kiosks vend," rhyming it with "hands." I changed "Market Square" to "marketplace" because I decided that my first instinct had been overly specific, limiting the moment to that one particular Market Square. The word *marketplace*, on the other hand, allows anti-Semitism to grow beyond Kraków and also carries implications of capitalism.

> In Kraków's marketplace, the kiosks vend   a
> carved men at thirty złotys each: a Jew   b
> who grips the Torah in his wooden hands,   a
> a beggar Jew, a bobble-headed Jew   b
> whose body sways and nods with just a pull   c
> against his jagged nose, a ~~foolish~~ Jew,   b
> a Jew who ~~throws~~ gold coins onto a scale,   c
> the balance tipping in his favor…?

Revision of the first eight lines came together quite quickly, once I knew how to handle the poem's end rhymes. I also decided on a strategy to deal with syntax. Beginning with the end of the second line, I alternated between short phrases like "a beggar Jew" and longer, more syntactically complex descriptions. I enjambed longer phrases as a way of concealing rhyme. By enjambing and by varying phrasal lengths, I could avoid the monotony that list poems sometimes suffer from.

Meanwhile, I made small changes to individual phrases. For instance, I turned the "foolish Jew" of the sixth line into the more evocative "singing Jew." In line 7, I replaced "throws" with "spills" to create internal rhyme between "spills" and "scale."

Having reached nearly the end of the eighth line, I didn't know how to proceed. While the eighth line would conclude with "Jew," as the rhyme scheme demanded, I wasn't sure about my next rhetorical move. I did intend, however, to include a volta — a rhetorical turn — after the octet. My eight-line list stopped precisely at the point in the sonnet where tradition demanded I alter the direction of my argument before beginning the final sestet.

In Kraków's marketplace, the kiosks vend	a
carved men at thirty złotys each: a Jew	b
who grips the Torah in his wooden hands,	a
a beggar Jew, a bobble-headed Jew	b
whose body sways and nods with just a pull	c
against his jagged nose, a singing Jew,	b
a Jew who spills gold coins onto a scale,	c
the balance tipping in his favor. These Jews	b
will be ~~brought home as Christmas gifts~~ to stand	a
on cluttered shelves. Children will clench the Jews,	b
the *ydki*, as ~~they like to~~ say…?	

When I'm stuck inside the drafting of a poem, I tell myself stories about the poem until I find a solution. In this case, I imagined the secret life of these figurines and visualized what must happen to many of them; they're bought as inexpensive gifts, carried home, played with, and eventually forgotten.

By the time I revised through the middle of the eleventh line, I had eliminated "Christmas gifts," which oversimplified the narrative, drawing too easy a binary between Christian and Jew. Instead, I stayed with the more intimate story of the figurines' travels from shop display to private residence: "These Jews / will be wrapped up and taken home to stand / on cluttered shelves." I placed the emphasis on inherited prejudices rather than religious beliefs, revising "as they like to say" to read "as their parents say." The word *ydki* is the Polish diminutive for "Jews," literally "little Jews," and should be pronounced condescendingly, disdainfully.

In Kraków's marketplace, the kiosks vend	a
carved men at thirty złotys each: a Jew	b
who grips the Torah in his wooden hands,	a
a beggar Jew, a bobble-headed Jew	b
whose body sways and nods with just a pull	c
against his jagged nose, a singing Jew,	b
a Jew who spills gold coins onto a scale,	c
the balance tipping in his favor. These Jews	b
will be wrapped up and taken home to stand	a
on cluttered shelves. Children will clench the Jews,	b
the *ydki*, as their parents say. How pale	c
their faces are, how dark the beards of Jews,	b
as black as coal dust ~~sitting on~~ new snow	d
(and ~~gone as shtetls from the fields~~ below).	d

The final four and a half lines of the poem arrived quickly, though I struggled with the parenthetical statement at the end of the sonnet. Until the last two lines, I had limited my rhyme scheme to three possible rhymes, but I knew that the final couplet needed to act as a discrete unit, both rhetorically and sonically. The closing couplet of an English sonnet should sing with the music and finality of an epigram. It is the sound of a door closing.

Eventually, I realized that the last line didn't work because its perspective differed from that of the rest of the poem. "[G]one as shtetls from the fields below" spoke of the wooden Jews as a town, a shtetl seen from a distance. But the rest of the poem held the figurines close, examining their details at less than an arm's length. It made no sense, therefore, for the final metaphor to approach its subject matter telescopically. Instead, I revised the line so that the metaphor sustained an intimate gaze. As for the parentheses, I used them like hands cupped around a mouth; some truths remain so painful they should be whispered like secrets.

That the wooden Jews needed to be forgotten in order to end the poem became apparent as I reflected on the word *souvenir*. I thought of my father, who had retired from the U.S. Foreign Service and was now a high school

French teacher. How often had he talked about the irony of souvenirs — silly tchotchkes bought to remember a visit to a foreign place — that we inevitably break, lose, or relegate to a closet? In French, "souvenir" is both noun and verb, making it an appropriate title for my sonnet, a poem that simultaneously speaks about a figure (or figurine) of memory and enacts memory itself.

At the end of the poem, coal dust evokes the Holocaust trope of chimneys but also refers to the fossil fuel that is ubiquitous to Eastern Europe in wintertime. I used the parallel contrasts of black beards against white faces and black soot against white snow to emphasize the irony of living in a post–Auschwitz universe, where life is anything but black and white, a state of existence that Primo Levi once called the "gray zone."

Souvenir

In Kraków's marketplace, the kiosks vend
carved men at thirty złotys each: a Jew
who grips the Torah in his wooden hands,
a beggar Jew, a bobble-headed Jew
whose body sways and nods with just a pull
against his jagged nose, a singing Jew,
a Jew who spills gold coins onto a scale,
the balance tipping in his favor. These Jews
will be wrapped up and taken home to stand
on cluttered shelves. Children will clench the Jews,
the zydki, as their parents say. How pale
their faces are, how dark the beards of Jews,
as black as coal dust covering new snow
(and lost like memory in the dirt below).

"Souvenir" first appeared in the March 2005 issue of *Poetry*.

Jehanne Dubrow was born in Vicenza, Italy, and grew up in Yugoslavia, Zaire, Poland, Belgium, Austria, and the United States. She earned her MFA in poetry from the University of Maryland, College Park, and is currently working toward a PhD in creative writing at the University of Nebraska–Lincoln. Her work has appeared or is forthcoming in *Poetry*, *The Hudson Review*, *Tikkun*, *The New England Review*, *Poetry Northwest*, and *Gulf Coast*.

The Winter Moths

FRANCIS BLESSINGTON

I'd seen winter moths surviving into January, and my wife told me some facts she had read about them in a newspaper article. Then a poem decided it wanted to be written. I always write the first draft longhand and uncritically. I put down anything, as in this draft:

The Winter Moths

Winter moths have blackened
and withered the strong red maple
that endured sixty scatheless winters.
The flickering white/brown wings sing
in the autumn gloom, asking admittance
to the early overlit room, alternating
on the window glass, divergent sharing
of possibility before melting into dark.
Three flicker in the room asking for death
exhausting their half-lives on carpet
and sofa, having no more purpose
no Realpolitik of wealth or power
mere figments of geography, leaf-
drawn into black tracks, twisting loose
from their insect bonds, dancing to rebel.

I noticed that the poem looked like a sonnet so I didn't break it into stanzas. Also I noticed that it wanted to be stress meter of three or four stresses to the line so I didn't loosen the lines (usually a bad idea), nor did I pull them into accentual-syllabic meter. The poem's about nature, not human nature, at least not directly, and I felt that too strict a form would make the moths too rigid. So I had a working form, and the poem had enough thickness for me to work on it.

As usual, I made one quick hand revision and put the poem on the computer. My revisions continue for days, maybe weeks, maybe longer, until I can't find anything to add or take away. My wife, also a poet, will read one or more drafts, depending on how much I change things. I think she read two drafts of this poem, making a few suggestions. My changes were rapid and instinctive, unless I had to puzzle something out, then I resorted to reason.

The original draft suggested that my purpose is to tell the biography of the winter moths as a force different from human experience and difficult to capture. In this poem, my overall meaning is clear early: the moths' fight against the law of death.

The first line was easy to fix. Craft, not art, tells me that poems usually work best in the present tense, so I changed the first line from "Winter moths have blackened" to "Winter moths blacken." I liked it, so it stayed. The new line pulled the accented syllables together, giving me a / ˘ / / ˘ pattern, which is strong because there are only two unaccented syllables in the line. The strong line fits the action of the invasive and predatory moths.

I put the second line in the present also and struck the word *strong* because the word is colorless, and the idea was already included in "red maple" and the action of blackening. In "Winter moths blacken / and wither the red maple," I liked the echoing of alliteration (*w*'s, *m*'s), consonance (*r*'s, *n*'s, *th*'s, *l*'s), and assonance (short *i*'s, suggestive of smallness) and the slant rhyme ("Winter," "wither") suggestive of struggle. The poem sings but not too much. The enjambment, or rove-over, I kept, the sentence going into the third line before a full pause in order to preserve tension and imitate the relentlessness of the moths.

My wife suggested the word *endured* is flat — much of my rewriting is fixing flats — and that called my attention to "sixty scatheless," which I sensed was following sound at the expense of elegance so "that endured sixty scatheless winters" became "that resisted sixty winters." As a part of speech, the adjective (and the adverb) is a hideous invention, so adjectives go if they can. Then I had:

Winter moths blacken
and wither the red maple
that resisted sixty winters.

The sound was good, even a little insect-buzzy, but "resisted" seemed weak. It stayed. I still hadn't found a better word, but it didn't wreck the poem. The moths are threatening, violent, and destructive, and the language reflects these qualities.

The flickering white/brown wings sing

Line 4 has four stresses, but I saw in the beginning that I was varying between three and four stresses and needed a change to avoid monotony. My wife struck out "white" in red pen. I checked the color of winter moths on the net and an obliging moth was flying around the room. It was brown-gray, though the ones on the computer seemed more whitish. But "gray/brown" is clearer than "white/brown," and I didn't want to puzzle the reader here. The slash was a bit academic so it became a hyphen, which was less noticeable. My wife underlined and put a question mark after "sing." This time I resisted, for her confusion about moths singing would be clarified as a metaphor later in the poem, for singing is vibrating the air, and they are "singing" their death song.

In line 5, I change "gloom" to "gloam" (from "gloaming") but days later change it back when I realize I'm sounding like Rabbie Burns. "asking admittance" stays for its understatement and takes some of the heavy poeticism off "autumn gloom" before the reader reaches the line end. I'm trying throughout the poem to mix some heavier words with Latin roots, "resisted," "autumn," "admittance," with the more Anglo-Saxon words, "sixty," "gloom," "asking," that predominate, but would make the diction of the poem too low without the contrast. A plethora of Latinate words would elevate the tone to that of an inaugural address.

"Room" in line 6 sounded too lowly and was in heavy middle rhyme with "gloom," so I changed it to "inside," which, more than "room," suggests the inside life of all creatures. "asking," "admittance," "overlit," "inside," and "alternating" gave me a schematic of *a*'s, *t*'s, and short *i*'s that I fancied is appropriate for the moths.

"divergent sharing / of possibility" was confusing, my wife thought. I meant the moths land and fly off the window glass at different times, hence sharing it. It's just bad writing and sounds like my early poems when I would overcondense because I wanted to jack up the diction at the expense of sense. This became "playing / the possibilities." By itself, this alliterating participial phrase would be too trite, but contrast will pull it off, for it dips only momentarily into the everyday conversational, and then bounces back. "before melting into dark" was trite, and again I was trying too hard and not listening to where the poem wanted to go. After all, this poem is not *Paradise Lost*. These guys are bugs, not Satan's army. "before melting into dark" becomes "before the greater cold." That has a basis in fact as well as metaphor. The poem then was:

The Winter Moths

Winter moths blacken
and wither the red maple
that resisted sixty winters.
The flickering gray-brown wings sing
in the autumn gloom, asking admittance
to the early overlit inside, alternating
on the window glass, playing
the possibilities before the greater cold.

The poem moved from the violence of the moths to their vulnerability and sense of need.

The poem naturally broke here between the generalized moths and the three particular ones that I pretended to see in the room. A stanza division still suggested the sonnet by its split into a sort of octave and sestet.

Line 9 has three moths "flicker." But this suggests the over-obvious candle-and-moth syndrome, and they certainly are not "asking for death." The "room" here is too vague so I risk "living room," which is a direct hit on the reader but I hope is unexpected and works. In my wife's version, I added "drunk" to the line, which she mercifully cut. I was getting insecure and re-iterative. "Three flicker in the room asking for death" became "Three flutter in the living room."

"exhausting their half-lives on carpet / and sofa" started out fine with "exhausting" being an active verb, which sets well with the combative nature of my moths. "their" just takes up a seat and can leave. I added "the" to "carpet" because of the domesticity of the scene, where the missing article seems a bit barbaric. "carpet" and "sofa" are too much the same thing, so "sofa" morphed to "lamp," which is vague where I want to be precise, so I added "shade" to "lamp." "Having no more purpose" is just "purposeless" because the word is stronger and because my moths never had a purpose. The moths I see now are more like people than I first thought.

The four cadences that end the poem were correct rhythmically in the first draft. They are in apposition with the moths and are meant to build in intensity. "mere figments of geography" had some wit about it but "mere origami of geography" was more vivid and widened the political arena of the previous line but kept the mothiness of the moths. "leaf- / drawn into black tracks" had a nice violence to it because of the extreme enjambment, perhaps suggesting hanging on, but "tracks" was hokey so "beds" picked up the human parallel again. "twisting loose / from their insect bonds" was incorrect. The moths were "twisting in their insect bonds" and failing to break out of their doomed mortality. "dancing to rebel" is pretentious and insensitive even to moths, so it became "reeling to rebel"; "reeling" is also a dance term, but the word conveys also assault and shock and combines with "rebel" to show the fight to live that is shared even by these benighted creatures. "reeling to rebel" sounded wrong to me while I revised the poem, but now the poem seems to have arranged itself around this summary phrase so the alliteration, assonance, and consonance have a finality about them that is not overdone. The participle has a floating quality about it, a state of being, that fits and focuses on the dying struggle of the moths that I want to capture. And, yes, they share something with us after all: they are a symbol of all creatures struggling to stay alive; hence they are relevant to us. But the poem stays their story.

One last twist of the knife.

I repeated the main part of the title "The Winter Moths" in the first line. I thought this was a weakness and hearkened back to before the seventeenth century when lyrics didn't have titles, just first lines or numbers. I looked up the scientific name of the insect and used that because *Oper-* (Latin for "deeds," "labors") suggests "opera," and *bruma-* sounds like thunder to me (it really means "winter" in Latin), and because the sterile, Latinate name scientists give the moths contrasts so sharply with the death-battling insects I wanted to portray.

I may still revise years later for a book or just for possible readings, as long as I can still relate to the feeling and circumstances of the poem. Here is the latest draft:

Operophterae Brumatae

Winter moths blacken
and wither the red maple
that resisted sixty winters.
The flickering gray-brown wings sing
in the autumn gloom, asking admittance
to the early overlit inside, alternating

on the window glass, playing
the possibilities before the greater cold.

Three flutter in the living room,
exhausting half-lives on the carpet
and lamp shade, purposeless—
no realpolitik of wealth or power—
mere origami of geography, leaf-
drawn to their black beds, twisting
in their insect bonds, reeling to rebel.

"Operophterae Brumatae" was first published in *Appalachia*.

Francis Blessington has published two books of poems, *Wolf Howl* (BkMk Press, University of Missouri–KC, 2000) and *Lantskip* (William Bauhan, 1987), as well as verse translations of Euripides' *The Bacchae* and Aristophanes' *The Frogs* (Crofts Classics, 1993; rpt., Authors Guild, 2003), a verse play, *Lorenzo de' Medici* (University Press of America, 1992), *Paradise Lost: Ideal and Tragic Epic* (Twayne, 1988; rpt, Authors Guild, 2004), *Paradise Lost and the Classical Epic* (Routledge and Kegan Paul, 1979), in addition to many essays, in such journals as *Arion*, *The Sewanee Review*, and *The Vocabula Review*. Short stories have appeared recently in *The Armchair Aesthete*, *The Dalhousie Review*, *Dream Fantasy International*, *The GSU Review*, *InLand*, and *Puckerbrush Review*. His most recent book is a novel, *The Last Witch of Dogtown* (Curious Traveller Press, 2001). His poems have appeared in *Appalachia*, *Arion*, *Arizona Quarterly*, *Cumberland Poetry Review*, *The Dalhousie Review*, *Denver Quarterly*, *The Florida Review*, *Frank*, *Harvard Magazine*, *International Poetry Review*, *Light*, *New Letters*, *The Sewanee Review*, *The Southern Humanities Review*, *The Southern Review*, *Southern Poetry Review*, *Willow Springs*, *Yale Literary Magazine*, *Yankee*, and in many other journals. He teaches at Northeastern University.

Jeans, Size Zero

This poem was created for a collaborative exhibit between seven fiber artists and seven poets in Madison, Wisconsin, who exchanged their work with the intention of creating a piece in response to each other's medium.

Ordinarily, I rely on the impetus for a poem to come from a sensory experience, memory or an overheard conversation. I knew that constructing something "at will" would be a challenge for me, and with enough other have-to's in my life, writing was my one oasis for dealing with things from an intuitive and emotional sense of place. I wasn't sure I could manage this expectation of writing-on-command.

However, my artistic partner had created a narrative wall hanging that depicted the history of Chinese foot-binding, a practice that effectively hindered women's ability to participate fully in society, and it touched an emotional chord in me. I saw a correlation between that former societal preference for small feet and our contemporary American worship of the minimalist female form: waistline trim, neither hips nor thighs spatially ample, that is, commanding. I'm old enough to remember the advent of the famous British model Twiggy, who, although a grown woman, looked like a 12-year-old in a perpetual state of arrested development, puberty and its curvaceous thickening delayed. Prior to the time of this artistic collaboration, I was raising a daughter to face the present-day media onslaught of messages that insisted the less of a woman there was, the more she was valued, and so was concerned with how she was coping with her sense of physical self.

Hence, my poem took a narrow and constricted shape in format with a clipped and abrupt tone to mirror the terse determination of a teenager who has become anorexic. I wanted this poem to express the enforced denial of pleasure, the quest for male acceptance and subsequent subservience, the willingness to trade physical strength and power for being deemed attractive and fitting in. I also wanted to show how it wasn't just men who encouraged this bone-jutting ideal, but other women as well.

Initially, I had titled this poem "Jeans, Size Ten." I assumed size ten jeans were fairly small because with a waist of 25 inches, those were the size I wore. I hadn't bought a new pair in years, and didn't know that the

41

clothing industry had since renumbered their sizes to make women think they are smaller than they really are. A size two in jeans is now considered average; size zero something to aspire to. Here's the original Version:

Original Version

Jeans, Size ~~10~~ Zero

Half an ~~apple~~ orange is breakfast
so the waistband slides
~~(to make the waistband slide)~~
a V-slouch off hips
Space enough for his hand
~~while~~ when pinning her to the ~~wall~~ brick
~~of the Star Cinema~~ of the cinema's back wall
Haltered not horsy / is what
the boys favor
Wrists ~~coltish~~ willow-thin
A vulnerable ~~neck~~ nape
~~Can she erase whittle herself to~~
Can she whittle herself ~~back~~ down
to ~~past pink~~ pastel acquiescence?
Forfeit Pillsbury biscuits
Skip the senior class picnic
Drink milk not water
for a shot glass waist
Run ~~to~~ the ~~Picnic Pt~~ Southwest Bike Path
before ~~soccer~~ BAND practice
Cinch sister's anklet
notch number ~~8~~ eight (A)
~~No slip of a thing / sits out a dance~~
~~gets gym dance sidelined at the dance~~
~~No girl one Pert and petite doesn't leave~~
~~any leaves the party alone (or A)~~
Every camera caresses
the swan silhouette
'Less is more' says Mother
in the stainless steel kitchen

as she lights dinner
one Winston cigarette

(A) Pert & petite ~~don't get is not not never sidelined at~~
~~dances~~
~~(sits out)~~
~~at the Saturday dance~~
~~A No slip of a thing never leaves~~
~~The a party alone~~
No ~~what~~ slip of a thing leaves
a ~~the a~~ party alone ~~? for~~

I changed "apple" to "orange" for an intense color at the start of the poem. Apples when halved are pale yellow.

I was considering "to make the waistband slide," hence, put it in parentheses, which is what I do when I'm considering an option. I like to get all the possibilities down on paper so I can see them and make a choice. I felt "so" was a faster shoehorn into the poem than "to make."

"When" was a better choice than "while" because it is one syllable and has the immediacy of right now. "Wall" was traded for "brick" because of the short *i* and hard *k* sound that gave the message more definition.

Usually, I prefer to use specific nouns, but "Star Cinema" didn't allow for another hard *k* sound, but "back wall" did.

I employ slashes to help me see where line breaks should go when I'm writing drafts in longhand.

"Coltish" didn't have the assonance of "willow-thin," though I liked its imagery. It also had more physical power in it than I wanted, suggesting the ability to leap, prance, and run away. "Willow-thin" suggested a frailer persona.

I chose "nape" with its long *a* sound because it echoed what boys "favor."

"Erase" I discarded for "whittle" because "whittle" implies a more willful act that involves tension, and I wanted willful tension to be expressed in this poem. I also liked the alliteration with "wrists" and "willow."

"Pink" I traded for "pastel" because it was only the second time the short *a* sound made an appearance, and it was echoed by "acquiescence." It also suggested an array of colors, allowing the readers to pick whatever hues they wanted. When readers are allowed to do that, they participate more fully in a poem.

I switched the next two lines because I wanted the biscuits to be a part of the class picnic and wanted specificity about the female's age.

I switched "milk" and "water" because that hard *k* sound worked better at the end of the line. (I often find a line will work better if two words swap places.)

Here I selected "Southwest Bike Path" because it's an actual place, and since this poem will be on exhibit in my town, I wanted the readers to be given a place they knew.

That hard *k* sound in "soccer" was out of place here, and I also figured it didn't make sense that she would run before playing soccer when soccer involves so much running itself.

I rearranged the lines where "slip of a thing" and "pert" appear so they'd have a snappier meter and keep the rhythm moving.

I tried putting the final four lines in the past tense, but everything before it was in present tense, and I also wanted to show how the influence of "Mother" was never-ending. Here's the final version

Jeans, Size Zero

Half an orange is breakfast
so the waistband slides
a V-slouch off hips
Space enough for his hand
when pinning her to the brick
of the cinema's back wall
Haltered not horsy
is what the boys favor
Wrists willow-thin
A vulnerable nape
Can she whittle herself down
to pastel acquiescence?
Skip the senior class picnic
Forfeit Pillsbury biscuits
Drink water not milk
for a shot glass waist
Run the Southwest Bike Path
before band practice

Cinch sister's anklet
notch number eight
Pert and petite
never sidelined at dances
No slip of a thing leaves
a party alone
Every camera caresses
the swan silhouette
Less is more says Mother
in the stainless steel kitchen
as she lights dinner
one Winston cigarette

Shoshauna Shy has contributed to poetry anthologies published by Random House, Grayson Books, Poetry Daily by Sourcebooks, and others. Her poems have been published by *Poetry Northwest, Wisconsin Academy Review, Cimarron Review,* and other journals. She is the author of three chapbooks produced by Moon Journal Press, Pudding House Publications, and Parallel Press, an imprint of the University of Wisconsin–Madison library system. She works for the Wisconsin Humanities Council.

The Penitent

MARK VINZ

As many of my poems do, this one began with a prose version, which simply tries to reconstruct an incident that, for no apparent reason, crept into my head one morning as I lay awake during one of my recurring stretches of insomnia. The incident itself went back to a time many years before when I was traveling in South Dakota with two other poets, taking part in a series of workshops and readings — another time when I was having trouble sleeping. What came to me first was the vivid image of a large black dog and the severed duck heads that he bore around his neck (and where I probably first discovered the meaning of the term *hang-dog look*). Especially to one who had spent very little time on farms, that image was startling. I had to wonder why I hadn't used it in a poem years before, and how it had managed to get lost, so to speak. Anyway, as I sat with my morning coffee that day, I tried to reconstruct the experience in a journal entry before it disappeared again:

> When they found out I hadn't been sleeping, Craig and Daniel dropped me off at their friends' farm so I might get a nap — we had a workshop to do that night and were 60 miles from our motel. All I really remember about that afternoon was the dog, a big black lab, with three severed duck heads tied around his neck — for punishment, the farmer told us, for killing the ducks in the muddy farmyard. He also said it was the only way that dog would ever learn. All afternoon I lay in the bed upstairs but I couldn't sleep. Maybe it was the unseasonable spring heat. Every so often I'd look out the window at the farmyard and whenever I did, that dog seemed to be looking up at me, duck heads swaying around his neck as he circled.

As Richard Hugo says in *The Triggering Town*, poems tend to have two subjects — what triggers or generates them and what the author discovers they're really about, which is what emerges through the process of revision. My first attempt to recreate the experience thus focused on a lot of information about what occasioned the poem — information that was important to me in the poem's genesis but wouldn't, finally, matter to a reader and would thus needlessly bog the poem down at the outset. As a result, the information about my friends disappeared quickly, once a poem began to emerge from my drafts, though the presence of insomnia did remain in some way important to the poem.

Insomniac   (Fourth or Fifth Draft)

This morning I remember a farm I visited once,
where there was a huge and hulking black labrador
wearing three severed duck heads, tied
around his neck with baling wire for punishment,
the farmer said, for killing mallards
which the family raised to sell.
It was a late March day as I remember,
and everybody went about their muddy business
except for me and that dog, watching each other
while he circled among the waddling ducks and geese,
heads flopping under his throat.

Why today should I remember that?
The angle of spring sun and thawing yard
I look out on? Or something else —
circling with lowered eyes, wearing some stubborn
grief it doesn't understand. The only way,
the farmer said, that some of us ever learn a thing.

As I worked through this draft, deciding to begin simply with "This morning I remember" to cut away that unnecessary exposition and move quickly to the image of the dog, I also sensed that this was an opening line that was flat and would soon have to be dealt with. But I was also discovering what the poem was really about, which seemed to begin with the line "Why today should I remember that?" (which wasn't in my first couple of drafts). The more I revised, the more it seemed this was why I was really writing the poem — to explore the question of why we retain such images, why they spring back into our heads long after they've been (supposedly) forgotten. And that seemed to be directly connected to the idea of *penance* — a penance I certainly didn't understand any more than the dog did. In this version, the penance, the "grief," is something "it" (the dog) "doesn't understand." As the revision process progressed, however, my focus became a *human* inability to understand, a link between what the dog was going through and what all of us have to go through in one way or another — bearing our own kinds of grief. Perhaps I was aware of a faint echo of Coleridge's ancient mariner at this point, too.

I also noticed, of course, some of the places where the language could be much improved — "hulking," for instance, is something better shown than labeled; likewise, ducks always "waddle," and the literal "heads flopping" is eventually to become the metonymy "penance flopping" (discovered long after the fact when pointed out by a friend). The poem's central subject has fully emerged at this point, calling for a new title. Insomnia still plays a part in the poem, though smaller than in earlier drafts; perhaps I saw insomnia itself as a kind of penance.

Looking back on this draft again, I can't stress the importance of the revision process enough; indeed, one of my favorite quotes is this one, from Dana Gioia: "Revision is an essential part of the creative act. Enter into revision with the same openness to inspiration you had while jotting down first lines. Remember, a first draft is a kind of doorway to a room where the poem is waiting in one of the corners." What happened in my own drafting process involved a lot of wandering through the house, so to speak, till I found the room I didn't know I was looking for.

The Penitent

What drives me from bed at first light is
a farm I visited once, and a huge black labrador
who wore three severed duck heads
tied around his neck with baling wire —
for punishment, the farmer said, for killing
the mallards his family raised to sell.

It was a late March day, as I recall, and
everybody went about their muddy business
except for me and that dog, watching
each other as he circled, head down
among those trusting ducks and geese,
penance flopping against his throat.

Why today should I remember that? Perhaps
it's the angle of spring sun and thawing ground
I look out upon. Perhaps it's something else,
circling with lowered eyes, bearing some stubborn,
incomprehensible grief — as that farmer kept repeating,
the only way that some of us will ever learn a thing.

The poem went through a few more drafts, a lot of tinkering, and this "final" version was eventually published in *Prairie Schooner* magazine (Spring 1998) as the last poem in a four-poem sequence called "Morning Watch" — which has to do with insomnia-provoked early-morning recollections in some way involving startling animals, as is also indicated by "drives me from bed" in the new first line. So, insomnia is still there as a "generator," and as I wrote more poems in some way relating to insomnia, I found I indeed had a small group that seemed to work together, though I think "The Penitent" is the strongest of the four and certainly the one I'm most attached to; that perhaps has something to do with the way it came to me.

Finally, in this version, I've also paid a lot more attention to form — for example, the six-line stanzas — and sounds, such as the rhythmic parallel provided by "Perhaps" in the third stanza, as well more regular four-beat lines, and even the almost onomatopoeic effect of the word *incomprehensible*, which is probably the biggest word I've ever used in a poem!

I've also paid more attention to the *s* consonance and alliteration that provides an aural pattern, especially in the third stanza. The last line has become strongly iambic, too, which adds, I think, to its finality.

As Michelle Boisseau points out, "Though it uses meter and rhyme non-systematically . . ., free verse is still organized around technical constraints." In my experience, these matters of technical constraint are what the final stages of the revision process focus on, once the basic movement and imagery have become apparent. Looking back on the poem, I have to wonder how conscious I was of those technical constraints in the early stages, being guided mainly by some sense of what "feels right" and then, in later drafts, paying more conscious attention to sounds and rhythms.

Finally, I believe what Paul Valéry said: "A poem is never finished, only abandoned." That's why, when it comes to poems, I always put the words *final* and *finished* in quotes. Poets can always do more tinkering with their poems.

Mark Vinz is professor of English and co-director of the Tom McGrath Visiting Writers Series at Minnesota State University–Moorhead. His poems, stories, and essays have appeared in numerous magazines and anthologies; his most recent books include *Long Distance, Late Night Calls: Prose Poems and Short Fiction*, and two collections of his poems in collaboration with photographer Wayne Gudmundson: *Minnesota Gothic* and *Affinities*. He is also the co-editor of several anthologies, including *Inheriting the Land: Contemporary Voices from the Midwest* and *The Party Train: A Collection of North American Prose Poetry*.

Revelry

ANNIE FINCH

If I had known, when I promised to write a poem for Cincinnati's Sitwells Café, how many revisions it would go through and how long it would take, I might have thought better of the offer. My friend Lisa, the owner of Sitwells, had been dislodged unceremoniously from her previous building by the landlord, and I was trying to give her moral support for the move to a new café space. After all, as I was in the habit of reminding my poetry students, poetry deserves a place in public and private life, not just on the bookshelves of other poets. And now, here I was, being offered a convenient chance to put my pen where my mouth was, right in the middle of one of the city's hippest artistic hangouts.

Actually, "around the edges" would be a more accurate prepositional phrase than "right in the middle," because as soon as we decided that I would write the poem, Lisa had the bright idea of painting it around the ceiling of the new café space. No wonder that I ended up putting it through over forty substantial drafts before it was finished. My aim was to write something that would be simple enough to be appreciated at first glance by someone walking into the café for the first time, and complex and rich enough that a hard-core Sitwells regular ("Sitwellians," they were called) could read it hundreds of times without getting bored, glancing up during deep pauses in conversation, from one of Sitwells' funky old school desks or the green-tiled round garden table. And it had to be short enough to fit in the space around the perimeter of the ceiling that Lisa referred to as the "ceiling soffit," in letters painted large enough to read from below.

I started with a warm-up Sitwells poem a few weeks after speaking with Lisa, in September. It wasn't good enough to revise. Then on a cold November day I went to work in earnest, sitting in the new café for inspiration. Since I had no ideas at all, other than the conviction that Sitwells is a great café, I began in idle free-association, hoping something would catch. The first drafts, most of them crossed out, are scrawled on the back of a fluorescent orange Sitwells poetry slam flyer. But I already had a sense of the music I wanted the poem to have. Only the tetrameter rhythm links the very first drafts with the final version . . . oh, yes, and one other thing. In the upper right-hand corner of one initial draft is a list of the rhymewords from Shakespeare's cynical attack on the consequences of physical passion, Sonnet 129: "shame," "lust," "extreme," "trust," "straight".... As a young poet drinking too-expensive lattes in San Francisco, I had read this beautiful, skillful sonnet over and over. It was painted in the archway of a North Beach café, the only poem I had ever seen painted on an eatery wall. And after reading it so often, I began to realize that I disliked it — not so much for its style as for its theme (I am a Wiccan, and part of my faith is to understand physical pleasure as a gift from the Goddess).

So today, hunched over my nicked wooden table from the deeply indented cushion of one of a pair of linked vintage red-velvet theater seats, panicking over how I was ever going to write a poem strong enough for Sitwells' ceiling, I started doodling down the rhyme-words off that long-ago calligraphied café wall and got an idea for my poem's focus at last. I would write a poem that celebrated the power and beauty of "lust" rather than its destructiveness — an anti-Sonnet-129 poem for the life-loving denizens of Sitwells. I don't know if I actually ended up doing this. I merely followed the revision process, which carried me through the poem in its own way. I do know, though, that one word from that original rhyme-list — "lust" — survived into the final version of the poem.

Even though I was beginning to zero in on a general theme for my ceiling decoration, I didn't move into the logical left side of my brain too soon. Instead, I continued to play for several more drafts, letting out plenty of kite string, letting the words flit where they wanted to go. I wanted my poem to be not only "accessible" to the businesspeople and other nonliterary types who often lunched at Sitwells, but also "experimental" enough in style and syntax to speak to the sophisticated avant-garde art student crowd who frequented it into the wee hours. So I didn't want it to be didactic or forced; I wanted the words to float to the surface of the poem of their own accord.

At home, I printed out successive drafts at my computer and dragged their electronic versions into the trash, then curled up with a pen to write revisions on the hard copies. I do this to save disk space and confusion and also to preserve the drafts in their actual state, resisting the temptation to tinker and improve them, in case I will want to use something from the early versions later (as a result, I've had to retype selected old drafts for the purpose of this, luckily highly unusual, book). After two months and fifteen drafts of playing with words (the next dated version is from January), I had come up with this:

This is the war that wills aloud,
in voices hushed or caved or wrung
out of the rack that sweetness hung
here for the measure of this crowd.
Profiles rock poised air. The proud
lips listen, voices feel. Eyes thrill
alive with words that blend their fill
seasoned through table, rung, or cloud.
Words pour and parry, spiral, among
the single and paired and multiple,
into the cups that will not spill.
Drink in the warmth that marks the tongue
that has been spoken here, and sung.

I don't know where the idea of war came from — whether it had to do
more with the edgy cultural vibrancy of Sitwells or my own internal dialogue with my Elizabethan precursor — but I recall the feeling that that
was the only way I could start the poem. And I find it interesting that not
only had I excised all of Shakespeare's rhyme words at this point, I had
also turned the poem into a sonnet, albeit one keeping the zesty, energetic
tetrameter rhythm that had come to me with the first free-associations and
that felt so appropriate for Sitwells. But already the poem is declaring some
independence from the battle by using an original hybrid sonnet form, ab-
baaccadeedd, instead of the Shakespearean sonnet pattern, ababcdcdefe-
fgg.

I liked the last third of the poem best, but the form seemed too stilted
and closed for the energy I wanted to create, the metaphors and imagery
too obscure, veering too far toward the literary, artsy end of the audience
spectrum. I needed it to be more concrete and accessible. Perhaps because
I felt a shorter, more punchy shape would put me in closer touch with that
concreteness, I would soon abandon the sonnet form for this project. First
it would serve its purpose, providing a capacious scaffolding within which
I built the imagery that would eventually shape the poem: lips, words,
voices, tables, cups, tongues.

Though only a few words from this stage (rung, alive, cup, cloud) will
survive into the final draft, the diction overall is already simple, mostly
monosyllabic, creating the urgent warm rhythm I also hear in parts of the
final version. The disyllabic words tend to be trochaic (sweetness, measure,

seasoned, parry, spiral, spoken), with the falling rhythm lending a slightly elegiac mood that would also characterize the final version of the poem. The double meaning of a "tongue" as a special language spoken at Sitwells would last for quite a few drafts, but in the final version it would seem redundant; my hope was that the poem itself would exemplify such a "tongue," which would no longer need to be referred to explicitly.

Many drafts and a month later, by the end of February, more of the language and imagery of the final version had emerged, and the rhythm had become even more of a falling rhythm, with trochees at the beginnings of more lines:

This is the hour that breathes aloud
over the mouths that slip and sing
where a new culture galloping
bends alive around cup and cloud.
Deep in this landscape that the dark
warms, and the morning light lets go,
chairs root and rung their hearts with snow,
curtains are velvet thick, like bark.
Blood warms the lips and moves the skin;
voices find hours to revel in.
In words all hushed or caved or wrung,
here for the measure of this crowd,
I drink in the warmth that marks the tongue
that has been spoken here, and sung.

Though it seems as if concrete imagery should logically appear first as a poem emerges, since it presents itself first to the senses, looking over this draft makes me understand that for me a poem can happen the opposite way: imagery can emerge with greater and greater definition out of a complex of feelings and thoughts. So, here, through a kind of cycling through of felt impressions of the feeling, mood, and meaning of the café, the concrete imagery of the chairs, curtains, and lips is beginning to solidify. These solid images were those I seized on and carried into later drafts. The tone of the poem was also becoming more direct and intimate, though perhaps going too far in that direction and beginning to seem too soft, too easy. But tone was not my main concern at this point. I was still trying to find the imagistic spine of the poem, and I knew the exact balance of tone was likely to fall into place after that.

At this point, the poem had gone back and forth several times between quatrains and a sonnet-like block of text. This variation on the sonnet rhyme scheme would be the last. For the poem's next incarnation, I made a definitive move into stanzas. I think this rejection of the sonnet form — partly spurred by the sense that a single block of text was too "literary" a shape for the broad audience I wanted to be able to enjoy the poem — was the moment that the poem began to have its own identity, its birth if you will; perhaps that is why, at this point, the poem has a title for the first time. Instead of the sonnet, I used an alternative form, a kind of "prayer," picking up on the hopeful idea of a "new culture" being birthed in the long conversations held nightly and daily over the tables of Sitwells. As appropriate in a public prayer, at this point I began to use the first person plural voice, the "our" that appears in the final version, rather than the "I" of the earlier drafts.

The genre of the prayer led to another breakthrough as well: around the middle of the next dozen (undated) drafts, where the poem has a title for the first time, the poem is temporarily back in a block form, but the sonnet rhyme scheme is gone, and an italicized couplet, like an utterance, has appeared in the middle of the poem:

A Prayer for Sitwells Café

Voices believe words and move free;
lust fills our lips; blood moves our skin.
Open our mouths to sip and sing.
Chairs root. Their hearts are runged with snow,
the curtains grow velvet thick, like bark.
Bend us alive around cup and cloud
through a new culture, galloping.
Passion is only revelry;
these are the hours to revel in.
Deep in this landscape ringed with dark,
warm us with the morning we let go.
This is the hour to breathe aloud,
to drink like the warmth of a learning tongue,
spoken and speaking, singing, sung.

As the poem gathered momentum and began to move toward its final shape, I tried repeating this italicized couplet as a refrain at the end of each stanza:

A Prayer for Sitwells Café

Voices believe words and move free;
lust fills our lips; blood moves our skin.
Passion is only revelry;
these are the hours to revel in.

Chairs root. Their hearts are runged with snow,
the curtains grow velvet thick, like bark.
Bend us alive around cup and cloud
through a new culture, galloping.
Passion is only revelry;
these are the hours to revel in.

Deep in this landscape ringed with dark,
warm us with the morning we let go.
This is the hour to breathe aloud.
Passion is only revelry;
these are the hours to revel in.

Open our mouths to sip and sing.
Drink like the warmth of a learning tongue,
spoken and speaking, singing, sung.

I have found that giving myself permission to write a bad draft, to play without fear of embarrassment, can help free a poem into its finished state. In this case, the repeating refrains were far too corny for the poem (not to mention that they would take up too much space around the ceiling), and they lasted for only a couple of drafts. But they helped bring the poem to its final structure, by isolating into the refrain the two lines that would become the last lines of the final version's two stanzas.

As I began to home in on the shape of the poem, I shortened it to eight lines, retitled it "Revelry," and added the question at the end of the first stanza to give it more of a dramatic plot. I cut out the hard-to-visualize "galloping culture" and moved "ringed landscape" nearer to "runged with snow," where consonance could create its magnetic field. The alliterating "lips" and "lust" had already found their way back in from an earlier draft, bringing the poem to root in the Shakespeare sonnet that had been part of its inception so many months earlier. The eight lines had the edge of simplicity and openness I wanted for the lunch-time crowd, but maintained surprise and mystery for the after-midnight crowd. Most crucially, the words felt as if they spoke to me, not from me. The poem was finished.

Lisa, true to her inspiration, had "Revelry" painted in artful lettering around the Sitwells ceiling by a young artist named Turtle. In exchange for my efforts, I was appointed Poet Laureate of Sitwells — a lifelong, unpaid office. The poem is still painted there today, some words red and some green, on a creamy background that darkened disturbingly during the three years before Sitwells finally went smoke-free. I haven't seen the painted version since moving away to Maine over two years ago, but I am prouder of it than of most other publications. And, though I am in the habit of marking up poems that appear in journals or even books with post-publication revisions, my patience in revising "Revelry" has been rewarded; luckily, I haven't felt the need to change a word.

Revelry

Chairs root. Their hearts are runged with snow.
Curtains grow velvet thick, like bark,
in this warm landscape ringed with dark.
Is passion only revelry?

Voices believe words and move free;
lust fills our lips; blood moves our skin.
We bend alive around cup and cloud.
These are the hours to revel in.

"Revising Revelry" first appeared in *American Poet*, Spring 2007.

Annie Finch is the author of four books of poetry, including *Calendars* (2003), shortlisted for the Foreword Poetry Book of the Year award. Her collection of essays, *The Body of Poetry: Essays on Women, Form, and the Poetic Self* was published in 2005 in the Poets on Poetry Series. She has also published poetry translations, libretti, and several anthologies of poetics. She is professor of English and director of the Stonecoast Brief-Residency MFA in Creative Writing at the University of Southern Maine.

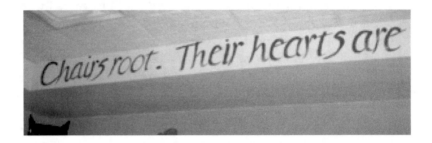

Three

LESLIE SHINN

I wrote "Three" after seeing a television news story — no more than a minute long — about a baby someplace in the world who had lately been born with a normal right arm and two abnormally formed arms on his left side. The story's gist was that one of the two left arms would be removed. Doctors were discussing which arm to remove, and why, based on which of the limbs' hands was deemed more viable. I found it a haunting circumstance, and on a walk one afternoon I "wrote" the first two words, "three arms," and made the decision to have the poem's first word serve as its title. The terse bald phrase is a fast and perhaps shocking entry into the poem, but I did want an immediate focus.

This tactic, incorporating the title directly into the body of the poem, and indeed this whole poem's arrangement, illustrates a recent experimentation of mine in making series of short and bare — but trailing and following — phrases, and in placing them on the page line by line, and here or there *across* the page, too. This I do according to the halting or more fluid manner I deem they fit the expression and — insofar as I feel I can direct the reader — the ways I want them to be read or spoken.

My draft shows the early disorganization of stanza and arrangement, as my own impetus struggled in emotion and tried to become less obstructed by pity and sadness — oh, many responses — and to become more clearly defined. By keeping closely to description, I felt a possibility might be opened for me — and for the reader — to best examine and explore the emotion inherent in this condition. Though the draft shows first my mentioning the "right arm," and his "face fair," my aim at that juncture later became to depict instead the beauty of the baby. I meant to illuminate more than just the fact of his pretty face. The short film footage I had seen of him revealed to me a mien typically soft and lovely, and also unforgettable for its seeming complete normalcy, its sweet and benign uncloudedness. His expression was that of any well-cared-for infant: untroubled, unthreatened.

Instead of just his face, then, I began to focus on that manner of his I described: an innocence undarkened. Trying hard to avoid disrespect and the poetic sin of banality left me floundering about until I found and settled on the word *countenance*. I liked its reference to the face and liked even

THREE

Arms, the baby has.

One, right,
+ a face fair real as any wish or dream
under a countenance   underneath   beneath
                                    + a countenance
                                    pure and clear of the shadsow
                        as hope
                    clear of the shadows
            clear of any shadows
                a countenance clear as any mother hopes

Of the two
left one is
a soft white clench,

small pearl bone cove held tight up
a new peony
of pearl
~~wrench of fresh~~
            held close

a few soft fingers in the shape
of a scissors
            small
of the special kind that
for
the fresh bud
or square of rose paper
                    cut
which is saved
                    + will flourish

more its tangential relationships, to calmness and composure (to keep one's countenance) and to forbearance (to countenance, or endure). As is seen in the draft, I struggled with how to speak beyond this one discovered and decided-on word: I tried on and discarded "pure" (too variously associative somehow), and seemed to settle on "clear," though then it was more work to say *how* it was "clear"; "clear" of what? Finally it seemed to be "clear of any shadows," though in the final draft, the singular (and more archetypal, comprehensive) "shadow" is the word I used for the evocation of darkness, a deep darkness that included, in draft, a bald and terribly banal (and therefore discarded) attempt to speak of this immense misfortune "any mother hopes" will not befall her child. I used both "underneath" and "beneath" as my conjunction here, deciding on the latter for its relative lack of clunk, and finally kept, "Three / arms / the baby has / beneath / a countenance clear of shadow."

I wanted to maintain a distance, a slight remove, in my manner of description when, next, the baby's three arms become the focus. I finally positioned the right limb completely without description, set alone on a line by itself, "one right," hoping to call attention to both its separation and its, well, rightness, or wholeness.

I consciously decided and then strove to compare each left hand to something, or some things, as winsome as the baby himself seemed to me to be. Composing these next few lines, though not easy, was a diversion, for I could momentarily dispense with the tight boundaries of the poem's construct and the arrangement of its parts. I allowed myself to swerve as far as I could from the skin and bone actuality, and tried to simply highlight the visual. (Concision, though, was here, as always, a requisite.) The "new peony" was a picture that somehow sprang from "small pearl bone cove held tight up" — an example of a useful, springboard-like conglomeration I often seem to employ. "New peony" seemed to depict accurately this hand's furl, and its simultaneous tightness and softness. Pushing beyond that phrase, I worked on color, and tried for a certain quality of coloration that transcended skin color, settling on "pearl," for its expansive referentiality and allusiveness. I further sought to reiterate and clarify this hand's fist-like appearance with "clench," moving that from the draft to join its new modifier, "pearl," and positioning this phrase before "a new peony," which I then indented for emphasis.

The second left arm's hand was completely different, as I recalled it, and proposed different comparative possibilities. The draft shows that I started graphically and prosaically with "a few soft fingers in the shape of a scissors." While "scissors" felt right, it seemed to need modification. I added "special" as modifier, but couldn't take that anyplace; the term is too broad. Finally I thought "small" was apropos; though not newly minted, it seemed suitably lucid.

Syntactically, I found it a big problem to introduce each of the two left arms. And I needed to be absolutely precise — and immediate — in focusing attention from the *arms* to the *hands*. I wanted to pare this nuts-and-bolts directional element as compactly as possible and still closely maneuver the expression. I rearranged the draft's "Of the two / left one is" in the final form so that it is perhaps more succinct: "and of the two / / left," but most essentially, I carpentered the clearer "one's hand is" that led to the description, followed later in the text by "and one's," which I hope plainly refers to the second left hand.

Amid the obvious confusion portrayed in the draft's last lines, it is probably visible that the poem's culmination begins there, with reiterations, or at least slightly different renderings, of the descriptions of each of the two hands: "the fresh bud / or fold of rose paper." "Fresh bud" is another phrase for the "new peony." I chose "fold" over the "square" or "cut" of the draft for what I hoped was its more easily imagined physicality (and the softer edge of a creased paper), though I kept the riskier use of the color, "rose," for its kinship with "peony" — and even more for its evocation of freshness and blooming than for its usually implied pinkness. The new (or second) descriptions move from the draft, but are placed a couple lines down in the poem's final form, to the right of the margin and, as upon the baby himself, one over the other and a little apart.

The last couplet is intended to be inexact. It can be read as a question about the left arms, though I never considered using a question mark. (In fact, I eradicated what little punctuation there was in the draft.) And it may refer (though perhaps disjointedly) also to the baby himself, in a declarative manner. To imply this expanded allusiveness, I switched the order of the phrases from the draft's "which is saved / + will flourish" to "which will flourish / and be saved." That arrangement seemed, sensibly, to follow more logically. It sounded more definite, or final. Whether read as a question or statement, the last couplet — essentially, and apart from the rest of the poem — can be read as incantatory, an entreaty. I wanted its lack of punctuation and arrangement apart on the page to allow this ambiguity, to suggest those syntactic possibilities of reference. I meant to express an allusion to choice, and a summary wish for well-being and life.

Three

arms

the baby has

beneath
a countenance clear of shadow

one right

and of the two

left
one's hand is

the pearl clench of
                                 a new peony

and one's

two bone fingers
a small scissors

                the fresh bud
                    or fold of rose paper

which will flourish
and be saved

Leslie Shinn received her MFA from the Program for Writers at Warren Wilson College. Her work has appeared in *Agenda* (UK), *Beloit Poetry Journal*,

The Cortland Review, Phoebe, DMQ Review, Tattoo Highway, Folio, and other journals. Leslie lives and works in Philadelphia.

Quiet Air

ANNE HARDING WOODWORTH

The origin of "Quiet Air" is a line from the Wallace Stevens poem, "Pieces": "Come home, wind, he kept crying and crying."

I tried to imagine under what circumstances a person might invoke wind to return. Certainly, no one who'd lived through a hurricane would, although a sailor might. Odysseus' journey, after all, was dependent on wind.

But I envisioned a man in a big old house in the interior of a land, not dependent on wind for his living but with a strange inability to withstand sanely the opposite of wind: quiet air. That idea appealed to my sense of opposites, of irony, of subversion of content — and I went with it.

Why does this man need the wind so badly? Because he can't tolerate the sounds of everyday life, especially the sound of time moving inexorably to the end. These sounds drive him mad. Wind covers them up, keeping him out of touch with reality — like so many extraneous sounds that bombard the brain today. So, when the next windlessness comes, he asks Elsa (wife? sister? housekeeper? it doesn't matter) to tie him into a rocking chair during the calm. He becomes an anti-Odysseus of sorts.

I began the poem with fidelity to the Stevens quote. I used an asterisk for the attribution, which eventually seemed awkward to me and intrusive to the poem. I tried an epigraph, "with thanks to Wallace Stevens," but that was uninformative. Finally, I thought: perhaps the poem has moved so far away from Stevens I can use my own words. I changed "Come home, wind," to "Come back, wind." This is a good example of how a line from one piece of writing can give rise to a whole new piece. As J. D. McClatchy wrote: "All poets have debts outstanding."* Giving up the Stevens quote allowed me to change the verb tense from past to present, something I do often (going both ways) in revision. This, I believe, quickened the pace of the poem. I also began to see in this new pace the possibilities of unobtrusive rhymes that would add to the new energy (heard-lurched-search-curled, ears-hears, faucets-pockets, tock-rocker, wicker-rocker).

In the first draft, I felt I had put the images of everyday life — that is, what is happening to the old man during the present lull — a little too

---

* J. D. McClatchy, "Writing Between the Lines," *The Practice of Poetry*, ed. Robin Behn & Chase Twichell (New York: Harper Perennial, 1992) 156.

early. The reader would not know soon enough what had happened the last time the wind had subsided (that the old man had run naked into the forest looking for wind). So, I moved some lines from stanzas three and four toward the beginning of the poem. Then I realized that rather than using three-line stanzas, which soon seemed unnatural to me in this case, I could link the chronologies into four parts: (1) what happened during the previous lull; (2) what the old man hears now in a lull; (3) how he's going to ride it out this time; and (4) old man gone mad again. The number of lines per stanza seemed to work in a natural new scheme: 7, 5, 3, 1.

I started with certain images in the first draft that I either changed or dropped: "window glass" became "sides of glass" for insects' onomatopoeic s sounds; "elephant" became "giraffe" in order to convey better the measure of a very tall pendulum and the ponderousness of time; I didn't like "salt words" sprinkling his brain and deleted it altogether — one of those moments in revision when one asks, "Whatever possessed me to write that?" and when the agony (or ecstasy) of delete is the only answer.

As for the title, I briefly changed the original "Stillness" to "Exposed," picking up on the old man's nudity in his crazed mindset during the previous lull, but I returned to the idea of stillness, settling on "Quiet Air," which is the essence of the poem. I liked the double-entendre of the word *air* that suggested wind and musical tune (a Siren's song, perhaps) and juxtaposed some kind of sound with the word *quiet*. Here is the first draft:

Stillness

Come home, wind, the old man cried,
aware of its absence when only the sun shone
and insects circled loudly in s-sounds

against the window glass, and looking
into the house through the screen door he saw
swing the pendulum in the front hall,

a gong on an elephant's neck. He heard again
everything he'd not heard since the last lull
when salt words sprinkled his brain, made him run naked
into the pine forest in search of the missing Boreas,
which up until then had been swirling

into his walls, hands, pockets, and his ears.

This time he asked Elsa to tie him into a wicker rocker
on the front porch where he would wait out the calm.
Come home, wind, he kept crying

*and crying,** rocked in frenzy.

*From Wallace Stevens

And here is the final draft:

Quiet Air

Come back, wind, the old man cries,
hearing everything he's not heard
since the last windless day when he lurched
naked into the pine forest in search
of the missing Boreas he loved,
protective tumult that curled
inside his walls, into his pockets, his ears.

In wind's absence now he hears
the drips of faucets, insects' s-sounds
against the sides of glass.
The pendulum drums out tock in the front hall
like a gong around a giraffe's neck.

He begs Elsa to tie him into a wicker rocker
on the porch where he'll wait out the lull.
Come back, wind, he cries out again

and again, rocking in frenzy.

Anne Harding Woodworth is the author of three books of poetry and has
an MFA in poetry from Fairleigh Dickinson University. Her work is pub-

lished or forthcoming in journals such as *TriQuarterly, Painted Bride Quarterly, Cimarron Review, Antigonish Review, The Dalhousie Review, SLAB,* and *Tiferet*. She lives in Washington, D.C., where she is a member and past chairman of the Poetry Board at the Folger Shakespeare Library.

Rose Devorah

Lyn Lifshin

To this day, I still write my poems longhand in spiral notebooks, often with various beginnings and endings, arrows and lines all over. When I type, I revise. And once the poem has been published, I often do a lot more revising when I decide to use it in a collection of poems. Lately, I have used more and more punctuation, so any poems selected for a collection are likely to have a lot more punctuation than the first and early versions. I do that to help the reader understand, feel, breathe the poem.

In graduate school, I majored in fifteenth- to seventeenth-century poetry, so I had that as a background. But after graduating, I read as much contemporary poetry as I could put my hands on. I also began to do poetry workshops in my house, in libraries, in colleges, and often I wrote poems along with my students. Some poems that I have continued to value have come from exercises like the one I am including here.

One exercise I've done is to ask my students to start with the name on their birth certificate and then list all the names they have ever been called, including nicknames, nasty names, names screamed at them when someone was angry, pet names, and so on.

I did the exercise myself, and for my poem I listed Rosalynn Diane Lipman, Lip, Lifshin, Mrs. Lifshin, Ros, Rosie, Rose, Lynnie, Fat, Kike, R. D. L., Gitana, Sherrie Liane, Lynn, Ms. Lifshin, Honey, Babe, Lady Lyn, Upstate Madonna, Skinny, Eric's wife, Bob's girl, hippy, stuck-up, gipsy, Le Bella E. Magra, Raisel Devora, Miss Middlebury High, Rose Deborah, The Black Rose, Devora, daughter, JAP, Cat, Lippy, Garnet Van Cortland, Foxy, Liane, Diane Sweety, Bebe, Frizzy, Curls, Brain, The Hair House.

I had no idea which name I would pick but ran my eye up and down the list and let one name "hit" me. I picked Rose Devorah and free-flowed with crayons ending up with a rose, a dark rose, almost a black rose, a rose with petals hardly connecting. I thought of it as a tattoo, a logo, something that might go on my stationery or on a T-shirt. I did this with my students, and it truly loosened my imagination; it made me feel freer and better able to see connections, patterns, and images that I might not have seen otherwise. It was easier to not worry about making sense — to just let what came to my mind flow. I could be crazy, outrageous, fantastic.

I wrote all of my images in a list:

> black hair and roses
> the fire that licked the bride
> the dreams of the old house
> ash and how the bride turned to ash
> fire from the candles
> the other sister stepping in
> the burnt roses
> the green dying from that wedding day
> the sun through old glass
> how that woman, whispered about, became part of me
> how she must have smelled of roses
> how she was intense
> how she was pale
> white lace scorched to yellow
> her cheeks and hair in flames

Then I wrote a diary entry about how I vaguely remembered a story about a relative in Russia who, at her wedding, caught a veil in a candle and burned to death. It was whispered, mysterious, something the children were not to hear. A great grandmother was named Raisel Devora, or Rose Deborah. I was named Rosalynn Diane for my great grandmother — a tradition in Jewish families to name a child after someone no longer alive.

Months later, I took out these scribbles, drawings, diary, notes, free-flowing associations, and wrote a poem about a mostly made-up woman. I let myself dream about someone I imagined from the images a little like the way dreams often emerge in a new, strange way from the things you might see during the day.

Rose Devorah

> Dreams of old wooden houses in Russian,
> of the blackest hair fire touched as the
> veil was scorched before the wedding.
> As the bride died, all that was green
> died too. It was as if the sun set before
> sunset. She might have been the aunt

I could have been named for. She burned
in a pale room as the walls dissolved.
Fire pulled her thru frames that were like
a mirror. Her cheeks were raw. It was
a cold rain. Her cheeks were the color of
cherries. Or maybe blood from something
wild and wounded. Rose Devorah pulls
into a fist of her name. It sounded like
sorrow. The light is blood and turns
the glass between where she is and where
she would be to ruby. She will never let
you near except for a price you
can't afford

I liked some of the images here, but it seemed the piece was too prose-like. I wanted to keep the dreamy, strangeness of the early free-flowing list. I liked the spontaneous, breathy, mysteriousness of that list. I've always liked things left out, spaces, sort of like in blues music. This version seemed to "tell" more than I wanted to. I wanted to let the reader experience the poem. I think I also was torn between making the poem about me — since in a small sense there is the connection to me, the name — and making it about this mysterious woman. I also wanted more air in the poem, and that is why I changed the line length. I wanted to show, not tell, more than this early version does.

In the next version, I think I plunged in faster. I used little punctuation, trying to give it more mystery, a dreamy, flowing feeling. Some of the lines are more pared down; most are imagistic and even fragmented. I also added images such as "tea roses or Rashmi Rose incense": I liked what those images suggested as well as their sound. I changed the emphasis from me to Rose Devorah. The past is in the present, which I think gives the poem something mysterious, too.

Rose Devorah

Dreams of old houses
in Russia, licorice hair
fire licks as lace is
scorched, turns ash

before the wedding
and the bride's bones
are dust in the roses
green dies from.
Sun sets in the
afternoon. Some
unknown aunt she
could have been named
for who might have been
wild, intense as rare
tea roses or Rashmi
Rose incense burnt in
a pale room walls
pulled from floats
thru frames that
are like mirrors, her
raw cheeks cherries
in the rain, or
blood from a wild
doe running turning
snow color of plums.
Devorah pulls into
a fist of her name,
it sounds like sorrow.
Blood light turns
glass between her and
what she reaches out
toward to ruby. She
won't let you near
except for a price
you can't afford

The biggest change I made in the next version was to cut the last ten lines. While I liked and still like some of those images, it seems the poem goes off in another direction. Ending the poem with the line "snow color of plums" seems more sharp, crisp, intriguing. There are a few other changes, some paring down and shortening of line lengths that I feel makes the poem tighter, breathless:

Rose Devorah

dreams of old houses
in Russia, licorice hair
fire licks as lace is
scorched, turns ash
before the wedding
and the bride's bones
are dust in the
rose light green
is sucked from as sun
sets in the after
noon. Some unknown
aunt she could have
been named for maybe
wild, intense as rare
tea roses or Rashmi
Rose incense burnt in
a room the walls
pulled from floats
thru frames that are
like mirrors, her
raw cheeks like
cherries in the rain
or blood from a wild
deer running, turning
snow color of plums

I think the change from "bride's bones are dust in the roses green dies from" to "the bride's bones are dust in the rose light green is sucked from" is tighter and more interesting. And "Some unknown aunt she could have been named for who might have been wild" seems wordier than "Some unknown aunt she could have been named for maybe wild, intense."

In a still more recent revision, I wanted to make the poem part of a group of seemingly autobiographical poems, so I changed the point of view from "she" to "I" to fit in with the other poems:

Some Nights I'm Raisel Devora
Dreaming of Old Houses in Russia

of licorice hair fire
licks as lace is
scorched, turns ash
before the wedding
and the bride's bones
are dust in the
rose light green
is sucked from as sun
sets in the afternoon.
Some unknown
aunt I could have
been named for maybe,
wild, intense as rare
tea roses or Rashmi
Rose incense burned in
a room the walls
pulled from floats
through frames that
are like mirrors, her
raw cheeks like
cherries in the rain
or blood from a wild
deer running, turning
snow color of plums

The most obvious changes here are the title and using "I" instead of "she."

As I have often done in the workshops I give, I have gone back to the other names and found there is something so evocative in them, something that connects me to a different time, place, and emotions that often surprise me with their immediacy and mystery, elements I value in poetry, and tried to uncover in Rose Devorah.

Lyn Lifshin has recently published *The Licorice Daughter*: *My Year with Ruffian* (Texas Review Press) and *Another Woman Who Looks Like Me* (Black

Sparrow). She has edited four anthologies of women's poems, is the subject of a documentary film, and has published over 120 books and chaps.

The Buck

SUSANNA RICH

Practically in its first draft (1989), my poem "The Buck" received an Honorable Mention in the *South Coast Poetry Journal* annual contest, and was published in June 1993. In 1995, "The Buck" — placed in the company of such poets as Margaret Atwood, Isabel Allende, Leslie Silko, and Sharon Olds — was reissued in a hardbound volume from Conari Press entitled *For She is the Tree of Life.* That the poem was so fully received so early in its development was both encouraging and, to me, misleading. While inventorying for a full-volume collection of my poems, I started, again, to edit "The Buck" and found confusions and missed opportunities. Although I will not attempt to fully digest all of what I have learned through this example of revision, I offer here some of my central concerns in crafting a poem: clarity of image, measures, the dismount. My main strategy for managing these concerns is anticipating alternative readings. Although in process my concerns are not always distinct, and I certainly don't revise in a linear, mechanical fashion, I distinguish them here.

Images

Because my poems are so visual, journals often choose to illustrate them. The *South Coast Poetry Journal* woodcut (below) both pleased and jarred me. In stanza four, the grandmother's hands are "reaching up to heaven." I had meant for the grandmother's arms and hands to be propped up and open, as if holding up an enormous bowl (as in popular religious iconography). The accompanying woodcut is a pair of gloved hands templed in prayer. Obviously, *reaching* in line 18 was vague. I hadn't fully anticipated variant readings of it — one of the constant and crucial challenges of writing.

The Buck

When I was ten,
Grandmother told me to get her
stuffed when she died
like the buck head by the door
catching evil in his antlers.

She was to be seated in the parlor,
on the sofa (or chair, our choice),
facing the piano where I would play
Brahms and Liszt and Chopin.

Her eyes were to be open
(maybe a little touch of glass,
for sparkle) and looking upwards
(slightly to the right)
like St. Theresa
or St. Sebastian pierced with arrows.
Her hands would be demurely gloved

in white lace fingerless gloves,
reaching up to heaven.
Her lips would be slightly parted to show
her silently parted pearlized teeth —
guardian angel, mouth of God —
telling me what to hear and speak.

We would never be alone at home.
When we went shopping for perfume,
or oil to treat her skin,
or maybe a new pair of gloves,
or a light bulb for her ever-burning lamp,
she and the buck
would wait for our return.
I'm four times the ten I was

but still banging at the keyboard all day:
dust floats up into my eyes, ears,
mouth, my nose and many pores —
shadow fingers reach
like antlers across the page.
She listens:
I sing.

In the Conari publication, the line about her hands reads "propped holding the dome of heaven," which makes it a more resonant, Atlasian burden. But some readers might object "How does that look? How do you hold a dome?" A too obvious way of visualizing *holding* is placing hands on top of a domed structure. Since "dome" is almost a cliché of sacred architecture — a word too easily glossed over in this context — I changed the word to "bowl" — "propped holding the bowl of heaven." This is clearer. If we imagine a bowl inscribing a half-circle, most people will hold it with two open hands placed at 4:00 and 8:00 o'clock. The bottom of a bowl is more like a grandmotherly breast. In addition, this image more clearly evokes statues of saints with hands open to catch heavenly blessings.

Conari Press Version

The Buck

When I was ten,
Grandmother told me
to get her stuffed when she died
like the buck head by the door
catching webs of evil
in his antlers.

She was to be seated
in the living room
on the sofa
(or chair, our choice),
facing the piano where I would play
Brahms, Liszt, and Chopin.

Her eyes were to be open
(maybe a little touch of glass,
for sparkle), and looking upwards
(slightly to the right)
like St. Theresa
or Sebastian pierced with arrows,

her hands — demurely covered
in white lace fingerless gloves —
propped holding the dome of heaven.
Her lips would be slightly open to show
silently parted pearlized teeth —
guardian angel, mouth of God.

When we went shopping for perfume,
or oil to treat her skin,
or maybe a new pair of gloves,
or a light bulb for her ever-burning lamp,
she and the buck would wait for our return.

Four times the ten I was,
I still bang a keyboard all day;
dust floats up into my eyes, ears,
mouth, my nose and many pores —
shadow fingers reach
like antlers across my page.
She listens: I sing.

Measures

Stanzas. In the *South Coast* draft, the stanza lengths vary from four, four, six, seven, and seven lines to the sprawl of the last stanza, eight lines. In a poem about evil, it would be much more effective to trade on the regular rhythms and repetitions of magic. It is through the focus on just such elements that the ancient Greeks believed the poet is able to receive *inspiration*. I often count lines to discern if any pattern is emerging. Intuitively, I had end-stopped all the first draft stanzas (periods and one enjambment on a comma), thus reflecting an unconscious need to contain a threatening idea. I knew I had to standardize stanza lengths as well. But how?

One clue was that the *South Coast* draft had six stanzas. Was that number significant? Another clue came from Revelations: the devil's number is 666. I adopted the number 6 as a formal device, to explore and enhance the feeling of evil in the poem. For the Conari version of "The Buck," I recast all but the last two of six stanzas into six lines. I had faltered in the penultimate and final stanzas, which had five and seven lines, respectively. There was something *tacked on*, overmanaged in that last stanza, even in revision. If, as in a crossword puzzle, there is a right answer, if a verse interprets itself — it might distance the reader. "She listens: I sing" is too obvious a reflection onto the poem: Look, I'm singing by writing this poem. The device of making the poem be about the poem has been overused. That kind of interpretation must be subtle, or a Billy Collins tweak, but not facile. Also, "She listens: I sing" lay the poem to rest, so to speak — condonable in the context of *writing* this poem, but not, perhaps, in realizing Federico Garcia Lorca's *duende* — that quality of great art that embraces danger, which "is a power and not a construct, is a struggle and not a concept." Most recently, I lopped that safe last line, and earned the poem its sixes and some more of its dangers. In the draft that precedes the current draft, there were six stanzas with six lines each.

Current Version

The Buck

Grandmother told me
to get her stuffed when she died
like the buck head by the door,
catching webs of evil
in his antlers.

She was to be seated
in the livingroom
on the sofa
(or chair, our choice).
facing the piano where I would play
Brahms, Liszt, and Chopin.

Her eyes were to be open

(maybe a little touch of glass,
for sparkle), and looking upward
(slightly to the right)
like Saint Theresa
or Saint Sebastian pierced with arrows.

Her hands would be demurely gloved
in white lace fingerless gloves,
propped holding the dome of heaven.
Her lips would be slightly parted to show
silently parted pearlized teeth—
my very own mouth, channeling God.

I would never be alone.
When I went shopping for perfume,
or oil to treat her skin,
or a bulb for her lamp in perpetuum —
she and the buck would
wait for my return.

Four times the ten I was,
I bang at a keyboard all day;
dust floats up into my eyes,
my mouth, my many pores —
shadow fingers reach
across this page.

Pronouns. I made another shift toward danger. In the previous drafts, the fifth stanzas include reference to a *we:* "We would never be alone. / When we went shopping." This late introduction of an unspecified *we* is confusing — up to this point, it had been just grandma and narrator. "We would never be alone" raises questions: Who is the *we?* It can't be the grandmother — she can't shop. Nor can the buck or God. Has someone else entered the poem? Who? Does the *we* include, without the reader's acquiescence, the reader herself or himself? Maybe. But the surface reading must imply a particular. In retrospect, it seems that the *we* was creating a proverbial safety in numbers (just as manipulating numbers, during writing, is a way to steady the psyche).

From the first person plural, I shifted to the first person singular — "I would never be alone" — and was rewarded with a chilling ambiguity. In the current draft, although the enjambment between the last line of stanza four and the first of stanza five means that the grandmother's mouth would channel God, syntactically "my very own mouth" collapses the grandmother's mouth into the narrator's. The stanza break on "my very own mouth" creates a syntactic tension that propels the reader on. No longer is there the relative security of the first three end-stopped stanzas — the last three each are unpunctuated cliffs precipitating the following stanza. No period ends the last.

Metrics. In the current draft, I scanned the poem's metrics, and was pleased to see that many of the lines move in trochees, the stressed–unstressed rhythm that governs, to use a popular example, the song from *The Phantom of the Opera*, "The Music of the Night." In the English language, in the human heartbeat, in the left-right of walking, the standard beat is the iamb — unstressed, stressed. To characterize it from a rightist perspective — start out weak, end up strong. Both "The Music of the Night" and "The Buck" reverse that tendency, as evil does, to the start-out-strong, end-up-weak metaphysics of the trochee and the dactyl. I was pleased, as well, to find that in the first stanza there were two terminal anapests — unstressed, unstressed, stressed — a skipping, exuberant, comic metric; a relief in the context of this poem. *The Music of the Night* also counterpoints trochees with terminal anapests. Humor and energy provide aesthetic relief and entertainment to enchant the reader, much as the beauty of "The Music of the Night" might disarm, allure not only the character Christine, in *The Phantom of the Opera*, but also the audience.

Another important metrical move for "The Buck" was the four comforting iambs in the exact central line of the poem: "Her hands would be demurely gloved." This is a resting place and launching point into the darkness of the last three stanzas.

"The Buck" had early found its music and its tone — which might explain its early acceptances. So there weren't as many changes to make metrically by the current draft. Nonetheless, I did drop the "St." before "Sebastian." Rhythmically, the extra unstressed syllable was more like a hiccup. Note also, the last line of stanza four. The caesura is flanked by two identical metric patterns: trochee / iamb; trochee / iamb. If I hadn't changed the line for the reasons mentioned — to create a horrible collapse of personal boundaries — this metrical pattern might, in the context of this poem, have inspired me to question this line. Two identical metrics haunt each other across the break between stanzas five and six, much as the grandmother and narrator do across the line between life and death.

The Dismount

The end of the poem, especially the last line, is analogous to a gymnast's dismount. This is where the reader is forever lost or, at least temporarily, won: Will the poem linger beyond this reading? To paraphrase Robert Frost: anyone can get into a poem. It takes a poet (or, I might add, a poetic reader, for it is the reader who ultimately brings the poem to life) to get out of the poem.

I had started the first drafts of "The Buck" with the information that the narrator is ten years old. Rethinking it, I felt that cast a political pall over the poem — How could the grandmother ask that a ten-year-old get her stuffed when she died? The line — at the outset of the poem, when the tabula rasa of the reader is being imprinted — might invite righteous indignation and not a deeper, more resonant reading. I transferred the line to the last stanza, compressing it with mention of the narrator's current age — to establish that time had passed. It is more chilling to discover, late in the poem — when the reader has become absorbed in the logic of it — that a ten-year-old had been told to have taxidermy performed on her grandmother. And since the knowledge comes so late — when the drive toward the poem's end should be most intense — it doesn't invite mere moralizing as it might have earlier on. This made me rethink the number of lines in the first stanza. Why not start the poem with five lines, a more comforting number — the number of digits on a healthy hand? The poem is, after all, filled with hands, and it is written with hands. Then the shift to six-line stanzas would feel more dissonant and disturbing. On another reading, the title of a poem can be seen as its first line. Thus, for "The Buck," the title/first line is followed by an ominous white-space chasm dropping us into a surreal experience — and the rest of the first stanza. So read, "The Buck" retains its devilish sixes.

The last stanza of a poem can also be thought of as a runway — can't have guy wires dragging the accelerating plane. The eyes, ears, nose of the earlier drafts were too many things up into which the dust was to float. Also, reference to *eyes, ears, nose* strung together is a cliché list seen on doctors' signs. To edit down to eyes, hands, and mouth creates a direct parallel to the stuffed grandmother: stanzas three and four focus on her eyes, hands, and mouth. This enriches the poem, implicates the narrator, and forgives the grandmother: *we are no different*. Realized poetry seeks to embody universals: what we bear in common.

I gnawed through several prepositions for the last line — *above, into, over* — before settling on *across* that page. First, the embedded "cross" is a religious symbol. But more important is what can be gleaned from a deconstructive reading of "across the page": (a cross, the page) = (the page is a cross). This satisfies the need to contain, and through writing, to defend against/manage the evil. Read thus, the reader is asked to note, or note again, that the grandmother in the story who, although asking for something bizarre and unnatural, is using religious imagery, is defending against the unnatural as well. I considered how I might anticipate "page" — with *my* or *that*.

To state that the shadow fingers are reaching "antlers" across the page is to tell the reader how to interpret the image — again, the overmanaging. It is too large of a knowing wink, and robs the reader of the pleasure of *getting it*. To allow the *specific* image to linger is to invite the reader not only to ask the questions *Whose? How? How long?* but to answer them for herself or himself — to be co-creator of the poem — to find resonances and depths I couldn't have anticipated. For the reader casts shadows on the page, as the narrator does. And those fingers reaching? Perhaps they are the shadows of the reviser. Perhaps they are also … well — the poem is entitled "The Buck." I pass it to you.

Professor of English at Kean University in New Jersey, Susanna Rich produces and hosts an online radio program, *Poets on Air*. Her work appears in dozens of publications, including *Birmingham Poetry Review, Carquinez Poetry Review, English Journal, Feminist Studies, Journal of New Jersey Poets, Kalliope, Nimrod, The Paterson Poetry Review, Phoebe* (both NY and VA), *Poem, South Carolina Review, Sulphur River Literary Review, Visions: International, Willow Review,* and *Zone 3*. She was awarded the first joint Fulbright and Collegium Budapest Fellowships in Creative Writing to complete "Still Hungary: A Memoir." "Lullaby: A Cradle Song" won first prize for personal essay at *Fugue*, and is listed as a "Notable Essay" in *The Best American Essays: 2004*. Her book *The Flexible Writer*, published by Allyn & Bacon, is now in its fourth edition.

Memorial Day Storm

Juleigh Howard-Hobson

First Draft

A sky gone white with cloud and flinging rain

This is the beginning of the poetic process, the writing down of what impelled me to start thinking, poetically. It is literal, it is factual, it is what I saw outside my window, it is written down exactly as it came to me. It does not last two seconds once I write it down. I re-read and rewrite instantly. Note that I wrote, instinctively, in iambic pentameter. It is not conscious at this point; it's simply how I, as a Neo-Formalist (some call me a "classicist") poet, think ... poetically speaking.

Second Draft

Under a sky gone white with cloud and flinging rain
Birds land on wet grass and shake their dripping wings

Here I play with the opening, adding iambs, going for the next line — this second rewrite has no proper meter, and does not rhyme yet. I decided that it was, in fact, much too concrete and trite to continue in this manner. I abandon this whole beginning, although I hold on to the idea behind it.

Third Draft

Damp petals wash from even damper trees
To fall along the grass and fence

This is closer to the poetical vision for me, less concrete, more imaginative, more aesthetic. Again, this is written in iambs, automatically. The consonance of the s sound and the assonance of the a sound add to the complete aesthetic I am innately searching for.

Fourth Draft

Damp petals washed from even damper trees
Fall along the grass and fence to cling,
White and

This is a continuation of the last rewrite, changing from the present tense ("wash") to the past ("washed") and expanding on the sentence. I have not included enough syllables in line two to make it true iambic pentameter, and I do not finish the sentence, although I add to the poetical feel by matching the *f* of "fall" to "fence." I ended up not liking this beginning; the image of wet petals washed up and clinging to various garden items just didn't match the inner vision I was attempting to reveal: how an untimely, unexpected, late hard rain affects everything.

Fifth Draft

Reflected in puddles, wet daffodils
Lean, pushed down by wind, held down by rain
Each yellow petal weighted in

This is my third start. I am beginning to see what it is that I want to relate: spring flowers, waterlogged and wasted, because a rain that should not have come, came anyway. I do not have the iambs completely correct — line 2 is one syllable short; line 3 is simply left discontinued.

Sixth Draft

Reflected in puddles, the daffodils

I decide that I want to switch "wet daffodils" to "the daffodils" since it goes without saying that the daffodils are wet. I discontinue this draft abruptly as I also decide that, poetically speaking, daffodils are too clichéd. Wordsworth had the final say on daffodils.

Seventh Draft

Reflected in puddles the flowers lean

Down against the pelting rain. Bright petals
Cast the more vivid against the grey still
Quality of the unmoving clouds, ill
Suited for this last spring storm — unforeseen
But arriving and down pouring

Here, changing the specific "daffodils" to the more general "flowers,"
I suddenly am able to realize a true draft of this poem. The consonance of
f is brought into play in line 1, as counterpoint to an abrupt *d*, which dramatically plunges the reader into the beginning of line 2. The assonance of
the short *a* and *e'* threaded throughout the poem, brings a compact conti-
nuity to the work, as well as ushering in a comfortable soft sound that is
jarred, like the flowers themselves, by the hard consonants of words such
as "pelting," "bright," "pouring." I discontinue this draft as I realize that
the rhyme scheme that I have chosen (abccab) will be difficult to sustain
when the last line must find a good, and seemingly effortless, rhyme for
"petals." I like the brevity of this poem, which I have decided not to extend to further stanzas; it is somewhat like a cloudburst, or a glimpse —
strong, forceful, yet very, brief. I do not have a title yet.

Eighth Draft

Reflected in puddles the flowers lean
Down against the pelting rain. Bright petals
Cast the more vivid against the stillness
Inherent in the wet stormy clouds, ill
Suited for this last spring storm—unforeseen
Arriving and down pouring none the less.

Here I play with alternative words within the poem. Substituting "stillness" for "greyness," and the words "inherent in the wet stormy clouds"
for earlier words.

Upon re-reading this, I instantly see that I have used "stormy" in line
4, followed by "storm" in line 5, which is much too repetitive. I make the
rhyme scheme abcbac. Also, the last word in line 5 is too jarring; it does
not flow as nicely as I would like it to. I want the very last words to stand
out; as it is, the word *unforeseen* stands out, and it should not.

Ninth Draft

Reflected in puddles the flowers lean
Down against the pelting rain. Bright petals —
Cast the more vivid against the grayness
Gathered up in the wet darkened clouds — ill
Suited for this last spring storm: unforeseen
By any, but arriving nonetheless.

Here I use the alliterativeness of hard *g* to sweep the reader along from lines 3 to 4, imitating the hard sweep of the rain itself. I like this version, the words flow, helped along by the consonances, assonances, and alliterative devices I've worked out in the various drafts, ending with the streaming *s* in line 5 that gives way, suddenly, to the hard *b* that opens the ending line. The sounds of the first two words in the last line are immediately echoed in the next two lines, which give the very last word *nonetheless* a standout feel, which is what I was after. But, still, I feel that this piece is not quite right, although I know now that it is a matter of fine-tuning rather than rewriting, now, to perfect this poem.

Tenth Draft

Reflected in puddles, the flowers lean
Down against the pelting rain. Bright petals —
Cast the more vivid against the grayness
Gathered up in the darkened clouds — are ill
Suited for this last spring storm: unforeseen
By any, but arriving ... nonetheless.

I have taken out "wet" and added "are" so that the sentence makes more sense. Adding the ellipses before the final word creates a poetical tension, and a sense that nature will do what nature will do ... nonetheless, which is the theme of this piece (and a favorite theme of this poet). Here, with the fine-tuning almost all done, I step back and notice that the vagueness of the poem doesn't work. It is too short a piece to be anything less than precise.

Final Draft

Memorial Day Storm

Reflected in puddles, red poppies lean
Down against the pelting rain. Their petals —
Cast the more scarlet against the grayness
Gathered up in the darkened clouds — are ill
Suited for this last spring storm: unforeseen
By any, but arriving ... nonetheless.

I decide that "the flowers" in line 1 is far too generic, and too much like other poems that share this theme. Changing it to "red poppies," I am able to make this a distinct scene, which the reader can see. I also change the vague "vivid" to the very specific "scarlet" in line 3, tightening up the imagery once again. Scarlet against grey is a nice dramatic picture. Titling this poem "Memorial Day Storm" brings the fact that the flowers are poppies to an ironic point. Poppies are symbolically used in memorials to our war-torn dead, which nature, always impartial, does not heed. "War is a problem of mankind, not nature" is one way to look at this poem's message. Another is "as we let warriors go to their wasted deaths, so nature disposes of her creations (this time, poppies) as heedlessly, too."

An Australian Anzac Day Award-winning poet, Juleigh Howard-Hobson's new formalist work has appeared or will appear in *The Raintown Review, On The Wing, The Australian Women's Weekly, Seven Cups of Coffee, Macquarie University's Arena, Focus, Odin's Gift, The Girl's Book of Success* (a child's poem; Little, Brown), *Bewildering Stories, Flipside Magazine, Shatter Colors Literary Review, Idunna, The Hypertexts, Strong Verse, Mezzo Cammin, Workers Write!,* and *Champagne Shivers 2007.*

Birthday Tulips

Elizabeth Farrell

The trigger for writing the poem "Birthday Tulips" was hearing the news that a friend's son had died in a drunk-driving accident. My own son, who was about to turn 24, was thriving and for the first time too busy to celebrate his birthday with his family. Every year as a young boy, he would pick out a pot of tulips for his birthday. I began to think about how one can lose a son from many kinds of possible deaths. It was from that perspective that I asked myself how one continues the rituals to mark a special day when the person you love is absent. I was feeling sorry for myself as a mother, and guilty for harboring those feelings when my son was alive, and another mother's son was dead. My intention was to write a poem to commemorate the annual event in which we would no longer participate together, in a manner that could invite anyone into the poem to relive birthday memories.

I began with the title, "Birthday Tulips," for in its simplicity that is what I thought the poem was going to be about. The title became a kind of guide that kept me close to the main idea of the poem. It instructed me to stay on the subject while allowing me the freedom to explore what the two words of the title suggested.

With those two words typed on the computer screen, I allowed a free flow of words to fall into their natural rhythm and line breaks as I typed full throttle on the topic of love, letting go, motherhood, and spring. In the first draft, I let the poem make itself, tell me what it wanted me to know, rather than the other way around. I continued typing until I reached the near end of the page, my preference being that the poem should be contained on one page only.

At that point, I rose from my seat, and allowed the poem to rest, like one puts a towel over bread dough to let the yeast do its work. I took a walk. I returned to the computer screen to read the first draft several times to see what small story might exist beyond my own personal lamenting, not wanting it to be a purely confessional poem. My objective was to begin from my own personal experience, but then to flesh out an emotional connection that might reach another person in a broader context. Working on the computer rather than writing on paper allows me to move words quickly and to immediately see the shape of the poem.

First Draft

Birthday Tulips

It is hard to know what color
the tulips will become without the tag
telling you. The buds are so tight
that without x-ray vision no one
can see through the green cover,
though my fingers try to unwrap
the tender bud packages to peek
for a hint of red, yellow, white.

This is like the boy who grows up
into a young man. Anxious to know
what he might become, how he would
look, what words he might say.

You can not hurry a marvelous thing,
especially where there is mystery
hidden inside the promise for a beautiful
pot of birthday tulips. I take my chances
and pick the one with the most buds,
the most possibility of blooms to come.

Today is the first birthday where he
is working and can not come home
for his mother's imperfectly made cake
with lighted candles for him to blow out.
He has his own wishes not lighted by
my match, his own ways to celebrate
how he has become a man.

The tulips, then, are for me this year.
I watch them daily unfold into a brilliant
blood red; the red of his birth, the red
of my memory for the passion of his coming.

The first draft is a kind of map for me to discover what is underneath the original layer of words. The tulips themselves as a metaphor for growth and change was an obvious image, and I decided to let it speak for itself without all the guessing-game words in the first verse: "x-ray vision," for example, was a young image, a fun idea, but no longer served the larger purpose of the poem. We all have experience of wanting to look at a tag or peek beneath the lid of a birthday box, and I was thinking of that with wanting to know the color of the buds. However, as I began to see the whole notion of growth and change coupled with the sense of the mysterious in our own growth as well, I wanted to eliminate words and ideas that were too specific. Therefore, the entire second verse about the boy growing into a man seemed unnecessary, and in following that line of thought I deleted most of the third verse. What became most important for the poem to communicate was found in the lines "You can not hurry a marvelous thing, / especially where there is a mystery." I realized from that point that I needed to remove the reason for my son's not being home for his birthday, and in the fourth verse withdrew the words "he is working," thereby returning to the trigger for writing the poem: a response to the death of another woman's son and the ongoing celebration of my own son's life. In this way, I wanted to further open up the poem to suggest there could be a number of reasons a loved one might not be present.

The lines "can not come home / for his mother's imperfectly made cake" became "is not home / to eat the cake his mother makes"; to be fed by the mother is an important universal image. Finally, a recognition that "He has his own wishes not lighted by / my match, his own ways to celebrate / how he has become a man" I edited for a broader interpretation to "He lights his wishes by his own match," which both affirms his independence and the mother's loss of being needed in the same way, hence the lament of the mother having to let go of her son, and in this case, the ritual of buying the tulips together.

"The tulips, then, are for me this year" became in the edited version, "The tulips, then, are a gift to myself," as I saw the gift of the son born to the mother as the ultimate gift, reflected in "the tulips" those "blood red skins of his birth" mirroring the physical act of giving birth and the memory of that reality come full circle in the birthday tulips themselves. Like the life process itself, I wanted the completed poem to offer and hold its own mystery.

Final Draft

Birthday Tulips

It is hard to know what color the tulips
will become, though my fingers try
to unwrap the tender bud packages.

You can not hurry a marvelous thing,
especially where there is mystery.

This is the first birthday he is not home
to eat the cake his mother makes.
He lights his wishes by his own match.

The tulips, then, are a gift to myself,
revealing the blood red skins of his birth.

Elizabeth Farrell's poems have appeared in many journals, including *Proposing on the Brooklyn Bridge, Animus, Penumbra, Calliope, The Onset Review, New Bedford Magazine,* and *Eleventh Muse.* Formerly, she was an advertising copywriter in Chicago, Illinois.

La Poir Hautaine

TRACY KORETSKY

Here is my original draft:

October's Last

You, who were too high,
have fallen.
Your blush now
browns toward bruise.
You, who dizzied the bees
with the sway of your bountiful bottom,
who flirted behind your green fan,
were not picked.
Your sweet messages,
at first coy then cloying,
were perfume for the sparrows
who mocked you with kisses
that opened you and scarred,
as those below you
offered themselves to hands
and were taken,
still warm, into grateful lips.

I was not satisfied with the line breaks in my first draft. The punctuation always appeared, rather predictably, I felt, at the end of the line. That meant that many lines began with weak, unengaging, words.

I experimented with two approaches to breaking my lines: counting stressed beats and counting syllables. For example, this draft has four stressed beats per line (the number following the line indicates syllables):

You, who were **too high**, have **fall**en. 8
Your **blush** now **browns** toward **bruise. You,** 7

who **dizz**ied the **bees** with the **sway** of your **boun**tiful 13
bottom, who **flirt**ed be**hind** your **green** 9

fan, were **not picked.** Your **sweet** 6
messages, at **first coy** then **cloy**ing, 9

were **perfume** for **spar**rows who **mock**ed with **kiss**es 11
that **op**ened and **marr**ed, as **those** be**low** you 10

offered them**selves** to **hand**s and were **tak**en, 10
still warm, into **grate**ful **lips.**7

And this draft has three stressed beats per line:

You, who were **too high,**
have **fall**en. Your **blush** now **browns**
toward **bruise. You,** who **dizz**ied

the **bees** with the **sway** of your **boun**tiful
bottom, who **flirt**ed be**hind**
your **green fan,** were **not**

picked. Your **sweet mes**sages,
at **first coy** then **cloy**ing,
were **perfume** for **spar**rows who **mock**ed

with **kiss**es that **op**ened and **marr**ed
as **those** be**low** you **off**ered them**selves**
to **hand**s and were **tak**en, **still**

warm, into **grate**ful **lips.**

These did not please me because the result was a squat, short poem
with irregular lines, whereas I was discussing a tall, shapely, tree. I decided
to try using equal syllables because that can often lead to lines of similar
lengths. I counted a total of ninety syllables. This version has five syllables
per line:

You, who were too high, have
fallen. Your blush now browns
toward bruise. You, who dizzied
the bees with the sway of
your bountiful bottom,

who flirted behind your
green fan, were not picked. Your
sweet messages, at first
coy then cloying were perfume
for sparrows who mocked with
kisses that opened and
marred, as those below you
offered themselves to hands
and were taken, still warm,
into grateful lips.

That is, it almost has five syllables per line, note that the line with "perfume" did not quite work, nor did the last line fill out. If I had chosen this arrangement, I might have cut or added words to make them fit or I might have decided to ignore my own rule.

Notice too that the problem of always beginning lines with weak words is completely fixed in this draft.

Ultimately, the only way to choose, after making a dozen or so similar experiments, is to put the poem away and come back to it later. So, in about a week, I looked at the poem again. With my vision refreshed, the choice seemed obvious. I liked the long narrow version with two stressed beats per line. I felt it looked elegant, created some interesting enjambments and allowed the punctuation and the stronger words to disperse unpredictably.

Two stressed beats per line gave me twenty lines, so I decided to divide them into five stanzas. My idea was that this was a poem about a pear that thought it was too good to be eaten, so imposing a sort of fussy, formal structure upon it seemed to support the meaning.

Finally, I needed a title. I thought of:

To an Unpicked Pear
To You Who Reached Over the Eaves
Late Fall
To a Pretentious Pear
La Poir Hautaine

The last, which means "The Haughty Pear" in French, struck me as rather funny. It seemed like a haughty choice. This, combined with the somewhat fussy structure of two stresses per line and four lines per stanza, serves to poke a little fun at the pear. My hope is that it pokes a little gentle fun at the kind of people who are like the pear as well, people who might choose a French expression over an English one just to show off. Here is my final version:

La Poir Hautaine

You, who were too
high, have fallen.
Your blush now browns
toward bruise. You,

who dizzied the bees
with the sway of your bountiful
bottom, who flirted
behind your green

fan, were not
picked. Your sweet
messages, at first
coy then cloying,

were perfume for sparrows
who mocked with kisses
that opened and marred,
as those below you

offered themselves
to hands and were taken,
still warm,
into grateful lips.

Tracy Koretsky is the author of *Ropeless*, a fifteen-time award-winning novel that offers fresh perspectives on disability. Tracy Koretsky's poetry and short fiction have been widely published in literary magazines, including *Potomac Review*, *Kalliope*, and *Phantasmagoria*. She earned more than fifty awards for her three novels and her widely published short fiction, poetry, and essays, including three Pushcart nominations. She is on the editorial staff of *Triplopia*.

A Letter from L.A.

RHODA GREENSTONE

Demolition of historical landmarks seems to be a frequent pastime in Los Angeles. When I heard of the demolition of The Hollywood Studio Club, my frustration and worry over history sacrificed for greed turned to anger and grief. For decades, the Hollywood Studio Club furnished room and board for girls from all over the country. While seeking their fame and fortune, the Studio Club girls were relatively safe under the watchful gaze of principled chaperones who made sure no men ever followed the starlets and young artists (some of whom actually became famous) past the lobby. "Our Studio Club" was the place two close girlfriends and I often congregated during those joyful first years of college, when life lay in front of us like an endless feast. It was the demolition of a landmark so vivid in my memory — on the heels of the terrible news that one of my oldest friends had suddenly died — that provoked "A Letter from L.A."

Composing a poem is a premeditated activity for me, an intense, disciplined process that is only briefly caressed by romantic inspiration. In plain words, crafting a poem is hard work. I'll admit the beginning of my poem was inspired. Lines 1–13 came quite easily, a lyrical marriage of idea and imagery. Initially, I let the remainder "write itself." It is important that I let the first draft come in any way it dictates, letting it flow freely without censorship or editorializing. Otherwise, there won't be a poem to work on.

From the start, I envisioned a poem that would juxtapose natural with artificial metaphors. The lyrical, nostalgic elements would be kept (I hope) from becoming trite by arrangement of oxymoronic images (the lovely hills choking on "dandruff chalk").

First Version

Letter to Lin Baum

In L.A.
The hills of the Ventura Freeway
Choke on dandruff chalk
Bordering Oxnard

Eucalyptus breathes
Greensilver mint all the way
To Montalvo

Near Santa Barbara
The clover and the cactus smile
Opening for a lover

The lover stops for a kiss
Hovers offering
Is won over

Remember when we picked out geography
From an airplane window
It can't be that long ago

The Santa Inez Mountains are purple
Their strong necks rub
Up against jayblue
The roads are vacant

Could it really be years
Since you dressed the view
Between L.A. and San Francisco

Fine time
Wish you were here
Always
Rho

The first draft seemed trite. Also, it didn't convey the message or feelings I intended. I am not a minimalist. Clearly, key ideas weren't represented. One of my goals in writing a poem is to make a point about something, or to bring something to light that might have been overlooked, or to create a fresh perspective so readers will look at an old thing with new eyes. My objective in the first draft of "Letter" is hidden in obscurity. I needed to add more concrete allusions, when my closest friend and I were drunk on life and on top of the world.

Therefore, I introduce the "Latin lover" who not only was an actual pivotal figure in both of our lives, but refers to the Latin influence seen on every historical mile of southern California from El Camino Real to the missions my friend and I drove through. Additionally, I met the friend of this poem when we both enrolled in a dynamic college geology class. Stanza five is infused with touches of reality that I believe help "ground" a poem, keeping it from becoming too abstract, while giving readers tangibles to visualize or smell or taste or hear or feel. I clarified the "geography" by alluding to the physical "monadnocks" and "horsts" in the third version. Instead of the impressionistic "jayblue" of earlier versions, I substituted "eternal blue" in stanza seven.

Because poetry is the condensation of language (more about that later), it is important to think economically. Redundancy really can't compete with Stein's "a rose is a rose is a rose" at this late date in literary history, unless there is some satiric or emphatic purpose for it (as is the case with "raise" and "raze" in line 25). Therefore, I wrestled with myself over which specific objects to include as vehicles to drive my points home (see the reductions from three to two relative objects between the second and final versions): "Rome and New York" were as effective as "Chicago or Rome or New York" (although I admit I'm not totally confident that choosing New York best conveys my meaning since Chicago was a watershed city for both my late friend and me, and since it is midpoint in the United States — tomorrow I might change my word choice to read "Rome and Chicago." It is difficult to know when to stop working on the thing).

Since a true free verse form would contradict the major themes of "Letter from L.A.," by the second version, I had manicured the freeform lines into tercets. Neater. Tighter. However, always alert to the economic selection of syllables or sounds that constitute a poetic foot, I feel my greatest responsibility is to *revitalize* the language of poetry. I find it exciting to run across a word like "monadnock" in a poem rather than bump into a dull old "bump." Which feels more alive? Again word choice is extremely subjective — some may think I'm nuts to include "monadnock" and "horst." Likewise, in line 22, how much more fun is the trope "dong dim" than the vaguely evocative "dawn dim" of the second version? Well, it was fun for me!

If I repeat a pattern that has been used for hundreds of years — which may well complement some other contemporary poem — it would subvert the action of "Letter from L.A." If I rely on traditional metric and rhyme schemes, not only will the poem show the stress of being stuffed into a whalebone corset, it will dress my message in antique lace when I want it to feel as contemporary as letting it all hang out in Saran Wrap. I take that back — I wouldn't like it quite that loosely idiomatic! How much pop culture does it take to overwhelm poetics? The answer not only depends on the writer's intentions, but how much the piece might date itself, snag itself on faddish terms that age quickly. An award-winning poet I respect has allowed the colloquial "you" to creep into his usually taut and neat verse. Frankly, his liberal adoption of "you" reduces his language to a far too common denominator for me to read his work with the same seriousness I once did.

To orchestrate unexpected sounds and accents may lead to a new way of seeing or hearing the language. Although my metrics are a conscious effort to allude to classical poetic forms, I labor over craft that won't be confined to or by too restricting a structure. Formalist constrictions shouldn't show here. Look at the first stanza: the poem starts with anapests, but the third line is nearly all spondees (as is line 12 and all the lines in the final stanza). Spondees are not only good when emphasizing words, but they slow down momentum. I remember reading that Shakespeare wrote in iambic pentameter because that was the most familiar speech pattern in his time. I find my writing patterns fall into spondaic and anapestic feet most of the time, but I'm not really interested in speech patterns in my poems. Most of the time I leave speech to my prose, although I have written a few dramatic monologues that relied heavily on speech.

Doggerel, such outworn patterns as a/a rhyming (dog/smog), or even abab (dog/root, smog/boot) carry inside them predetermined readings. For example, we have comic expectations from a scheme that goes "There was a young boy from New York / Who had to eat all food with a fork...." For the sake of a refreshing harmony and unity, I push for interrelated internal rhymes, which I feel create much livelier patterns than end rhymes. Mostly I am interested in achieving the unexpected, in achieving a surprise that will jolt a reader out of complacency. However, I do have the occasional lyrical end rhyme that I include for the purpose of bringing natural images into strong relief with corrupted ones in this piece. The "L.A." of line 1 and "Freeway" of line 2 are struck immediately against the hard "chalk" and "Oxnard" of the following lines. It should be evident that my poems often break their own rules if the broken rules result in an interesting new juxtaposition of words or conjuring of images.

Once the working parts that carry the message seem to be in the right order, I orchestrate by reaching for sounds (near rhymes) that will connect one word to another ("breathes" in line 4 to "Greensilver" that begins line 5), or connect a word to another line ("lover" of lines 9 and 10 to "Hovers" beginning line 11), or connect one stanza to another ("L.A." echoing in the first, seventh, and tenth stanzas). I labor over sounds that will harmonize with the diverse parts, often turning to dictionaries and thesauruses. Notice how I avoid the harshness of sibilance in my repetitive soft s-word endings: *cactus*, stanza 3; *kiss* and *immortalizes*, stanza 4. Often internal *a* or *o* or *e* serve to tie lines together. Notice as well how stanzas six and seven and stanzas seven and eight exhibit enjambment, so they elide, building momentum toward the end.

Second Version

Last Letter to Lin Baum

In L.A.
The hills of the Ventura Freeway
Choke on sage-gray dandruff chalk

Bordering Oxnard
Eucalyptus breathes
Greensilver mint all the way to Montalvo

Near Santa Barbara
The clover and the cactus smile
Opening for a Cuban lover

The lover stoops for a kiss
Hovers offering
Is temporarily won over

Remember when we selected our own geography
From an airplane we dubbed monadnocks
And horsts as they pointed up to us

The Santa Inez mountains are purple

Their strong necks rub against the jayblue
Their back roads are vacant and still waiting

For that square song ("The Hussle?") we hummed that sum-
mer and
Fall, ingenues attuned to L.A. and San Francisco
Was it after Chicago or Rome or New York the music diffused

During those dawn dim infrared a.m.s
During those thinlipped p.m.s that made us women
The Pan Pacific Auditorium went up in flames and

They razed Carthay Circle to raise a parking structure
Some things change that much; try to forget
There was enough wild marjoram then to deodorize The Valley

Fine time Wish we were there
Signed A Friend in L.A.

Third Version

A Letter from L.A.

In L.A.
The hills of the Ventura Freeway
Choke on sage-gray dandruff chalk

Bordering Oxnard
Eucalyptus breathes
Greensilver mint all the way to Montalvo

Near Santa Barbara
The clover and the cactus smile
Opening for a Latin lover

The lover stoops for a kiss
Hovers attempts to implant
A scrapbook memory

Remember when we preempted geology
From an airplane we fingered monadnocks
And horsts before they pointed up to us

The Santa Inez Mountains are purple
Their strong necks rub against eternal blue
Their back roads are vacant and still awaiting

That square song ("The Hussle?") we ta-dummed all
Fall, ingenues attuning to L.A. and San Francisco
Was it after Rome or New York we dropped the chorus

During those dong dim infrared a.m.s
During those thinlipped p.m.s that chiseled us
The Pan Pacific Auditorium went up in flames and

They razed Carthay Circle to raise a parking structure
Our Studio Club implodes today; forget then wild marjoram
At the tar pits was plentiful enough to deodorize Van Nuys

Fine time
Wish we were there
Signed A Friend in L.A.

The final draft is difficult to determine. Some of the words, maybe even whole lines, won't shut up, won't allow me to put the poem to bed. Some won't stop rubbing my psyche the wrong way. I feel uneasy because a word isn't a good fit or it is imprecise, both of which are absolute no-no's for a poem. Ambiguity, which is good because it stimulates the imagination, is not the same as fogginess, which is bad because it obscures or bores the reader, the worst thing a poem can do.

Sometimes it turns out words miss the mark and need to be reconsidered. Notice stanza five. I hope you can see why I struggled for weeks before settling on "spoke" over "selected" or "defined geology." And after all has been done and redone in the body of the poem, the title requires scrutiny since the poem has grown so much from its inception.

Then a poet may look at the end result of weeks of poetic deliberation only to say, "But that's not what I meant at all. That's not it at all!" The irony of ironies is that the finished poem, perfected or otherwise, ends up the reader's property anyway. Yes, while I am composing, I am controlling the process, but it is the reader who will read or misread, the reader who will give the poem life or kill it.

Let us make sure a great poem doesn't die from anonymity. Write, read, circulate before executing one more poem!

Final Version

A Letter from L.A.

In L.A.
The hills of the Ventura Freeway
Choke on sage-gray dandruff chalk

Bordering Oxnard
Eucalyptus breathes
Greensilver mint all the way to Montalvo

Near Santa Barbara
The clover and the cactus smile
Opening for a Latin lover

The lover stoops for a kiss
Hovers immortalizes
A scrapbook memory

Remember when we spoke geology
From an airplane we fingered monadnocks
And horsts before they pointed up to us

The Santa Inez Mountains are purple
Their strong necks rub against eternal blue
Their back roads are vacant and still awaiting

That square song ("The Hussle?") we ta-dummed all
Fall, ingenues fine tuning L.A. and San Francisco
Was it after Rome or New York we dropped the chorus

During those dong dim infrared a.m.s
During those thinlipped p.m.s that chiseled us
The Pan Pacific Auditorium went up in flames and
They razed Carthay Circle to raise a parking structure
Our Studio Club implodes today; forget then wild marjoram
At the tar pits was plentiful enough to deodorize Van Nuys

Fine time
Wish we were there
Signed Your Friend in L.A.

In a former life, Rhoda Greenstone was a photojournalist and freelance writer who wrote articles, features, editorials, interviews, and reviews for most of the magazines and newspapers in the L.A. area, including the *Los Angeles Times, Hollywood Reporter, Beverly Hills Independent,* and *Malibu Times.* Her poems have appeared in *The Rag, Samisdat, Wascana Review,* and other literary journals. For the last two decades, she has instructed college students in the joys of language arts and humanities. Currently, she is seeking an agent for her novel, *Names Will Never Hurt Me.*

Singing On

Diane Halsted

"Singing On" came out of a new writing experience. I wrote it midway through my participation in Poem A Day sponsored by Poetry Evolution on the web. Eight poets wrote a poem each day for a week, sent it to the other poets by email, and received seven comments on the poem. None of the poets knew each other except through the emailing of poems and comments.

I gave myself the prompt before I got out of bed that morning: I would take whatever was the first line of the poem given by Garrison Keillor on *Writer's Almanac* that morning. Keillor's selection was a poem by Emily Dickinson so the first line of her poem became the first line of my poem. I had no choice about how I started, but I had every choice about where I went from there. Where I went was informed by two coincidences.

That a line of Dickinson's chose me was striking: I had made just the day before a reservation to stay in Amherst in October. When I told the hotel keeper we were coming to see Emily, he told me her house opened by arrangement only. I would need to make an appointment.

Looking for the poem and its number in my teaching anthologies, I found instead letters from the poet to Thomas Wentworth Higginson. Her comment about a mother caught my attention with all the highlighting, underlining, and starring in several colors prompting me to discuss it with classes over the years.

The poem came quickly, in less than thirty minutes, and surprised me as my poems often do. I had told myself I would not revise my contributions to the daily poems until after I had sent them to the others. I didn't even catch the repeated "of her" until after the poem was out in email land and I had printed it for myself.

I sought to acknowledge what has always appeared to me to be the very base from which Dickinson's work comes — the absence of a mother. Her mother was present physically but not emotionally, and Emily Dickinson, then, did not have a mother in the usual sense of the relationship. This absence of maternal connection, I feel, feeds her work. I called her Emily *D* and used Amherst, *Mass,* so there could be no mistaking about whom I wrote but also to convey my own familiarity with her. It amazes me that she was able to sing at all, let alone so bountifully, without all-important maternal love and attention. Here is the first draft:

Singing On

I shall keep singing!
says Emily D. from her front porch
in Amherst, Mass, and
I hope she sings still

for we poets have a date
with Emily in October
to see her father's house,
her desk, her chair,

perhaps letters to
Higginson, a journal,
her Shakespeare, her
pudding pans,

to feel the *ecstasy*
in living, her slant
truth telling, the circumference
of her business,

to hear her singing
and hope it drowns out
the pathos of her of
her saddest words:

"I never had a mother. I
suppose a mother is one
to whom you hurry when
you are troubled."

Revision began the week following, but the draft will show I made mostly cosmetic changes. I often move whole stanzas around, cut numerous sentences, change stanza shape, but here I was generally satisfied with the poem as it happened. The four-line stanzas and the short lines I used as a bow to Dickinson. The poem is all one sentence. I changed only little words, working from the printed copy of the first draft. This too is unusual for me. More often I work on the computer and although I print regularly, I can't say I have a record of every revision as I can in this case. I removed "front," in part because the line was too long and in part because it was unnecessary. I changed "at" to "in" because it sounds better. In the second stanza, I took out "we poets" because the identity confused. I was being too accurate. Even though two of us are going to see Emily, using the singular "I" eliminates confusion and is consistent with the "I hope" of line 4. In stanza four, I removed "the" in front of *ecstasy in living*. Removing the word *the* from a poem is one of the first things I do when I start revising. Nearly every line reads better without the word *the*; some do not. The good poet knows the difference. And I took out "telling" because the idea works better without it and so too does the line. A note here about the italics — always a question for the poet. I used italics to show phrases that were in Dickinson's poems. Where I took the idea but didn't use her exact words, as in "her slant / truth" and "the circumference / of her business," I used no italics. And where I quoted her prose sentence that came directly out of a letter, I used quotation marks.

The only point I reconsidered was the idea I wanted to convey about the prose quoted at the end. Ultimately, I decided that I wanted to set the reader up for sadness, giving no other judgment from the speaker in the poem. Therefore, I removed "it drowns out / the pathos of her" and replaced it with "it sounds / louder than." This revision I puzzled over, considering using some Eliot or allusion to Eliot or something else from Dickinson and a few other possibilities but settled on the simple. I didn't want to complicate a simple idea.

Revised Draft

Singing On

I shall keep singing!
says Emily D. from her porch
in Amherst, Mass, and
I hope she sings still

for I have a date
with Emily in October
to see her father's house,
her desk, her chair,

perhaps letters to
Higginson, a journal,
her Shakespeare, her
pudding pans,

to feel *ecstasy*
in living, her slant
truth, the circumference
of her business,

to hear her singing
and hope it sounds
louder than
her saddest words:

"I never had a mother. I
suppose a mother is one
to whom you hurry when
you are troubled."

Diane Halsted has taught college writing and literature at several colleges and universities for many years. At present, she teaches writing poetry, creative nonfiction, and memoir to older learners in the Cuesta College Emeritus College program. She has published prose in *North Atlantic Review, Chrysalis Reader, Mochila Review, Ride!,* and *The Journal,* among others. Her poetry has been published or is forthcoming in *Lynx Eye, Carquinez Poetry Review, Gargoyle, Aethlon, The Cape Rock, Drumvoices Review, English Journal, Louisville Review, 13th Moon.*

A Magazine of Bare, Naked Ladies

Janis Butler Holm

Putting together a collage poem is often harder than starting with one's own words — the writer is limited to what others have written. But some language begs to be played with. For me, Walt Whitman's Leaves of Grass is a treasure-trove of linguistic pleasures. I love the energy, excess, and downright camp of Whitman's phrasing — his catalogues and crescendos and repetition, his "shouting aloud."

"A Magazine of Bare, Naked Ladies" is one of several poems I've constructed from Whitman's language, but how the process of construction actually begins remains a bit mysterious. For this poem, I scanned the full text of "I Sing the Body Electric," looking for phrases that, for whatever reason, grabbed my attention. "The sprawl and fulness of babes, the bosoms" immediately struck me as humorous, given current referents for "babe." But I didn't set out to write a funny piece. I simply highlighted phrases that appealed to me in some way — as sound, concept, whatever — without reflecting on my choices. Here is "I Sing the Body Electric" with my selections in bold:

From *Leaves of Grass* (1871–1872)

I Sing the Body Electric

1
1 I SING the Body electric;
The armies of those I love engirth me, and I engirth
    them;
They will not let me off till I go with them, respond to
    them,
And discorrupt them, and charge them full with the
    charge of the Soul.
2 **Was it doubted that those who corrupt their own
    bodies conceal themselves?**
**And if those who defile the living are as bad as they who
    defile the dead?**
And if the body does not do as much as the Soul?

And if the body were not the Soul, what is the Soul?

2

3 The love of the Body of man or woman balks account
— the body itself balks account;
That of the male is perfect, and that of the female is
perfect.

4 **The expression of the face balks account;**
But the expression of a well-made man appears not only
in his face;
It is in his limbs and joints also, it is curiously in the
joints of his hips and wrists;
It is in his walk, the carriage of his neck, the flex of his
waist and knees — **dress does not hide** him;
The strong, sweet, supple quality he has, strikes through
the cotton and flannel;
To see him pass **conveys as much as the best poem,
perhaps more;**
You linger to see his back, and the back of his neck and
shoulder-side.

5 **The sprawl and fulness of babes, the bosoms and heads
of women, the folds of their dress, their style as
we pass in the street, the contour of their shape
downwards,**
The swimmer **naked in the swimming-bath,** seen as he
swims through the transparent green-shine, or lies
with his face up, and **rolls silently to and fro in
the heave of** the water,
The bending forward and backward of rowers in row-
boats — the horseman in his saddle,
Girls, mothers, house-keepers, in all their performances,
The group of laborers seated at noon-time with their
open dinner-kettles, and their wives waiting,
The female soothing a child — the farmer's daughter in
the garden or **cow-yard,**
The young fellow hoeing corn — the sleigh-driver guiding

his six horses through the crowd,

The wrestle of wrestlers, two apprentice-boys, quite
   grown, lusty, good natured, native-born, out on
   the vacant lot at sun-down, after work,

The coats and caps thrown down, **the embrace of love
   and resistance,**

The upper-hold and under-hold, **the hair rumpled** over
   and **blinding the eyes;**

The march of firemen in their own costumes, **the play of**
   masculine muscle through clean-setting trowsers
   and waist-straps,

The slow return from the fire, the pause when the bell
   strikes suddenly again, and the listening on the
   alert,

**The natural, perfect, varied attitudes — the bent head,
   the curv'd neck, and the counting;**

Such-like I love — I loosen myself, pass freely, am at the
   mother's breast with the little child,

Swim with the swimmers, wrestle with wrestlers, march
   in line with the firemen, and pause, listen, and
   count.

3

6 I knew a man, a common farmer — the father of five
   sons;

And in them were the fathers of sons — and in them
   were the fathers of sons.

7 This man was of wonderful vigor, calmness, beauty of
   person;

The shape of his head, the pale yellow and white of his
   hair and beard, and **the immeasurable** meaning of
   his black eyes — the richness and breadth of his
   manners,

These I used to go and visit him to see — he was wise
   also;

He was six feet tall, he was over eighty years old — his
   sons were **massive,** clean, bearded, tan-faced,

handsome;

They and his daughters loved him — all who saw him
loved him;

They did not love him by allowance — they loved him
with **personal love!**

He drank water only — the blood show'd **like scarlet**
through the clear-brown skin of his face;

He was a frequent gunner and fisher — he sail'd his boat
himself — he had a fine one presented to him by
a ship-joiner — he had fowling-pieces, presented to
him by men that loved him;

When he went with his five sons and many grand-sons
to hunt or fish, you would pick him out as **the
most beautiful and vigorous of the gang,**

You would wish long and long to be with him — you
would wish to sit by him in the boat, that you
and he **might touch each other.**

4

8 I have perceiv'd that **to be with those I like is enough,**
To stop in company with the rest at evening is enough,
**To be surrounded by beautiful, curious, breathing,
laughing flesh is enough,**
To pass among them, or touch any one, or rest my arm
ever so lightly round his or her neck for a mo-
ment — **what is this, then?**
I do not ask any more delight — I swim in it, as in a sea.

9 **There is something in staying close to** men and women,
**and looking on them, and in the contact and
odor of them,** that pleases the soul well;
**All things please the soul — but these please the soul
well.**

5

10 **This is the female form;**
A divine nimbus exhales from it from head to foot;
It attracts with fierce undeniable attraction!
I am drawn by its breath as if I were no more than a

helpless vapor — all falls aside but myself and it;
Books, art, religion, time, the visible and solid earth,
  the atmosphere and the clouds, and what was
  expected of heaven or fear'd of hell, are now
  consumed;
**Mad filaments, ungovernable shoots play out of it — the
  response likewise ungovernable;**
**Hair, bosom, hips, bend of legs, negligent falling hands,
  all diffused** — mine too diffused;
Ebb stung by the flow, and flow stung by the ebb —
  love-flesh swelling and deliciously aching;
**Limitless limpid jets of love hot and enormous, quiver-
  ing jelly of love, white-blow and delirious juice;**
Bridegroom **night of love,** working surely and **softly
  into the prostrate dawn;**
Undulating into the willing and yielding day,
Lost in the cleave of the clasping and sweet-flesh'd day.

11 This is the nucleus — after the child is born of woman,
  the man is born of woman;
This is the bath of birth — this is the merge of small
  and large, and the outlet again.

12 Be not ashamed, women — your privilege encloses the
  rest, and is the exit of the rest;
You are the gates of the body, and you are the gates of
  the soul.

13 The female contains all qualities, and tempers them
  — **she is in her place, and moves with perfect
  balance;**
She is all things duly veil'd — **she is both passive and
  active;**
She is to conceive daughters as well as sons, and sons
  as well as daughters.

14 As I see my soul reflected in nature;
As I see through a mist, one with inexpressible com-
  pleteness and beauty,

See the bent head, and arms folded over the breast —
  the female I see.

6

15 The male is not less the soul, nor more — he too is in
  his place;
He too is all qualities — he is action and power;
The flush of the known universe is in him;
Scorn becomes him well, and appetite and defiance be-
  come him well:
The wildest largest passions, bliss that is utmost, sor-
  row that is utmost, become him well — pride is
  for him;
The full-spread pride of man is calming and excellent to
  the soul;
Knowledge becomes him — he likes it always — he brings
  everything to the test of himself;
Whatever the survey, whatever the sea and the sail, he
  strikes soundings at last only here;
(Where else does he strike soundings, except here?)

16 The man's body is sacred, and **the woman's body is
  sacred;**
No matter who it is, it is sacred;
Is it a slave? Is it one of the dull-faced immigrants
  just landed on the wharf?
Each belongs here or anywhere, just as much as the
  well off — just as much as you;
Each has his or **her place in the procession.**

17 (All is a procession;
The universe is a procession, **with measured and beautiful motion.**)

18 Do you know so much yourself, that you call the slave
  or the dull-face ignorant?
Do you suppose you have a right to a good sight, and
  he or she has no right to a sight?

Do you think matter has cohered together from its dif-
   fuse float — and the soil is on the surface, and
   water runs, and vegetation sprouts,
For you only, and not for him and her?

7
19 A man's Body at auction;
I help the auctioneer — the sloven does not half know
   his business.

20 **Gentlemen, look on this wonder!**
Whatever the bids of the bidders, they cannot be high
   enough for it;
For it **the globe** lay preparing quintillions of years,
   without one animal or plant;
For it the revolving cycles truly and steadily roll'd.
21 **In this head the all-baffling brain;**
In it and below it, the makings of heroes.

22 **Examine these limbs,** red, black, or white — **they are
   so cunning in tendon and nerve;**
They shall be stript, that you may see them.

23 **Exquisite senses**, life-lit eyes, pluck, volition,
Flakes of breast-muscle, **pliant back-bone** and neck, **flesh
   not flabby,** good-sized arms and legs,
And wonders within there yet.

24 Within there runs blood,
The same old blood!
The same red-running blood!
**There swells and jets a heart — there all passions, de-
   sires, reachings, aspirations;**
Do you think they are not there because they are not
   express'd in parlors and lecture-rooms?

25 This is not only one man — this is the father of those
   who shall be fathers in their turns;

In him the start of populous states and rich republics;
Of him countless immortal lives, with **countless embodiments and enjoyments.**

26 How do you know who shall come from the offspring
of his offspring through the centuries?
Who might you find you have come from yourself, if
you could trace back through the centuries?

8

27 **A woman's Body at auction!**
She too is not only herself — **she is the teeming mother
of mothers;**
She is the bearer of them that shall grow and be mates
to the mothers.

28 **Have you ever loved the Body of a woman?**
Have you ever loved the Body of a man?
Your father — where is your father?
Your mother — is she living? **have you been much with
her? and has she been much with you?**
— Do you not see that these are exactly the same to all,
in all nations and times, all over the earth?

29 **If any thing is sacred, the human body is sacred,**
And the glory and sweet of a man is the token of man-
hood untainted;
And in man or woman, a clean, strong, firm-fibred body,
is beautiful as the most beautiful face.

30 Have you seen the fool that corrupted his own live
body? or **the fool that corrupted her own live body?**
**For they do not conceal themselves, and cannot conceal
themselves.**

9

31 **O my Body!** I dare not desert the likes of you in
other men and women, nor the likes of the **parts**

of you;
I believe the likes of you are to stand or fall with the
    likes of the Soul, (and that they are the Soul;)
I believe the likes of you shall stand or fall with my
    poems — and that they are poems,
Man's, woman's, child's, youth's, wife's, husband's,
    mother's, father's, young man's, young woman's
    poems;
Head, neck, hair, ears, drop and tympan of the ears,
Eyes, eye-fringes, iris of the eye, eye-brows, and the
    waking or sleeping of the lids,
Mouth, tongue, lips, teeth, roof of the mouth, jaws, and
    the jaw-hinges,
Nose, nostrils of the nose, and the partition,
Cheeks, temples, forehead, chin, throat, back of the
    neck, neck-slue,
Strong shoulders, manly beard, scapula, hind-shoulders,
    and the ample side-round of the chest.
Upper-arm, arm-pit, elbow-socket, lower-arm, arm-sinews,
    arm-bones,
Wrist and wrist-joints, hand, palm, knuckles, thumb,
    fore-finger, finger-balls, finger-joints, finger-nails,
Broad breast-front, curling hair of the breast, breast-
    bone, breast-side,
Ribs, belly, back-bone, joints of the back-bone,
Hips, hip-sockets, hip-strength, inward and outward
    round, man-balls, man-root,
Strong set of thighs, well carrying the trunk above,
Leg-fibres, knee, knee-pan, upper-leg, under-leg,
Ankles, instep, foot-ball, toes, toe-joints, the heel;
All attitudes, all the shapeliness, all the belongings of
    my or **your body**, or of any one's body, male or
    female,
The lung-sponges, the stomach-sac, the bowels sweet and
    clean,
The brain in its folds inside the skull-frame,
Sympathies, heart-valves, palate-valves, **sexuality,** ma-
    ternity,

Womanhood, and all that is a woman — and the man
  that comes from woman,
**The womb, the teats, nipples, breast-milk, tears, laugh-
  ter, weeping, love-looks, love-perturbations and
  risings,**
**The voice, articulation, language, whispering, shouting
  aloud,**
Food, drink, pulse, digestion, sweat, sleep, walking,
  swimming,
**Poise on the hips, leaping, reclining, embracing, arm-
  curving, and tightening,**
The continual changes of the flex of the mouth, and
  around the eyes,
The skin, the sun burnt shade, freckles, hair,
The **curious sympathy one feels, when feeling with the
  hand the naked meat of the body,**
The circling rivers, the breath, and breathing it in and out,
**The beauty of the waist, and thence of the hips, and
  thence downward toward the knees,**
The thin red jellies within you, or within me — the bones,
  and the marrow in the bones,
The exquisite realization of health;
**O I say, these are not the parts and poems of the Body
  only, but of the Soul,**
O I say now these are the Soul!

From Whitman's "I Sing the Body Electric" (1871–1872)

Then I typed these phrases in a list, to isolate them from the rest of the poem. Here is my list, with the phrases I ultimately chose in bold:

Was it doubted that those who corrupt their own bodies conceal themselves?

And if those who defile the living are as bad as they who defile the dead?

The expression of the face balks account;

dress does not hide

conveys as much as the best poem, perhaps more;

You linger to see

The sprawl and fulness of babes, the bosoms and heads of women, the folds of their dress, their style as we pass in the street, the contour of their shape downwards,

naked in the swimming-bath

rolls silently to and fro **in the heave of**

The bending forward and backward

cow-yard

The wrestle of wrestlers,

the embrace of love and resistance,

the hair rumpled

blinding the eyes

the play of

The slow return from the fire

The natural, **perfect, varied attitudes** — the bent head, the curv'd neck, and the counting;

the **immeasurable**

massive,

personal **love!**

like scarlet

the most beautiful and vigorous of the gang,

You would wish long and long **to be with**

might touch each other

to be with those I like is enough,

To be surrounded by beautiful, curious, breathing, laughing **flesh** is enough,

what is this, then?

I do not ask any more delight — I swim in it, as in a sea.

There is something in staying close to

and looking on them, and in the contact and odor of them,

All things please the soul — but these please the soul well.

This is the female form; A divine nimbus exhales from it from head to foot;
It attracts with fierce undeniable attraction!

Mad filaments, ungovernable shoots play out of it — the response likewise
ungovernable;

Hair, bosom, hips, bend of legs, negligent falling hands, all diffused

love-flesh swelling and **deliciously aching;**

Limitless limpid jets of love hot and enormous, quivering jelly of love,
white-blow and delirious juice

night of love,

softly into the prostrate dawn;

Undulating into the willing and yielding day,

Lost in the cleave of the clasping and sweet-flesh'd day

she is in her place, and moves with perfect balance

she is both passive and active

The **wildest largest passions**, bliss that is utmost,

the woman's body is sacred

Is it a slave?

her place in the procession.

with measured and beautiful motion

Do you suppose you have a right to a good sight,

Gentlemen, **look on this wonder!**

the globe

In this head the all-baffling brain; In it and below it,

Examine these limbs,

they are so cunning in tendon and nerve;

Exquisite senses

pliant back-bone

flesh not flabby,

And wonders within there yet.

There swells and jets a heart — **there all** passions, **desires, reachings**, as-pirations;

countless embodiments and enjoyments.

A woman's Body at auction!

she is the **teeming** mother of mothers;

Have you ever loved the Body of **a woman**?

have you been much with her? and has she been much with you?

If any thing is sacred, the human body is sacred, And **the glory and sweet of**

the fool that corrupted her own live body? For they do not conceal them-selves, and cannot conceal themselves.

O my Body!

parts of you

Broad breast-front

All attitudes, all the shapeliness, **all the belongings of**

your body,

The brain in its folds inside the skull-frame,

sexuality,

Womanhood, and all that is a woman

The womb, the teats, nipples, breast-milk, tears, laughter, weeping, love-looks, love-perturbations and risings,

The voice, articulation, language, **whispering, shouting aloud,**

Poise on the hips, leaping, **reclining, embracing,** arm-curving, and tight-ening,

curious sympathy one feels, when feeling with the hand **the naked meat of the body,**

The beauty of the waist, and thence of the hips, and thence downward to-ward the knees,

O I say, these are not the parts and poems of the Body only, but of the Soul,

O I say now these are the Soul!

My phrase list was long, as might be expected with a source text of 2,548 words. Though Whitman's poem celebrates both the male and the female bodies, my selections favored the female. I began grouping some of the phrases that seemed to fit together. "Lost in the cleave of the clasping and sweet-flesh'd day" seemed to go with "bosoms," and I was still chuckling over "babes." Reviewing the list again, I knew I didn't want the seriousness or clinical effect of "womb, the teats, nipples, breast-milk." But "beautiful, curious, breathing, laughing flesh" struck me as a wonderful sequence. And it became clear that "babes" would have to be part of the poem — the joke was just too delicious — so I began to think in terms of something hu-morous.

At this point, I focused on "Limitless limpid jets of love hot and enor-mous, quivering jelly of love" because of its (now) comic excess, and sud-denly I had the tone and theme of my poem if not the language. I wanted to write something funny about lust — maybe adolescent lust and its pas-sionate intensity. And where do adolescents find babes and bosoms but in girlie magazines?

My list of phrases yielded several that could apply to nude poses, and Whitman's exclamatory "look on this wonder!" was the perfect opening. From there, it was fairly easy to pick phrases that correspond to the ado-lescent girlie magazine experience. But I tried to choose language that would underline the innocence, sweetness, and excitement of that first ex-perience, rather than its inherent cheesiness. Whitman's "The glory and sweet of" and "wildest largest passions" fit together nicely to that effect. And his "O," for me, captures the yearning of the adolescent body.

Once the poem was constructed, I made sure to check its phrases carefully against the original, as poetic need often overrides what the eye actually sees. I also had to think about whether to "mark" the poem as a collage, whether to use slashes after phrases so that the reader would be (especially) aware of the poem as a construction. Doing so seemed a good idea, as much of the humor of the piece derives from its recontextualized language.

Here is the final poem:

Magazine of Bare, Naked Ladies

)ok on this wonder! / The sprawl and fullness of babes, the bosoms /
e bending forward and backward / the / perfect, varied attitudes /

)u linger to see / love-flesh / lost in the cleave of / in the heave of /
ımeasurable / massive / naked / bosoms /

ıere swells / softly / the naked meat of the body / there all / desires, reachings /
e glory and sweet of / wildest largest passions /

/ to be with / to be surrounded by beautiful, curious, breathing / flesh /
ł the belongings of / a woman /

/ to be / whispering / reclining, embracing / teeming / shouting aloud /

/ deliciously aching / exquisite senses /

/ love!

The body of this poem is composed of words and phrases from Walt Whitman's Sing the Body Electric."

First published in *The Gay and Lesbian Review*, 12.2 (March–April 2005), p. 42.

Janis Butler Holm teaches experimental writing in Athens, Ohio, where she has served as Associate Editor for *Wide Angle*, the film journal. Her essays, poems, and stories have appeared in both small-press and national magazines.

o.j. simpson in the ford bronco on the los angeles freeway (on NBC Television, June 17, 1994)

Brian Gilmore

The following short draft of what was to become a poem I scribbled down on a note pad. This is how the poem began. I always write on note pads. I make changes as I sit there working through my thoughts whether on the bus, at work, in meetings, at home, anywhere really; it is how I like to write poetry, in a simple manner and with convenience. I revise as I write too, at least initially.

I typed my notes when I got home because I liked what the poem was trying to say overall and wanted to save the essential thoughts of the poem. I also liked the small phrasings like "on the freeway," and "guns to our heads." I knew I didn't have a poem yet, but I had a beginning, a working draft, if I may say, of what I wanted to say. I had been dwelling on the idea that for black men, nothing seems to be enough no matter what. There is always a need for more intervention to try to turn things around. Even with the days of pride in the 60s and 70s, the changing of laws, the liberalization of society for a certain time, it was not enough, and now things are certainly moving in another direction where the condition of black men, of which I am one, is perilous. The use of the O. J. Simpson incident is just metaphoric; it is not to suggest that he is a victim. The poem, however, was an exercise in short, quick phrases, thoughts, all connected by the metaphor and all working off that point, this idea of being trapped. The short phrasings are intentional.

o.j. simpson in the ford bronco on the los angeles freeway

in the white ford bronco,
on the freeway, all the cops
in the world behind us, driving
real slow.

guns to our heads. a.c. is

driving us down the road.
we have no money or
passport, we don't know
why we are here.

all of that important stuff can't
really stop the madness. fred d,
harriet t, huey p, we never had
free breakfast anyway, we remain
hungry.

two dead white people? we didn't
do it but we still have a disguise we
want to wear all the time. maybe
it is halloween or carnival but
we aren't in a krewe, not from new orleans,
we don't say "trick or treat"
when doors open because we don't
expect any candy.

we really just want to leave like richard
wright tired of all the threats.
say it loud
i am not bigger thomas
i am not bigger thomas.
i am not bigger thomas.

it doesn't matter; we are in
the white ford bronco.

it should be a great life here.
the men, the women, rise from their
beds make an honest living, praise the Lord, tell
us of not so long ago when we overcame
the work of the devil and made our world.

it is still not enough

the devil is a mother,
and fake mustaches and guns
is all we are given
when what we asked for is
free breakfast and some more books
about harriet tubman.

The second completed draft, which is a series of smaller edits and changes, brought the poem to its first finished form. It is a complete thought at last and captures the true emotion of the poem — frustration. I wanted to expand my thoughts and add specific references to certain occurrences that made the poem become a complete experience for the reader. I also wanted it to read better, such as where I added "it seems" to the first stanza. It is clear the first draft is only a beginning; the story does not have an ending.

I expanded the final paragraph (though I knew I was having trouble) to bring the poem to an end. What did I want to say, I kept asking myself. What was the poem about? The stanza that begins, "it is a great life here" is a good example of the type of changes I wanted to make. I added lines there to demonstrate the efforts of ordinary men and women to provide examples of hard work and discipline to overcome seemingly impossible odds. It was important to convey the idea that people were trying to resolve these issues; it just hadn't worked yet. However, I still didn't like some parts of it. Some of it seemed too wordy, too familiar. I knew I had to chop down some phrases. I wanted vagueness. It wasn't over, though I was happy that I was able to expand the stanzas and the thoughts. The poem still feels too full. The chant in the middle, "i am not bigger thomas" is a thought, but it never worked for me. Yet I put it there to remind myself of what I wanted to do. However, the rhythm it achieves is not working; it is overkill.

o.j. simpson in the ford bronco on the los angeles freeway, nbc
television, june 17, 1994

in the white ford bronco.
on the freeway. all the cops
in the world, it seems,
behind us driving slow.

guns to our heads. a.c. is
driving us down
the road. we have no money or
passport, we don't know
why we are here.

all of that important stuff can't
really stop the madness. fred d,
harriet t, huey p, we never had
free breakfast anyway, we remain
incredibly hungry.

two dead white people?
we didn't do it but we
still have a disguise we want
to don most days. maybe it is
halloween or carnival;
we aren't in a krewe, not from new
orleans, don't say "trick or treat"
when doors open, we
don't expect any candy.

sometimes we just want to leave like
richard wright tired of all the threats
say it loud:
i am not bigger thomas
i am not bigger thomas
i am not bigger thomas

it doesn't matter; we are in
the white ford bronco.

it should be a great life here;
such a nice place to be born, to live,
to become; one would think all of us
would love ourselves like nelson loves
mandela, like nina loves simone.

the men, the women, rise from their
beds make an honest living, praise the Lord, tell
us of not so long ago when we overcame
some of the best work of the devil and
made our world sing something wonderful
like aretha franklin's "respect."

it is still not enough.
the devil is a mother,
and fake mustaches and guns
is what we are
given.

what we want is
free breakfast
books about harriet tubman
and evening drives in
something other than
the bronco.

and tell the police to stop following
us on the freeway.

I searched the Internet for the date of the O. J. Simpson slow chase on the freeway, and several sources stated that it was June 17, 1994. This was important to me because I remember actually seeing the slow chase. I was watching NBA basketball between the New York Knicks and Houston Rockets, and NBC cut into the game with a split screen and showed the chase as we watched the game. I didn't remember the exact date, but as the poem festered inside me for weeks it had to be part of the title to give it a cinematic quality that I wanted.

In my changes to the second draft, I purposely sought to make the poem read easier by taking out words that seemed unnecessary, and I also tried to eliminate phrases that seemed too familiar. The second draft was bulky. The words need to carry weight but be economical. Most of the stanzas received such a treatment. The poem reads easier now.

I also chose two literary references that are more exact but more elusive to the reader. This was to force the reader to think differently about the poem's overall meaning. The first is the disguise reference. Where the previous drafts mention a disguise (O. J. had a fake mustache in the Bronco), the final draft alludes to Paul Laurence Dunbar, the celebrated black poet of the turn of the nineteenth century. His poem, *We Wear the Mask*, is well known, and I wanted the disguise reference to invoke the thoughts of that poem. Thus, it is no longer, "we still have a disguise," but "like dunbar we still have a disguise we want to don most days."

This stanza also experienced a change in the reference to "halloween" and "carnival." Where before it was an either–or proposition, this new version combines them to again focus on the idea of frustration, as if to suggest, what difference does it make?

The second big change is the Richard Wright reference. In previous drafts, I allude to Richard Wright wanting to leave the country because he was under threat from his own government; however, that seemed too general. I decided that the real metaphor I wanted was "Big Boy," a famous character from a Richard Wright story who escapes the horror of the Jim Crow south. It is much more specific and literary. It also enabled me to eliminate that "i am not bigger thomas" chant that I did not like.

Overall, this final version reads much better for me; it is simpler but conveys the same thoughts. Another good example of my desire to alter the language is displayed in changing the word "great" to "wonderful" in the seventh stanza. It is a subtle reference to the famous movie, *It's A Wonderful Life*. The manuscript in which this poem appears is called "The George Holiday Rodney King Video." The poems are cinematic biographic journeys. This one is just one of them.

> o.j. simpson in the ford bronco on the los angeles freeway
> (on NBC Television, June 17, 1994)
>
> in the white ford bronco.
> on the freeway.
> all the cops in the world, it seems,
> behind us driving real
> slow.
>
> guns to our heads. a.c., our man, is
> easing us down
> the road. we have no

money or passport, we
don't know why we are
here; we didn't do it.
all of that important stuff can't
stop the madness. fred d,
harriet t, huey p, we never had
free breakfast anyway.

like dunbar we still have a disguise
we want to don most days. it is
halloween and carnival;
we aren't in a krewe, not from new
orleans, don't say "trick or treat"
when doors open
don't expect candy,
beads, or naked women
waving their
breasts.

we just want to leave like
Big Boy in the back of a
truck.

we are in the white ford
bronco.

this should be a wonderful life.
such a nice place to be born, to live,
to become; one would think all of us
would love ourselves like nelson loves
mandela, like nina loves simone, like
stevie loves
wonder.

men, women, rise from their
beds make honest wages, praise
the Lord, tell us all the time of
not so long ago when we

overcame the best work of the
devil, made the world sing
aretha franklin's
"respect."
it is not enough.
the devil is a
'mother.'

fake mustaches and guns
is what we have. we need
free breakfast
books about bannaker
and evening drives in
something other than
a white bronco.

and tell the police, please
don't follow us slowly
on the freeway.

Brian Gilmore is the author of two collections of poetry, *elvis presley is alive and well and living in harlem* (Third World Press 1993) and *Jungle Nights and Soda Fountain Rags: Poem for Duke Ellington* (Karibu Books 2000). He is a columnist with the Progressive Media Project and contributing writer for *Jazz Times Magazine*.

Ornithology 101

DEREK SHEFFIELD

My muse is a wild one who reaches me at all hours, in any place, through all kinds of mediums: images, phrases, memories, and more. Typically, she leads a poem in through the backdoor of consciousness. "Ornithology 101" arrived differently, however. For this poem, I flung open the front door, called, clapped, and whistled, and that sweet lady of the lyric sent it fluttering down out of the blue.

After I took an ornithology class from a colleague at the college where I teach, I realized that I had been introduced to some amazing language, and I wanted to work that language into a poem while evoking my newly hatched biologic awareness. A month or so after the class ended, I began working on the poem by combing through my notes to create a word cache with terms like "plumulaceous," "keeled sternum," and *"Carduelis tristis."*

From the cache, I wrote a draft of the poem. And then I revised that draft, and the next and the next. The early version shown here is the fourth or fifth.

Ornithology 101
for Dr. Stephens

Now you have staked their skeletons,
eyed the scope of a hollow leg, prodded
strutted, white ribs, pinched
a wishbone to feel resilience, thumbed
a keeled sternum's edge still attempting
to steer the absent feathers, stroked
a hummingbird's mum iridescence, ruffed
the plumulaceous white breast of a great egret
slit and stuffed as last spring's final project,
sprinted with a severed wing to catch
the physics, given new vision
to a blackbird with two dabs of cotton, breathed
mothballs for three memorable months of study,
you can leave with an "A" in class *Aves.*
Now you know the American goldfinch in Latin

is thistle-eating sadness, you can walk out
into green trembling, and the air,
with blind fingers remembers your face.
Now you have looked into birds
the undulant streak at the edge of sight
calls your new song:
                         Carduelis tristis.

As I began revising this one, I realized the dedication, "for D r. Stephens," was a private reference. It came from my gratitude to my colleague for allowing me to take his class. Since it didn't add significant substance to the poem, I cut it.

In lines 1 and 14, I inserted "that" in order to narrow the meaning to more precisely create as sense of "after the fact": not "now you have" but "now *that* you have." In the second line, I replaced "a hollow leg" with "digit number four." Not only does the revision specify the image using scientific language, but more importantly, it sounds better, at least it does to me. It sounds cold and removed, especially "digit," which feels right for this poem.

There are a few places in the poem where I omitted deadwood — words that weren't adding much and only served to impede the pace. Poet William Stafford used another metaphor for this when he spoke of "cutting out the fat." In lines 12 and 13, I deleted "breathed / mothballs for three memorable months of study." And in line 8, I cut "plumulaceous." This one was a difficult choice because it's such a lovely, polysyllabic, ornithological word. But it had to go. It made the line too sluggish and tended to trip my readers, none of whom seemed to know how to pronounce it. In line 4, I didn't just omit language, but replaced two words with one. In place of "to feel" I put "for," making the lines "pinched / a wishbone for resilience" more concise and less clunky. Also, the "for" here conveys the tactile image just as well as the infinitive "to feel."

My most significant revisions appear in the last nine lines. Between line 14 and the end, I replaced two repetitions of the poem's opening phrase, "now you," with one. I felt that the third instance slowed the pace too much. I like the poem's tone of urgency and onwardness created by fewer sentences, and I wanted to sustain that as much as possible.

In this same section, I replaced some more general and expected natural imagery — "green trembling," "undulant streak" — with more sciential and surprising details — "diagrammatic movements of geese," "dotted

135

lines," and "Latinate streaks."

Lastly, I altered what is arguably the most important part of any poem, the last line. Initially, I wanted to finish on the scientific name for the American goldfinch, the Latin binomial, "*Carduelis tristis*," which means "thistle-eating sadness." (It eats thistle seeds and someone thought its song sounded gloomy.) Beyond sharing the simple beauty of the name itself, my impulse here was to emphasize the scientific. Also, the name evoked for me one of the outcomes of my newly acquired knowledge. The more I learned about birds, in one sense, the sadder I became. I discovered that most of our songbird populations are in steady decline owing primarily to massive habitat loss up and down the American continent. However, I determined that I was violating a cardinal (yes, a pun) rule: show, don't tell. I therefore decided to end with an image.

In place of a scientific name no one except birders and Latin teachers can pronounce, I came up with "the air is feathers / measuring the bones of your face." This image is visual *and* tactile. I like that. I also like the heavy *s* sounds. Poet Robert Creeley said, "Form is never more than an extension of content," and I think the sibilant *s*'s evoke the touch of feathers — in other words, or rather, word, onomatopoetic.

And beyond the imagery and texture of this passage, I like what it *suggests*, that the world (not just the air, but "air" — through synecdoche — as entire world) returns humanity's analysis. In other words, if our interaction with the world comes entirely through the lens of a scope or the tongs of tweezers, maybe an animated world examines us? Put another way, perhaps it is a matter of becoming our attentions: as we *are* so *is* our environment.

Of course, there are other ways to read these last few lines, and I wouldn't have it any other way. One last caveat: even though I consciously set out to write this poem, to work with the scientific language of birds, I had absolutely no idea where that language, those rhythms and sounds, would lead me. It is most often a deadly proposition to write a poem with the end in mind, deadly in the sense that the language can be lifeless, a collection of hollow shells (many overtly political poems suffer from this). Poet Richard Hugo, in his vital text, *The Triggering Town*, writes that "all truth must conform to music." And that New England farmer and versifier, Robert Frost, advised, "No surprise for the writer, no surprise for the reader."

Therefore, a golden bird with pepper-black wings lights on a green-nee-

dled branch and sings and sings all morning. Do you hear the melancholy?
Can language contain it?

Final Version

Ornithology 101

Now that you have staked their skeletons,
eyed the scope of digit number four, prodded
strutted white ribs, pinched
a wishbone for resilience, thumbed
a keeled sternum's edge still trying
to steer scattered feathers, stroked
a hummingbird's mum iridescence, ruffed
the white down of a great egret
slit and stuffed as last year's final project,
sprinted with a severed wing to catch
the physics, given new vision
to a blackbird with two dabs of cotton,
you can leave with an A in class *Aves*.
Now that you have looked through birds, you see
the diagrammatic movements of geese
across the blue sky, dotted lines
narrowing a million years. You expect
from every American goldfinch thistles
and sadness, and when you walk out
among the world's perches and Latinate streaks
at the edge of sight, the air is feathers
measuring the bones of your face.

Chosen by Li-Young Lee as the winner of the James Hearst Poetry
Award and published in *The North American Review*.

Derek Sheffield's poems have appeared in the *The Georgia Review, The North
American Review, The Seattle Review, Crab Creek Review, Poetry Northwest,
Swink, Margie: The American Journal of Poetry, Ecotone, Puerto del Sol, Passages North*, and several anthologies. His poems have also been included in
the *Anthology of Magazine Verse & Yearbook of American Poetry*, nominated for

a Pushcart Prize, and selected as finalists for the St. Louis Poetry Center Award, the Pablo Neruda Award, and the Elinor Benedict Poetry Prize. He has received a Washington State Artist Trust Grant, and David Wagoner chose nine of his poems for *Poet Lore's* Poets Introducing Poets. Blue Begonia Press published his chapbook, *A Mouthpiece of Thumbs* (2000). He teaches at Wenatchee Valley College, where his classes include creative writing and a learning community called Northwest Nature Writing, which he teaches in cooperation with noted ornithologist, Dr. Dan Stephens.

Sleeping Through the Fire

PETER SCHMITT

Sleeping Through the Fire," published in *The Hudson Review* in 1998 and appearing in my 2007 collection, *Renewing the Vows*, was begun at least as early as 1988, so far as I can tell. It's hard to be sure since I don't attach dates to my drafts. Maybe I should, though I suspect poets do so sometimes with one eye on their biographers. But "Sleeping" seems to have first emerged as a pair of exploratory quatrains, alongside the draft of an unrelated letter whose date can be placed.

At some point thereafter, probably sooner rather than later, developed the semi-narrative poem beginning with the lumbering pun, "I lumbered downstairs." That I have on file (old-fashioned manila file, that is) significantly revised, *typed* versions of a complete poem is, for me, unusual since I prefer not to type a poem up until confident that it's closely approaching, or has reached, its ultimate shape. As many writers no doubt can attest, something about the formality of typescript imposes a certain finality on a work, which tends to discourage or inhibit revision — and thus can be illusive and dangerous. Or so it is for someone who did not come of age with computers and word processors, who still favors — and likely always will — working in longhand, right up until the poem simply demands at last to be set in print and dispatched in the mail (U.S. mail, that is).

In fact, even before a poem is committed handwritten to the page, a good deal of it will probably have been composed in my head — as many lines as possible until some threaten to spill from my memory. So by the time the first words touch my lined yellow pad, they've typically been revised already a few times, though I wouldn't say polished. That process is for the page.

Thus, for whatever reasons now lost to time, the long, nascent version of "Sleeping Through the Fire" was banged out on my old electronic typewriter, in its now-quaint, Elite 10-point font. Compared to its final form, this draft is much more faithful to the actual experience, as my early work tended to be, regardless of whether those details are crucial to the *poem*. There's the family chiding, and dialogue (brief), and exposition ("I trudged / through the yard"). What will remain constant through to the completion of the poem is the "ghost pentameter," the ten- or eleven-syllable line I

Sleeping Through the Fire

I lumbered downstairs and found the family
already at breakfast. No one looked up,
but they started snickering. Finally,
my father said, "You missed the fire." "What fire?"
He nodded toward the door. "Across the road,"
he called. The screen door swung behind me. I trudged
through the yard, and heard more tittering inside.
Then there it was:
                    just beyond the narrow lane,
where the pines came as far as the gravel
turnaround for cars, the blackened patch of ground.
Needles charred and damp. And lifting the eyes,
the singe climbing the trunks past where the first
branches began, about the height of a man.
I noticed muddied black tracks winding out
toward the lane, as if the fire had begun
to lick its way toward the house. But the grass,
flattened there, revealed what had to be the tread
of the volunteers' truck, and the whole scene
flashed up, as if out of a dream:
                                    the neighbors
gathered around, debating the merits
of a bucket brigade, the hoses too short:
were there enough to make a chain from the lake?
And the nervous laughter, and the glancing
for wind, and wondering, where was the truck?
And no one noticing, until long after,
my absence:
              for there I slept, above that scene,
at a height where the flames must just that moment
have been reaching. What was I dreaming, that night
of that 16th summer, for I had to be
locked in a dream so far away, whatever
one dreams when one is 16. Unless my sleep
was the kind said to be deep beyond dream,
where the body is left behind, and the soul
trails away like smoke.
                          I could never know,
but as I stood staring at the sooty earth,
I suddenly felt selfish for having slept
so soundly, or soundlessly, for having left
my family to face the fire alone.
How could the clamor through the open window
never have reached me? And when the day came
when the family was no longer there first,
would I be sleeping then, too? I told myself
someday instinctively I would know, and wake.
But still sometimes today, staying a night
in my parents' house, the burglar alarm
howling out of the dark, tripped by a wind
and faulty connection, I stay there still
in bed. Not moving. Not wanting at all
my parents to be the very last to wake.

140

have used considerably from about that time forward.

Almost all the key images of the eventual poem are already in place: the charring of the trees, the volunteers' truck, the bucket brigade, me asleep at sixteen. But much, in time, would be stripped: several speculative questions ("What was I dreaming ... How could the clamor ... And when the day came..."); my guilt made explicit ("I suddenly felt selfish"); a flurry of over-alliteration ("as I stood staring at the sooty earth"); and a movement *away* from the moment, from past to present ("But still sometimes today") that defies one of my core principles in composing poems: *stay in the scene!* To put it another way: observe the dramatic unities of time and place.

If I tucked this draft away for a while — years, it would turn out — it probably had to do with such reasons, and a sense that the experience described was somehow too private, insufficiently resonant — or that I had failed to make it relevant to anyone but myself.

But the scene stayed with *me*, or at least the notion that a poem could be made of it, and by the typeface of the next installment, we move ahead to the middle 1990s. The print looks like the product of my first computer, an aged Leading Edge that a friend just gave me — lamenting my Luddite tendencies — rather than toss to the junk heap. "Sleeping" is now considerably compressed; where there was white space airing out the lines, has now condensed — been melted down? — to a solid block. This reduction has been accomplished primarily through a single abstract phrase beginning the poem: "the oblivion of adolescence."

Gone now are the questions, the vague wondering about my dream life, and the scene never shifts from the small space enclosing house and woods. The poem has taken a quantum step toward its final form; it's actually reached its ultimate length, and after the abstraction, images control the movement and provide whatever "comment" one might claim is found here. An ending has been arrived at — an ending about a beginning, you could say — one that felt right, that seemed to evolve naturally out of the details, and that just might speak to others: about growing up, responsibility, an adult sort of "wakefulness."

What had never seemed sufficiently a narrative poem — not enough "story," no true beginning, middle, and end — now no longer pretended to be, though it retained certain narrative aspects: an event *is* described. And I seem to have decided that the poem really wasn't about losing my

Sleeping Through the Fire

```
In the oblivion of adolescence,
I slept through it all: the fire across the lane
at the edge of the woods, just beginning
to involve the pines.  There in that second
story bedroom, not once did I waken
to the neighbors' first shouts, to their running
with extinguishers and later, their chain
of buckets from the lake.  Though the walls were thin
I never felt my family downstairs,
their bolting from rooms and slamming of doors.
And through an open window, somehow I missed
the volunteers' truck taking the corner,
the squeal of its brakes and dispersal of men.
Instead, I floated like smoke above the scene,
there at sixteen, even with the flames rising
to the next level.  And no one looked for me.
In the morning, I would see the black ring--
the damp needlebed, and charred limbs--but that night
they left me in my room, where I might sleep
a little longer, before unexcusing
daylight called me down at last into the world.
```

parents — a legitimate fear anyone might have — or that such a fear was not embodied in the images of *this* poem, in *these* details.

Having made headway, it's likely that around this time I began thinking of sending the poem out to magazines. My old logbook of submissions — which I *have* kept faithfully since 1992 — confirms that by 1996 "Sleeping Through the Fire" was indeed in the mail, if without initial success. And the next substantial revision can be pinned with accuracy to April 1997, since in those days I attached the date to my submissions (partly to remind the magazine just how long they'd been sitting on my work).

You can see that it's back to the trusty Smith-Corona with the 10-point type. The Leading Edge, or its printer, or both, may finally have expired and it would be three more years until (to ring in the millennium!) my first new computer — too late for this poem. But before I stuck this particular copy in an envelope, my mind clearly changed about the second line (think of all that retyping). Substituting "failed to move" for "kept sleeping" emphasizes a deficiency on the speaker's part, if not an actual betrayal: a revision that would survive the final cut.

Sleeping Through the Fire

When the flames lit up the woods across the lane
                    failed to move,
I ~~kept sleeping,~~ lost in some adolescent

slumber. Soon the tallest pines were involved,

but there in that second story bedroom

not once did I waken to the neighbor's shouts--

not as the wind shifted toward the house,

and they ran with CO_2 and buckets

spilling from the lake. Though the walls were thin

I never felt my family downstairs,

their bolting from rooms and slamming of doors.

And through an open window, somehow I missed

the volunteers' truck taking the corner,

the squeal of its brakes and dispersal of men.

Instead, I floated like smoke above the scene,

there at sixteen, even with the fire rising

to the next level. And no one looked for me.

In the morning, I would see the black ring--

the damp needlebed, and charred limbs--but that night

they left me in my room, where I might sleep

a little longer, before unexcusing

daylight called me down at last into the world.

By now "Sleeping" has unclenched from the solid block into quatrains with a concluding, standalone line, a feature of several of my poems. The "oblivion" abstraction has been sent to oblivion — show, don't tell — and the poem gets right to it, involving the reader immediately in the scene: "When the flames lit up the woods." Still at twenty-one lines, the shift to quatrains (back to its most embryonic form) provides a little breathing room on the page, similar to the first typed draft. Slant-rhymes seem more apparent now, particularly as the poem goes along (lane/adolescent, shouts/house, doors/corner, men/scene, ring/unexcusing), though they've changed little from the previous version. Additions include the ominous wind shift, and the "extinguishers" have been replaced by CO_2, saving a syllable — if not the trees.

Not only did I rethink the second line, but evidently the quatrains too, as the logbook records the copy sent out April 30, 1997, was accepted by *The Hudson Review* two months later, and the poem as printed is in tercets. It's likely I questioned what might be called the stanzaic integrity of the quatrains: did they comprise coherent units, and were they end-stopped, with some form of punctuation? A little "rule" of mine at the time was that a majority of stanzas in a poem (including the last) had to be end-stopped with punctuation: the partitioning felt better rationalized that way. Instead of two of five quatrains, five of seven tercets were now end-stopped: more in my comfort zone. Today, for better or worse, I'm less strict. Or, like a middle-aged spread, I have a wider comfort zone.

When a poem is accepted for publication, it doesn't mean it won't be revised again, but I haven't with "Sleeping" and I usually don't. The adage, "poems are never finished, just abandoned" applies, but acceptance is a kind of permission to devote what time I have to newer work still in progress.

That a poem can take nearly ten years to finish is for me not unusual. Some have taken longer. It's a matter, always, of patience: waiting for the right image, the right conclusion, however long it takes. True poems can't be forced, or rushed, or willed into existence. Eventually, and when you least expect it, they will yield their truths and lead you out of the darkness. If you're alert, and ready, they will point the way to their own resolutions. So many things have to come together to make a successful poem; they likely won't happen all at once. I don't trust poems written quickly, probably because I don't write many of them. And my students are required to revise at least once, before handing in, every poem or story they submit to

Sleeping Through the Fire

When the flames lit up the woods across the lane
I failed to move, lost in some adolescent
slumber. Soon the tallest pines were involved,

but there in that second story bedroom
not once did I waken to the neighbors' shouts—
not as the wind shifted toward the house,

and they ran with CO_2 and buckets
spilling from the lake. Though the walls were thin
I never felt my family downstairs,

their bolting from rooms and slamming of doors.
And through an open window, somehow I missed
the volunteers' truck taking the corner,

the squeal of its brakes and dispersal of men.
Instead, I floated like smoke above the scene,
there at sixteen, even with the fire rising

to the next level. And no one looked for me.
In the morning, I would see the black ring—
the damp needlebed, and charred limbs—but that night

they left me in my room, where I might sleep
a little longer, before unexcusing
daylight called me down at last into the world.

class so that they can begin to appreciate where writing's real work is so often accomplished. "Revise, revise, revise," Elizabeth Bishop wrote in "North Haven," her elegy for her friend Robert Lowell, and it's a motto we know she might have spoken of herself. It should be *every* writer's motto, and happily, anyone can make it their own right now.

Peter Schmitt is the author of three full-length books of poems: *Renewing the Vows* (David Robert Books, 2007), *Country Airport*, and *Hazard Duty* (Copper Beech); and a chapbook, *To Disappear* (Pudding House). He has received two Florida Arts Council grants, most recently for the year 2007.

Apology, to a neighbor who lost his place

Phil Hey

I awoke one morning with a couple of lines in my head:

> They told me you were going broke. I knew.
> I heard their words, but what was I to do?

Paul Valéry said "God gives us the first line; we have to do the rest." At least I knew where the background came from, the farm crisis, so I knew there was more to say. But indeed, what was I to do, especially with a rhyming couplet? Couplets are so peremptory and predictable, as John Keats called them "the little rocking horse," so if I didn't want to follow a string of couplets down the page, I had to find something else to do. (Rule 1: Finish what you start.)

Momentarily I thought about the blues, just a couplet with the first line repeated before singing the second, but the story really wasn't blues country. What else? Well, if the lines were worth repeating, I could do a villanelle. (Rule 2: Sometimes all you're going to get is an exercise, but even that is worth doing.) I knew the challenge right away: You get nothing, not even a gold star, for the ability to write a technically perfect villanelle — that's just tools of the trade. Maybe a (nonwriting) literature teacher might be impressed, but serious poetry readers wouldn't be.

After breakfast, sitting at the computer with no excuses to put off the writing, I typed out the first tercet:

> They told me you were going broke. I knew
> you'd had hard times, losses more than gains;
> I heard their words, but what was I to do?

So far so good; I liked the tone and the rough variation against the iambic-pentameter norm of the second line, and almost without thinking I had enjambed the first line. But could I stand to see those two lines again? And what about the middle rhyme — let's see, direct rhyme *planes, skeins, trains?* Well, it wasn't necessary to remain technically perfect. I forged onward to the next tercet:

> With beans near down to five, corn at two,
> the crop's not worth picking or the time
> it takes to plant

That came out easily from background (Rule 3: You really ought to know about what you're writing about), but it struck me: How could I give up two beats of the repeated line? The second line didn't sound good if end-stopped, so I had to cut-to-fit the repeating line:

> it takes to plant. Of course you went broke. I knew

Again I had set up an enjambment; this time into the next tercet. What to say next? Here I had to stop and take a reflective break — coffee, petting the dogs, whatever — because if I kept that second tercet, I'd be fully committed to making a purposefully irregular villanelle. As a young wannabe, I had been immersed in Dylan Thomas's villanelle "Do not go gentle into that good night," with accompanying praise, but I was shocked by Mark Strand's saying that it wasn't a very good villanelle. Now I agree; though it has splendid diction, the form generates a predictable series in the middle stanzas (*wise* men, *good* men, *wild* men, *grave* men) that makes them read as separate stanzas strongly end-stopped, with little cumulative value except the direct repetition. How could I handle some repetition — close enough to recognize — and yet escape being locked into the form? Back to Rule 1.

I had set up a slightly different change in the persona with his saying "Of course you went broke." What did he know, and how could he explain, after that admission? From background, I knew that farmers don't go broke like the rest of us — they keep expanding their debt (with kindly help from the bank) until they run out of credit. When you're talking about needing a new combine for over $100,000, you hit that line pretty hard. As is usual in the farm belt, my persona didn't hear it directly from his neighbor, more likely from the group around the table at the local café … a safe distance that would keep him from having to look his neighbor in the eyes. Thus the next tercet:

you were in trouble when they told me you
couldn't refinance and get that new combine.
Sure I heard the words, but what else could I do?

Yes, that's how they'd talk about it, but oh my, I'd chanced on another revealing of the persona. Was I going to end up with a whiner, an excuse-maker on my hands? His "what else could I do?" pointed in that direction. I didn't like it at all, especially since Edmund Burke's saying popped into my head: "The only thing necessary for the triumph of evil is that good men do nothing." I didn't want to follow this guy around anymore, and yet there seemed to be a terrible rightness to his attitude and excuse-making. Time to stop again — enough for coffee and household chores and puttering around in the garage, almost hoping that if I could engage my mind enough in something else, this whole creative experience would disappear and wipe the slate (and computer memory) clean.

No such luck. When I returned, there it was, hanging in mid-screen waiting to be grounded in completion. Damn; how do people like him argue, anyway? Um, being rational, defensive, hoping to find something the neighbor could agree with? Or just whatever spills out of his mouth, maybe. So:

You know what I mean. I had tough times too.
We're not our neighbor's keeper. So when they came
to tell me you'd gone broke, I always knew

you wouldn't ask for charity.

Another enjambment, this time a very strong one across the stanza break, and (I felt) necessary to follow his voice. Background told me it was right, too; you don't really ask for charity in that situation; if your neighbors feel it, they'll show up, as they always will to bring in the crop, for example, if the farmer gets sick or disabled or dies. There it hung, and I was still stuck. I'd included plenty of variation from technically perfect, and I felt obliged to follow the persona to whatever end the poem took, but the repetition was still getting to me. As was the coffee, bringing in an edge of heartburn, sometimes a sign that I'm approaching saying something of worth, *sigh*. When Baudelaire was talking about poetry to a woman's club, he described what it was like to be poor and struggling as a writer. When one asked "But how do you live?" he replied "As for that, we let our servants do it for us." I'm not all that poor, but I was struggling and had no servants to bear heartburn and incomplete poems. I kept asking myself why this person would repeat so much; I've always found it useful to imagine a scenario where the persona is actually talking.

After a few hours of stuck it hit me, with a force a good deal less manageable than heartburn: he's talking to someone who isn't listening, who can't listen anymore, but he has to spit it out at last:

> ...And now
> you don't need it anymore. They've seen you home
> with a few last words and nothing more to do.

I truly had no idea that the villanelle would lead me to his neighbor's grave. But sometimes poems have to lead that way, to an unexpected discovery (maybe Rule 4, something like if you know what you're going to say before you start writing, and if the poem doesn't contain a discovery, you probably should write an essay instead). It would be easy and false to say that the last stanza was just piecing out, completing the form. The first two lines of the closing quatrain were easy enough, plain carpentry:

> This little space of earth they gave your name
> is all that's left. The rest goes on the same.

Still the obligation, though. I couldn't let him go — the repeating lines had to happen, and again a small discovery that he finally admits more to himself than his late neighbor:

> They told me you were going broke. I knew
> before the words. But what was I to do?

What are any of us to do when it's too late to apologize? But the villanelle was done. I remembered that Elizabeth Bishop had drafts of her great villanelle "One Art" above her desk for over a year. I can only hope that mine is worth the days it hung unfinished on my computer screen.

Apology, to a neighbor who lost his place

They told me you were going broke. I knew
you'd had hard times, losses more than gains;
I heard their words, but what was I to do?

With beans near down to five, corn at two,
the crop's not worth the picking or the time
it takes to plant. Of course you went broke. I knew

you were in trouble when they told me you
couldn't refinance and get that new combine.
Sure I heard the words, but what else could I do?

You know what I mean. I had tough times too.
We're not our neighbor's keeper. So when they came
to tell me you'd gone broke, I always knew

you wouldn't ask for charity. And now
you don't need it anymore. They've seen you home
with a few last words and nothing more to do.

This little space of earth they gave your name
is all that's left. The rest goes on the same.
They told me you were going broke. I knew
before the words. But what was I to do?

From *How It Seems to Me: New & Selected Poems.*
Fairwater, WI: Midwest Writers Publishing House, 2004.

Phil Hey has been writing and teaching at Briar Cliff University since 1969.
He received an MFA at the University of Iowa Writers Workshop in 1966.
In 1998, he was given the Literacy Award for college English teachers by
the Iowa Council of Teachers of English and Language Arts. Published in
numerous magazines and anthologies, Phil is the author of six collections
of poetry, most recently *How It Seems to Me: New and Selected Poems.*

Shampoo

ERNIE WORMWOOD

In 2001, at a workshop at Anam Cara in Ireland, I was given a copy of *Not Far From the River*, poems from the Gatha Saptasati, translated by David Ray. The poems as translated from the ancient Prakrit are quatrains written by various poets over two thousand years ago. The first one translated by David Ray is the first one I read:

> Now that I see these dancers
> I recall how much I enjoyed
> that shampoo
> you gave me with your feet.

I was absolutely seduced and immediately intrigued by how such a shampoo would take place. I had never seen a single foot shampoo. The first response poem I wrote was entitled "Deciding How to Give a Foot Shampoo" and, although I didn't intend it, people laughed when I read it. I wrote the poem with the single speaker giving directions on deciding how to give the shampoo. Some images from the first version survive in the final poem "Shampoo," such as the mechanics for the shampoo, who sits where, and the provision that hair was not required for the shampoo, lending credibility to the not so hidden eroticism of one person giving another a foot shampoo. I confess to much swooning as I imagined this. But my first version engendered laughing, not swooning.

I let the poem rest. In 2003, at the Southampton Writer's Conference, in a workshop with Marie Howe, I was introduced to poems written as dialogues and up popped the final version of the poem as an interrogation between the shampooee and shampooer. This version was not at all funny, but used simple language to mask and enhance the mystery, apprehension, and excitement between the two who are about to indulge in a shampoo given with the feet. It seemed to flow from the original quatrains.

I also simplified the title, giving the poem an edge, drawing the reader into the interaction. The previous title had acted as a kind of "hat" for the poem and was relegated to the place where old hats go.

So the different concept for the poem came after a time and on reading the work of others under the tutelage of a poet of great subtlety. I have quite happily found the poem on a couple of lists of people's favorite poems on the Internet.

"Deciding How to Give a Foot Shampoo" was never published. "Shampoo" appears in *Rhino*, 2006.

Deciding How to Give a Foot Shampoo

> "Now that I see these dancers
> I recall how much I enjoyed
> that shampoo
> you gave me with your feet."

> *Not Far From the River*,
> poems from the
> Gatha Saptasati,
> translated by David Ray

Think on your technique, how you will lie down,
whether you will lie down,
on top or bottom
or end to end or side to side,
or might you have the shampooee on the floor
while you sit in a lovely chair with wings?

Will it be totally no hands?
What to wear, not wear.
It is not necessary to have hair to receive a shampoo.

Remove calluses, toe rings. Consider a pre-pedicure with hot wax. At
least trim toenails.
How about a bright polish, for zest?

Practice holding tiny brushes between your toes.
Mechanics of rinsing?
Egyptian towels?

Shampoo

"Now that I see these dancers
I recall how much I enjoyed
that shampoo
you gave me with your feet."

Not Far From the River, poems from
the Gatha Saptasati, translated by
David Ray

How will you give the shampoo?

*You will lie down. I will lie down, either on top of you or underneath you.
My feet must be near your head. Or we may lie end to end. I might sit
in a lovely chair with wings with you at my feet.*

Will you use your hands?

*My hands will help to pour, but the form of the shampoo is my feet on
your hair.*

What will I wear?

Whatever you like.

What will you wear?

Whatever you like.

Must I have hair?

Hair is not necessary for a foot shampoo. Many shave their heads after.

What if I want more than one shampoo?

*This happens often and it is quite acceptable to have another shampoo,
and another, and another.*

Ernie Wormwood is a member of the Squaw Valley Community of Writers,
a recipient of the Southampton Writer's Conference Poetry Scholarship

(2003), and was a finalist in the Dogfish Head Poetry Contest in 2005. Her poems have appeared in *Yawp, The Antietam Review, The Cafe Review, Rhino, Beltway Poetry Quarterly, InnisfreePoetry Journal, Convergence, Raintiger, Writer's Alliance, Poetrybay, Upstage Magazine*, and in the anthologies *Poetic Voices Without Borders* and *Only the Sea Keeps: Poetry of the Tsunami*. She lives in Maryland, teaches at several local colleges, and is an activist for peace.

Life List

Janet McCann

L ife List" was written in memory of a colleague and friend, a Milton
specialist who died of bone cancer just after retirement — actually, the
first symptoms of the disease caused the retirement. My intent was to write
a small elegy for him. The first line in the draft came first. He did, indeed,
know everything there was to know about birds, and taught me the names
of the birds who visited the campus.

Draft Version

Life List

My friend who knew the name of every bird
is dying, after a quiet regular life
of Milton and birdwatching, and if I could
imagine him a farewell, it would be this,
to look out back into the tidy yard
he tended for forty years, to where
he placed the martin house he'd built
and the hummingbird feeder,
just in time to see a sweep of air
curve in and take form, the giant bird
not on his life list, there on the sill,
to be recognized by beak, feathers and pinions
and final knowledge, Adam's homecoming
after the story's end, better than Eden.
May he leave in his hand a feather, so that his wife
would know where he had gone.

After I finished the draft, I realized that I hadn't identified him clearly
enough initially, so I changed the first line to be a full identification. I
changed "tidy" to "small" because the word *tidy* seemed to suggest fussi-
ness. As for the next lines, I wanted it clear that there were a bunch of bird
houses, not just two.

The major change for me was the elimination of the "giant bird." I don't know anything about birds, except the names of the few my colleague had identified for me, and I did not want a reader to visualize something from Sesame Street. So I took a bird book, and looked through it until I found something with enough presence to make it a possible symbol of the transcendent. I looked at the book for a long time before choosing.

I wanted to make the religious slant of the poem clearly accessible but not to hit the reader over the head with it. I think some of the tinkering I did was with that in mind.

I changed "leave in his hand" to "have in his hand" because I did not want too many confusing "he" references: the first to the bird, the second to the scholar. It is still a vague reference but I think the "he" is now intuitively identifiable without too much thought.

I changed the spacing to tercets because I have always liked tercets; they make me think of Dante. Additionally, the poem seemed to read too fast without those breaks. My last decision had to do with the dedication — to use the name? His family might be offended, so I used initials.

Final Version

In memory of S. A.

My friend the scholar-birdwatcher
is dying, after a quiet regular life
of Milton and birds, and if I could

imagine him a farewell, it would be this:
to look out into the small yard
he tended for forty years, to where

he placed the bird houses, the martin
house and the hummingbird feeder,
just in time to see a sweep of air

curve in and take form, the great arctic gyrfalcon
not on his life list, there on the sill,
to be recognized by beak, feathers and pinions

and final knowledge, Adam's homecoming
after the story's end, better than Eden.
May he have in his hand a feather, that his wife

might know where he has gone.

Janet McCann's poems have been published in *Kansas Quarterly, Parnassus, Nimrod, Sou'wester, New York Quarterly, Tendril, Poetry Australia, McCall's,* and elsewhere. She has won three chapbook contests, sponsored by Pudding Publications, Chimera Connections, and Franciscan University Press. She has co-edited two anthologies, *Odd Angles of Heaven* (1994) and *Place of Passage* (Story Line, 2000). Her most recent poetry book is *Emily's Dress* (Pecan Grove Press, 2004). A 1989 NEA Creative Writing Fellowship winner, she has taught at Texas A & M University since 1969.

Exodus

JAY RUBIN

In the spring of 2006, I enrolled in a midrash poetry-writing class offered at the Jewish Community Center in San Francisco. Midrash, for those unfamiliar with the term, is simply a genre of literature that re-examines or, as is often the case, reinterprets biblical stories, mining those ancient texts for contemporary subject matter. This particular class was led by award-winning poet Dan Bellm, who not only spoke Hebrew but was also quite knowledgeable about the Bible, especially the book of Exodus, which was the focus of our class.

During each class meeting, we spent the first hour reviewing a specific section of Exodus, usually a few chapters that we'd been assigned to read ahead of time. Our discussions were quite lively, each of the half-dozen students in class often having very different interpretations of particular biblical passages. After an hour, we'd stop our discussions, open up our journals, and begin freewriting for thirty to forty minutes. Once done, we read our freewrites aloud to one another. Often, but not always, our freewrites wound up being revised into poems.

Here's a copy of the freewrite I wrote one night in class:

Exodus (Freewrite)

What did those Hebrews talk about, wandering out in the desert? Did they debate the existence of God? Did one Hebrew point to the morning's wealth of manna, another pointing out the sand in his cup of wine? Hundreds or thousands or hundreds of thousands camping out in the dark desert. Burning Man, at its height, draws maybe thirty thousand, a temporary city on the Nevada moonscape, the sun beating down all day like a dry-skin drum, at night the moon rising among a diamond-crusted velvet sky. What did these Hebrews talk about? Did they long for their days in Egypt? Did they come to find pleasure in

159

captivity, the guardian who feeds them, clothes them, chides them into submission. This God is our new Egypt, one Hebrew shakes his fist. *Quiet*, says another, *He'll hear you*. Who did the healing out in the desert? Did the doctors and the nurses mock all the midwives? Who played the part of apothecary? Who sold the health insurance? What did those Hebrews talk about? Did their children go to school, perform in plays? Which one portrayed Pharaoh? Which one stuttered like old man Moses? Who played straight man Aaron? Was Miriam, even at her advanced age, the first public sex symbol, the desert Madonna, holding her hip-hop court? At night sometimes, I stand alone in my backyard, the fog spilling down from Twin Peaks. I can hear the cedars creak, the palm fronds rustling. Are they speaking to each other? Are they pointing at me, giggling, a Moses still unsure, still uncertain why the fog has called my name?

After I decided to work this freewrite into a poem, the next step was to type the freewrite directly onto the computer. The typed version looked much as it does above. Then I went through the text and began breaking it into lines. As you can see, the first sentence of the freewrite is a question. After breaking that question into two lines, dividing it at its internal comma, I liked the visual length of both lines. Therefore, I based the remaining line lengths on more or less the same visual length. The first draft looked like this:

Exodus (Lineation)

What did those Hebrews talk about,
wandering out in the desert?
Did they debate the existence
of God? Did one Hebrew point
to the morning's wealth of manna,
another pointing out the sand

in his cup of wine? Hundreds or
thousands or hundreds of thousands
camping out in the dark desert.
Burning Man, at its height,
draws maybe thirty thousand,
a temporary city on the Nevada
moonscape, the sun beating
down all day like a dry-skin drum,
at night the moon rising
among a diamond-crusted velvet sky.
What did these Hebrews talk about?
Did they long for their days in Egypt?
Did they come to find pleasure
in the captivity, the guardian who feeds them,
clothes them, chides them into submission.
This God is our new Egypt,
one Hebrew shakes his fist.
Quiet, says another, *He'll hear you.*
Who did the healing out in the desert?
Did the doctors and the nurses
mock all the midwives?
Who played the part of apothecary?
Who sold the health insurance?
What did those Hebrews talk about?
Did their children go to school,
perform in plays? Which one
portrayed Pharaoh? Which one
stuttered like old man Moses?
Who played straight man Aaron?
Was Miriam, even at her advanced age,
the first public sex symbol, the desert
Madonna, holding her hip-hop court?
At night sometimes, I stand alone
in my backyard, the fog spilling down
from Twin Peaks. I can hear
the cedars creak, the palm fronds
rustling. Are they speaking to each other?
Are they pointing at me, giggling,

a Moses still unsure, still uncertain
why the fog has called my name?

As I reread the first draft, I immediately noticed a repeated pattern in the first nine lines: With the exception of line 4, each of the first nine lines contained exactly eight syllables. That syllabic count then became the standard measurement as I proceeded to revise the poem.

In the first line, I changed "Hebrews" to "ancients," hoping it would help center the poem in the long-ago past. In the second line, by changing "out" to "lost," I was able to keep the eight-syllable line while adding more information to the poem: After all, the ancient Hebrews weren't simply *out* in the desert, as if on some holiday outing; they were lost. I left the third line alone. In the fourth line, the one that was only seven syllables, I added the adjective "vain" to describe the Hebrews, extending the line to eight syllables. Line 5 was fine as it was. In line 6, I changed "pointing out" to "pointing to." Though this made no difference to the line's length, it slightly changed the intention of the pointing Hebrew, allowing him, perhaps, to be noticing the sand for the first time, rather than pointing it out as previously discovered evidence. At this point, the first major cut occurred. I decided to delete all references to the Burning Man arts festival. While the digression had been interesting to me during the freewriting process, it seemed like an unnecessary diversion for the poem. With those ten and a half lines removed, the eighth line was two syllables short. I fixed that problem by making the sand "floating" in the wine. And I wound up ending the first stanza with the refrain-like question: "What did these Hebrews talk about?"

At this point, I noticed that the first stanza not only comprised eight-syllable lines, it was also eight lines long. I liked that structural pattern — eight lines of eight syllables each. It was sort of boxy. And the box-like stanzas reminded me of the ancient Hebrews, themselves boxed in by the desert. Having this stanza pattern set, I was able to approach the rest of the poem.

To reduce the first line of the second stanza from nine to eight syllables, I removed the superfluous "their" from "their days." The next line, though, required a complete rewrite. By putting a dash at the end of the first line, I could use the second line to describe those "days in Egypt." What I came up with — "The sweet surety of bondage" — was exactly eight syllables. Perfect! I replaced "guardian" in the next line with "Pharaoh," referring to the guardian by his precise title, and changed the verb "feeds" to the past tense. Since I'd removed the phrase *in the captivity* from the start of the third line, I needed two more syllables to bring the line to eight. I fixed this by bringing the first two syllables of the next line, "clothes them," up to the end of the third line, changing again the present-tense verb to the past tense. To keep the fourth line eight syllables, too, I added the word *blind* before "submission"; and, to change the verbal abuse of the Hebrews to physical abuse, I changed "chides" to "beat." Because the fifth line was a line of dialogue, I allowed its syllabic count to vary. And to signify the line as dialogue, I italicized it rather than put it quotes — just because I liked the way it looked. In the next two lines, to indicate the tension between the arguing Hebrews, I let the syllabic variance continue. I changed "Quiet" to "Sheket," which is Hebrew for "Be quiet." And I put an exclamation point at the end of the line. Finally, after cutting out all the questions about doctors and nurses and health insurance salesmen, the eight-line stanza was left to close with the near-repeated refrain "What did those Hebrews talk about?"

Since I'd already removed the digressions about Burning Man and the references to the health industry, I decided to remove the next eight lines about the Hebrew schoolchildren performing in theatrical plays about their exodus from Egypt. That meant the third and final stanza would begin with me, the speaker in the poem, standing in my backyard.

After removing "the" from before "fog," I was able to keep the third stanza's second line the standard eight syllables. To add a couple syllables to the following line, I put "almost" before "hear." With the fourth line short by a syllable, I brought "rustling" up from the next line, making the fourth line one syllable too long; even so, the variation introduced some new tension (the speaker, after all, feels as if he's been gossiped about), so I allowed it. For the fifth line, I replaced "speaking" with "talking" to echo the talking Hebrews in the refrain lines. I then added dashes to offset the "giggling," and turned "giggling" into "laughing." Finally, I switched around "unsure" and "uncertain" so that the line would end with the longer *ur* sound rather than the short *un* sound. The revised draft looked like this:

Exodus (Revised)

What did those ancients talk about,
Wandering lost in the desert?

Did they debate the existence
Of God? Did one vain Hebrew point
To the morning's wealth of manna,
Another pointing to the sand
Floating in his Sabbath wine?
What did those Hebrews talk about?

Did they long for days in Egypt —
The sweet surety of bondage:
The Pharaoh who fed them, clothed them,
Beat them into blind submission.
This God is our new Egypt,
One Hebrew shakes his fist.
Sheket! says another. *He'll hear you!*
What did those Hebrews talk about?

At night sometimes, I stand alone
In my backyard, fog spilling down
From Twin Peaks. I can almost hear
The cedars creak, the palm fronds rustling.
Are they talking to each other?
Are they pointing at me — laughing
— A Moses still uncertain, still unsure
Why the fog has called my name?

During the spring of 2006, I was an MFA candidate in New England College's low-residency MFA in Poetry program; so I sent this draft of "Exodus" to my semester mentor Jeff Friedman, a poet who's written quite a few midrash poems — both his own and others that he's translated from Hebrew. His main criticism of "Exodus" was that the third stanza didn't seem to fit in with the other two, that it seemed like part of another poem. As with most criticism I get, I ignored it at first. A couple months later, when I brought the same draft to be workshopped at the New England College MFA Program's summer residency, the workshop leader and the other MFA candidates in the group all agreed with what my mentor had said — the poem needed some sort of transition between the second and third stanzas.

I found my solution by going back to the original draft. While keeping out the lines referring to the Hebrew schoolchildren and their theatrical productions, I reinserted lines and ideas related to Moses, Aaron, and Miriam. Essentially, the project of the poem was to meditate on the Hebrews in the desert, then draw a comparison between how Moses must have felt being called by God and how I sometimes feel, wondering if there's a divine calling meant for me. To meet this end, I started a new third stanza by asking several questions about how Moses must have felt. To contrast Moses' reluctant obedience, I asked another question about his brother Aaron and sister Miriam. Of the eight lines in this new stanza, only one matched the standard eight-syllable pattern. This was okay with me since this stanza now introduced the most tension of the poem — tension reflective of Moses' fear and his siblings' disobedience. In fact, while the one standard eight-syllable line referred to Moses' obedience, the stanza's last three lines, those breaking out of the boxy pattern, refer to Aaron and Miriam who, in their disobedience, were breaking out of a box of their own.

Although this new stanza, like the original three, was eight lines long, I felt as if the transition to the final stanza was still somewhat weak. To indicate a shift, I added a single centered asterisk between the third and fourth stanzas. This is a technique often used by poet Louis Simpson who, in the first part of many short poems, sets up a narrative situation, then, after a stanza break with a single centered asterisk, concludes with another short stanza that reflects on the first part of the poem. Further, following some other suggestions from the NEC workshop, I changed "The Pharaoh" to "A Pharaoh" in the second stanza, and I changed the verb in the refrain line at the end of the second stanza from the general "talk" to the more specific "fight." ("Argue" might have been a more accurate word, but it had one too many syllables.) Finally, in the third-to-last line, I switched "pointing" and "laughing," then removed one dash, offsetting the final image of me as Moses wondering what my call might be. Here's the final version.

Exodus (Final)

What did those ancients talk about,
Wandering lost in the desert?
Did they debate the existence
Of God? Did one vain Hebrew point
To the morning's wealth of manna,
Another pointing to the sand
Floating in his Sabbath wine?

What did those Hebrews talk about?
Did they long for days in Egypt —
The sweet surety of bondage:
A Pharaoh who fed them, clothed them,
Beat them into blind submission.
This God is our new Egypt,
One Hebrew shakes his fist.
Sheket! says another. *He'll hear you!*
What did those Hebrews fight about?

And what of Moses, up on that mountain?
What did he make of burning bushes,
Bitter fog and lighting strikes?
Did he beg for God's good pardon?
Did he plead for prophecy?
And what of Aaron, down among the flock,
His sister Miriam singing songs,
Dancing for a golden calf?

*

Sometimes at night, I stand alone
In my backyard, fog spilling down
From Twin Peaks. I can almost hear
The cedars creak, the palm fronds rustling.
Are they talking to each other?
Are they laughing at me, pointing —
A Moses still uncertain, still unsure
Why the fog has called my name?

Of course, a piece of writing is never quite finished. I could keep making changes to this poem after each time I read it. Eventually, though, a poem is simply abandoned, released to the world — warts and all.

Jay Rubin teaches composition and creative writing at the College of Alameda in the San Francisco Bay Area. He is also the editor and publisher of *Alehouse*, an all-poetry literary journal. His own poems have been published in journals across the country.

Writing Eye

David Radavich

I was originally moved to write "Writing Eye" upon learning of the death of Pramoedya Ananta Toer, the great Indonesian writer and novelist who passed away in spring 2006. "Pak Pram," as he was affectionately known, endured incredible hardships during years of incarceration and torture, including losing his hearing as a result of a vigilante attack in his home. Yet he somehow never lost his commitment to books and to writing, and he refused to become cynical or hateful: "That would be an intolerable burden" (*Rhein Neckar Zeitung*, April 2006).

I wanted to capture something of that admirable courage and commitment in my own poem, which I originally called "The Writing Eye." But I never felt quite at ease with the result, especially the final section; I did not feel the poem lived up to either its subject or its promise. Fortunately, I have since been able to revise it into something that approaches my initial vision.

The Writing Eye
In memory of Pramoedya Ananta Toer, 1925–2006

One night they came
to his house masked, beat him
to the floor, then carried
him away to jail.

All his books torched,
papers burst into flames
like ideas
being first born.

More than a decade
without waiting.

Yet he kept
putting pen into paper,

sneaking out leaves with
visitors, nurses, missionaries.

How could he
think we would turn

his pages now,
open our eyes as telescopes
in the long, black, forgotten night?

In our smooth leather
chairs under halogen light,
how could we

remember
what words are

whose heads
have not been fired
in the hands of the street?

Behind masks
with dark ideologies.

Here we are

consuming to death
like zombies, dominoes,
drugged-out vandals

of green life

that has lost
its mind in many

private cells

so silent
they no longer

see beyond striated walls

or even try
to escape the torture

they no longer acknowledge.

My first change involved the title: removing the simple word *the*
seemed to tighten the import, avoiding an unnecessary word but also suggesting that the word *writing* could serve either as an adjectival participle
("the eye that writes") or as a verb ("writing the eye"), with multiple meanings. I kept the first section virtually the same except for one small word in
the second line of stanza four. In the first version, I had written "putting
pen into paper," hoping to escape the obvious cliché, "putting pen to
paper," while also suggesting a physicality in the act of writing, even a
kind of ferocity. However, upon reflection, that seemed too cute or precious
by half, so I opted for "putting pen on paper," which still avoids the cliché,
suggests physicality, yet doesn't call too much attention to itself.

The second section remains intact, but the third section I altered sub-
stantially. I added "Yet" at the outset of that final section as an intensifier
implying contrast. In the early version, the ending stanzas twice mention
"they," which refers grammatically to "private cells," while the "its" in the
fourth stanza of this section refers to "green life." These references are problematic on at least two levels: (1) it's not clear in each case what exactly is
referenced; and (2) strictly speaking, "green life" doesn't have a mind and
"private cells" do not see or acknowledge. Sometimes such metaphorical
leaps can be justified in poetry — I do it all the time, strategically — but
these simply did not work.

Instead, I changed all the pronominal references to "we," which unites
the final section from beginning to end and adds considerable power. So
it's no longer the vague "green life" that has lost its mind but "we." (I also
rearranged the middle lines of that section to emphasize "minds" and
"cells.") The final two verbs are a great deal more accusatory than before:
"we no longer see" and "we no longer acknowledge." Thus the revised
version points an indicting finger at the comfortable West, imprisoned in

its own commercialist bubble that doesn't see either its own enslavement or the abuse of committed voices like Pramoedya Ananta Toer.

Writing Eye
In memory of Pramoedya Ananta Toer, 1925–2006

One night they came
to his house masked, beat him

to the floor, then carried
him away to jail.

All his books torched,
papers burst into flames
like ideas
being first born.

More than a decade
without waiting.

Yet he kept
putting pen on paper,

sneaking out leaves with
visitors, nurses, missionaries.

How could he
think we would turn

his pages now,
open our eyes as telescopes
in the long, black, forgotten night?

In our smooth leather
chairs under halogen light,
how could we

remember
what words are

whose heads
have not been fired
in the hands of the street?

Behind masks
with dark ideologies.

Yet here we are

consuming to death
like zombies, dominoes,
drugged-out vandals

of green life

having lost our
minds

in many private cells

so silent
we no longer

see beyond striated walls

or even try
to escape the torture

we no longer acknowledge.

The revised poem, "Writing Eye," unlike the preliminary version, ends on a note of protest and witness, implicitly critiquing recent American policies regarding torture in Guantanamo Bay and rendition programs that violate international law yet are regarded by large segments of the national public as justified and acceptable. In so ending the poem, I continue the legacy of Pak Pram into our own time and place in a manner I feel he would applaud.

David Radavich is the author of *Slain Species* (Court Poetry Press, London), *By the Way: Poems over the Years* (Buttonwood Press, 1998), and *Greatest Hits* (Pudding House, 2000). He has also published a full-length comedy, *Nevertheless* ..., several short dramas, and a wide range of poetry in journals and anthologies. His plays have been performed across the United States, including five Off-Off-Broadway productions, and in Europe. His new book, *America Bound: An Epic for Our Time*, was published by Plain View Press in 2007.

Depth of Field

WINIFRED HUGHES

This poem began as a response to the extraordinary pioneering photographs of Julia Margaret Cameron, taken mostly during the 1860s. The
first draft attempted to get at the intensity and revelatory quality of her
portraits of "famous men," as well as her allegorical and mythic tableaux.
What fascinated me most was the long exposure time — three to ten minutes — and its effect on Cameron's sitters. The material seemed to call for
a spacious, largely narrative form, which I broke into six-line stanzas with
alternate indented lines, in order to keep the poem moving and to create
moments of tension through the use of enjambment at the ends of both
lines and stanzas ("the time required to hold / / one pose," lines 6–7, for example).

(1)

Victorian Portraits
Julia Margaret Cameron, 1815–1879

They never smiled. Not that they
    were naturally stiff, priggish,
whale-boned or stock-collared,
    but no one could keep it up
five or ten minutes at a stretch,
    the time required to hold

one pose, one set expression,
    until the slow-motion
shutter shut them down, and they were
    thoroughly exposed.
A sigh, absentminded shift
    or eyeblink, and the image

blurred successive selves together,
    mismatched chronologies.
Old Julia Cameron, her black dress

stained with silver nitrate,
preferred to stage her sitters,
        costumed them as knights

or angels, hardly bothered to disguise
        the broomstick mast
above King Arthur's longboat —
        courted illusion and got
reality in the form of her Madonna's
        boredom, the unfeigned

sulkiness of her infant Christ.
        She brooded her "famous men" —
Browning, Herschel, Carlyle,
        Tennyson as the "dirty monk" —
in a converted chicken-coop,
        terrorized them into

looking truth right back at her,
        gazing at time's measured
passage without a flinch,
        their characters deepening
visibly as they sat and waited
        for nothing more

than to stop the waiting. Julia
        gave them no escape
from her tightened focus
        on cheek bones, brow ridge,
taut mouth, eyes anguished
        or remote – a presence

surfacing they hadn't known
        was kept inside them,
as they became composites
        of themselves, each disparate
moment at once suspended
        and left behind.

After reading the first draft at a meeting of U.S.1 Poets' Cooperative, I decided that I needed to make the situation more immediate for today's readers — to get "us" into the poem, so to speak. I let it sit for a month or so, until I came up with a more compelling way into my material by re-phrasing the line "no one could keep it up" as a question, "Could we keep it up ...?" At that point, I went back and underlined the passages that seemed most essential, that I really didn't want to let go of. Right away, the structural framework of a new, much tighter and denser poem seemed to leap out at me. In putting together the underlined passages, I shortened the line and stanza lengths, increasing the overall tension, while still allowing for a full stop — and stanza break — after the crucial line "shutter shuts them down." Both verbally and thematically, I was interested in the juxtaposition of "posed and exposed" (the new line 4) but on second thought, gave it a twist by replacing "posed" with "poised" (which still contains "posed"). In the new third stanza, I needed to rearrange the "sigh" and the "blink" for rhythm and for assonance (long *i*'s in "sigh" and "absentminded," short *i*'s in "shift" and "blink").

(2)
Victorian Portraits
Julia Margaret Cameron, 1815-1879

They never smiled. Not that they
        were naturally stiff, priggish,
whale-boned or stock-collared,
        but no one could keep it up
five or ten minutes at a stretch,
        the time required to hold

one pose, one set expression,
        until the slow-motion
shutter shut them down, and they were
        thoroughly exposed.
A sigh, absentminded   shift
        or eyeblink, and the image

blurred successive selves together,
        mismatched chronologies.

175

Old Julia Cameron, her black dress
    stained with silver nitrate,
preferred to stage her sitters,
    costumed them as knights

or angels, hardly bothered to disguise
    the broomstick mast
above King Arthur's longboat —
    courted illusion and got
reality in the form of her Madonna's
    boredom, the unfeigned

sulkiness of her infant Christ.
    She brooded her "famous men" —
Browning, Herschel, Carlyle,
    Tennyson as the "dirty monk" —
in a converted chicken-coop,
    terrorized them into

looking truth right back at her,
    gazing at time's measured
passage without a flinch,
    their characters deepening
visibly as they sat and waited
    for nothing more

than to stop the waiting. Julia
    gave them no escape
from her tightened focus
    on cheek bones, brow ridge,
taut mouth, eyes anguished
    or remote — a presence

surfacing they hadn't known
    was kept inside them,
as they became composites
    of themselves, each disparate
moment at once suspended
    and left behind.

(3)
Victorian Portraits

Could we keep it up
as they did, five or ten
minutes at a stretch,

posed and exposed
before the slow-motion
shutter shut them down?

An eyeblink, absentminded
shift or sigh, and the image
blurred haphazard

selves together, mismatched
chronologies. Could we have
gazed at time's measured

passage without a flinch,
looked truth right back at it,
our characters deepening

visibly as we sat and waited
for nothing more
than to stop the waiting —

taut mouth, eyes anguished
or remote, a presence
surfacing we hadn't known

was kept inside us. Could we
become composites of
ourselves, each disparate

moment at once suspended
and left behind? We know
why they never smiled.

It took a few more drafts to get the tenses right and to complete the shift from third to first person. The somewhat distanced present perfect of "Could we have / gazed" (lines 11–12) and the completed past of "we sat and waited" (line 16) became instead the more direct and inescapable present. The change of tense at line 11, along with the decision to omit the words *mismatched chronologies*, left "Could we" at the end of the line, placing emphasis on "we" in comparison with Cameron's subjects. Where I had kept the original wording of "shutter shuts them down" (line 6), I realized it had to be "us" who get shut down. From the start, I had wanted to suggest something more than just a literal picture-taking session; I felt I was able to evoke a larger sense of the passage of time and more definitive endings by putting "us," the living, into the same position as the long-dead Victorians. Finally, I had the sense to cut out the last two stanzas, which seemed unnecessarily wordy and complex, even though I lost my original first and favorite line — the starting point for my thinking about Cameron's photographs ("they never smiled").

(4)
Looking at Victorian Photographs

Could we keep it up
as they did, five or ten
minutes at a stretch,

poised and exposed,
before the slow-motion
shutter shuts us down?

A sigh, absentminded shift
or eyeblink, and the image
blurs successive

selves together. Could we
gaze at time's measured
passage without a flinch

look truth right back at it,
our characters deepening
visibly as we sit

waiting for nothing more
than to stop the wait —
mouth taut, eyes remote

or anguished, a presence
surfacing we hadn't known
inside us.

When I read the revision at U.S.1, I found myself trying to explain the photographic process behind Cameron's startling images and decided that the term *depth of field* would make a more intriguing title. I also had to admit, as one colleague pointed out, that the long exposure time was not technically "slow-motion" (line 5), which I replaced with "slowed." Someone else suggested moving the detailed description of the sitting in the last two stanzas up to the beginning of the poem, where the process of exposure is more generally referred to. I did try that suggestion but concluded that I couldn't, and in fact didn't want to, make it work. The final version was published in *Poetry* in April 2002.

(5)
Depth of Field
   (Victorian Portraits)

Could we keep it up
as they did, five or ten
minutes at a stretch,

poised and exposed
before the slowed shutter
shuts us down?

A sigh, absentminded
shift or blink, and the image
blurs successive

selves together. Could we
gaze at time's measured
passage without a flinch,

look truth right back at it,
our characters deepening
visibly as we sit

waiting for nothing more
than to stop the wait —
mouth taut, eyes remote

or anguished, a presence
surfacing we hadn't known
inside us.

Winifred Hughes is a writer and editor living in Princeton, N.J. Her poems have appeared in *Poetry, Poetry Northwest, Ars Interpres, Dalhousie Review,* and *The Literary Review,* among other journals. Her critical book, *The Maniac in the Cellar: Sensation Novels of the 1860s,* was published by Princeton University Press.

Last In

JANNETT HIGHFILL

This poem was prompted by a conversation with my mother about a year ago. My aunt had recently fallen on the landing, and my mother had had to call the fire department to rescue her. The image of what my mother must have seen stayed with me until the first four stanzas emerged in the first draft. As I was musing on that beginning, I had the idea of treating humans as a kind of inventory problem, and the ending emerged as well (from "In the middle of the night / wedged between the Newell" to the end). With a beginning and an ending, I needed a middle — as you see in the first draft. I situated my aunt as a widow with a detail or two and then described an incident that I've often heard about from my mother's childhood.

Last In

The upstairs landing is so small lying
on the floor is a stunt in space

management — turning yourself
into a human jigsaw puzzle,

or playing twister with a giant
fiddle-leaf fig. The middle of the night

takes the edge off the game —
it's all been a sick joke anyway

since your husband slumped over
a stack of invoices and never

sat up by himself again — you
called 9-1-1 enough then.

You don't much care this time whether
it's firemen or angels, or your sisters

(you've been the baby of the family
for fifty years now), the sisters who

spent their childhood playing
road trip to New-York-Boston

in a salvaged-out chassis abandoned
in the windrow, your mother

having packed potato salad (chunked,
not mashed) for the road.

Your sisters played road trip
without you, not missing you,

not born yet. How could you forgive
them? In the middle of the night

wedged between the Newell
post and a cast stone planter

you wait for your sisters,
or whatever, if God manages

a family like inventory —
last in, first out.

When I came to revise the poem, it seemed to me that the dominant feeling of the poem, especially at the end, was acceptance tinged with something else, resentment, perhaps. In the body of the poem, I'd given two independent reasons why my aunt might be feeling resentment: her time of being a widow, and her relationship with her sisters as the much younger child in a large family. I couldn't help noticing that the latter seemed more interesting to me, so I gave it more space and filled in more details. In my revision, the most important decision I make is to scrap the matter about the deceased husband.

The second thing I noticed about the poem when I came to revise it was its movement through time. The first draft begins *in medias res*, moves to the continuous present, then comes a brief flashback (the husband's stroke). Then the poem returns to the present moment, then another bit of continuous present, and then a longer flashback (the sisters' childhood game), one moment of ambiguous time, and finally the return to the present. Beginning a poem *in medias res* creates drama and immediacy, which are hard to sacrifice. But drama must be weighed against clarity (or the lack thereof), and I think clarity in this poem is best served by a more chronological timeline. So the second change I made was to revise the structure of the poem. (The revision also eliminates a lot of repetition and scene setting: "The middle of the night / / takes…" and "In the middle of the night / / wedged…"; "…the sisters who spent their childhood playing / road trip…" and "Your sisters played road trip….")

The structural changes between the first and final drafts are shown in the accompanying table. Although much of the final draft is in the first draft, the table demonstrates the complete structural reworking of the poem when I applied the simple rule of recounting things chronologically. (The table, however, obscures the choice to abandon the couplets of the first draft for an organic stanza with more dramatic possibilities.)

Between the first draft and the final draft, I had only to add three things. The first is a bit of scene-setting, "A lifetime ago." The second is a bit of exposition, "who find you," which is certainly implied in the first draft but the economy and arrangement of the revision let me make it explicit. The third and thematically most important is "and sicker than any of them" to give more weight to the resentment my aunt might be feeling.

And of course there are other choices in the revision. I trade one kind of sound for another in "thorny / ornamental orange" for "fiddle-leaf fig" because I want "thorny" and the assonance with "contorting" from the previous stanza, the change in that word being prompted by my desire to use the word *turning* earlier in the stanza. But these kinds of revisions — the fun part of working on a poem — are made possible by the major structural work on the poem.

The most important effect of the structural reworking of the poem — simplifying the time line into only a long ago (the sisters' childhood) and the present moment — is the fulcrum between the two times: "How could you forgive them?" This question applies equally well to the past, the continuing present, and the moment of crisis on the stairway landing. The revision highlights this emotional center of the poem and delivers it to the reader much sooner.

Last In, First Draft

Last In, Final Poem

The upstairs landing is so small lying
on the floor is a stunt in space

management—turning yourself
into a human jigsaw puzzle,

or playing twister with a giant
fiddle-leaf fig.

The middle of the night

takes the edge off the game—
it's all been a sick joke anyway

since your husband slumped over
a stack of invoices and never

sat up by himself again—you
called 9-1-1 enough then.

You don't much care this time whether
it's firemen or angels, or your sisters

(you've been the baby of the family
for fifty years now)

the sisters who

spent their childhood playing
road trip to New-York-Boston

in a salvaged-out chassis abandoned
in the woodrow,

your mother

having packed potato salad (chunked,
not mashed)

for the road.

Your sisters played road trip

without you, not missing you,

not born yet. How could you forgive
them?

In the middle of the night

wedged between the Newell
post and a cast stone planter

you wait for your sisters,
or whatever, if God manages

a family like inventory—
last in, first out.

A lifetime ago

your mother

having packed potato salad (chunked,
not mashed)

your sisters

in a salvaged-out chassis in the windrow
played road trip to New-York-Boston

without you, not missing you,
not born yet. How could you forgive
them?

Now, the baby of the family
for fifty years

and sicker than any
of them

you don't much care whether
it's firemen or angels, or your sisters

who find you

wedged between
the Newell post and a cast stone planter

on the upstairs landing, a turning
so small that lying on the floor is a stunt
in space management—contorting yourself

into a human jigsaw puzzle,
or playing twister with a thorny
ornamental orange tree.

You wait for your sisters,
or whatever, if God manages

a family like inventory—
last in, first out.

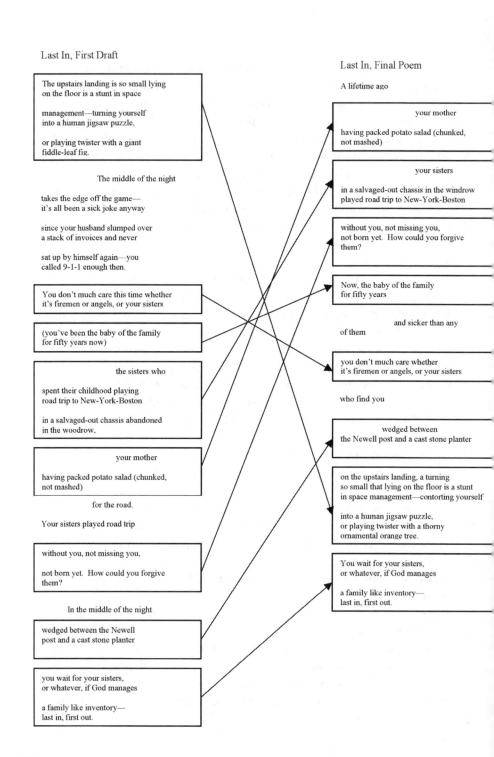

184

Final Version

Last In

A lifetime ago your mother
having packed potato salad (chunked,
not mashed) your sisters

in a salvaged-out chassis in the windrow,
played road trip to New-York-Boston

without you, not missing you,
not born yet. How could you forgive
them?

Now, the baby of the family
for fifty years and sicker than any
of them

you don't much care whether
it's firemen or angels, or your sisters

who find you wedged between
the Newell post and a cast stone planter

on the upstairs landing, a turning
so small that lying on the floor is a stunt
in space management — contorting yourself

into a human jigsaw puzzle,
or playing twister with a thorny
ornamental orange tree.

You wait for your sisters,
or whatever, if God manages

a family like inventory —
last in, first out.

This poem is for my Aunt Sue, and for my mother who tells me the stories.

Jannett Highfill received an MFA from Warren Wilson in 2001. Her poems have appeared in *The Iowa Review, Tar River Poetry, The Greensboro Review, Rhino, The North Stone Review*, and elsewhere. She has had poems nominated for an Illinois Arts Council Award and a Pushcart Prize, and was a runner up for the Iowa Award in Poetry.

On the fly-leaf of Goethe's
Venetian Epigrams

Ken Cockburn

I wrote this poem in response to an invitation from the editors of the anthology *Love for Love*, "to choose a favourite love poem and compose a response." I had been translating Goethe's *Venetian Epigrams*, written in 1790
and which, despite their charm and subtlety, are not my favorite love
poems; but it did seem feasible to write a response to them in the time
available. I had recently come across a review of a biography — the first I
think — of Goethe's lover and later wife, Christiane Vulpius, from whom
his duties in Venice kept him unhappily separated. (This mentioned the
couple's surprisingly frequent purchases of new beds, leading the biogra-
pher to speculate on her enthusiasm during sex.)

I had first read Goethe's poems in Venice in 1986 when I spent a short
holiday in the city, and still had the book I'd taken, though it was now
rather battered. One strong memory from that trip is of visiting the grave
of Ezra Pound. I was reading a biography of him at the time as well, but I
didn't know he was buried in Venice until I arrived at the graveyard and
saw his name on a sign.

So I had two moments in the past as starting points — my visit and
Goethe's — with words and images suggested by memory, and by the texts
of Goethe and Pound. To connect the poem with the present, I brought in
the setting of an Italian café in Edinburgh, on a street called Elm Row,
where I would often spend an hour writing before going in to work.

I was also wondering how to develop this material as a love poem,
given that my Venice trip wasn't connected with an affair. I introduced my
wife, but negatively, or by way of contrast with Goethe's situation, as we
weren't getting on well at the time.

I handwrote some notes trying to pull these ideas together, and typed
up the first draft of the poem. This takes these ideas and outlines them
somewhat schematically: present location, my edition of Goethe's poems,
my link with the poems, associations suggested by the present location,
Pound in Venice. Images (rather than quotes) from epigrams are woven in
as well (the waitress, "water to wine," "the benevolence of rain").

First Draft

Elm Row Epigrams
Edinburgh, October 1999
To J.W. Goethe

The waitress brings me *un Americano*
to an Italian soundtrack, paintings of the *campagna*.
Time, before the day's business kicks in. Stir the sugar, sip
strong black coffee, then the lukewarm milk to assuage its bitterness.

Opening this tatty discoloured classic, the *Venetianische Epirgramme*
going back so: read *in situ* '86; a 50p purchase, Cardiff '85;
annotated "Berlin, December 1966", published Reinbek bei Hamburg
1961; and the poems composed, Venedig, *anno* seventeen hundred and
ninety.

Considering a translation. The mercurial felicity
of their composition, your unrestrained *amore*,
my hesitant uncertain equivalents which lack your wealth.

Memories of Venice. Love was at a distance,
and the encroaching revolutions, the guillotines and the golden arches,
die Vulpius, breaker of beds, and my unrestrained dancing girl
who lately, I've done nothing but argue with.

I put the arguments with her out of my mind to contemplate
the waitress, her grace between the tables, could she
turn water to wine, and remember a friend, again maybe '86 or so,
on another occasion, another waitress: *there's a face to leave home for.*

Not to mention the unrestrained American E.P., who'd
sat on the Dogana's steps / For the gondolas cost too much that year
a lizard on his simple stone, an alert stillness
in the *cimitero evangelico*, a laurel-leaf picked, pressed

between *The Cantos*; fireworks above the lagoon, at Salute,
there for an instant and the flame is gone.
Back, it's past one. The unshuttered window. The night
is saturated with the benevolence of rain.

I could see there was a lot of extraneous material. The poem came to suggest itself as a sonnet, the octet describing reading Goethe in the café, and the sestet the range of associations this triggers. Its love theme came into focus more clearly, not as disappointment, but in a present attraction that leads to a renewed sense of possibility, a clearing or a cleansing after rain.

Second Draft

Elm Row
To J.W. Goethe

The waitress brings me *un Americano* —
bittersweet. The *Epigramme* before me,
its discoloured pages and cracked spine,
read *in situ*, back in '86;

their mercurial composition, amidst
the onrush of revolution and of love
as irresistible as the *acqua alta*
and all those broken beds in the years to come! —

The waitress moves her grace between the tables.
Could she turn water to wine? I recall another,
a friend's remark, *there's a face you'd leave home for,*

recall Pound's grave, chanced upon that morning,
before the fireworks above the lagoon, and later,
night filled with the benevolence of rain.

Edinburgh, November 1999

The content, and the order in which it is presented, has been settled, the lines are all broadly speaking pentameters, and the stanzas are the right length. But to adhere to the discipline a sonnet demands, it had to rhyme, and this is what I worked on in the final draft.

I wanted a light kind of rhyme that didn't draw attention to itself and didn't dominate the phrasing, but that added a sense of constructedness, of deliberateness, to the whole. Finding suitable rhymes involved rethinking the poem, honing the imagery and the phrasing. Many of the rhymewords are present in the second draft, but are not placed at the end of the line; others are brought in by way of a reconfiguring of certain images.

The poem was published in *Love for Love: An Anthology of Love Poems*, edited by John Burnside and Alec Finlay (Edinburgh: pocketbooks, 2000) with the title "Elm Row," a street-name evoking the natural world in an ordered form, which seemed apt. As the poem was presented with some of the Goethe epigrams, there was no need to refer to them in the title. I have since added the poem, without the translations, to a new sequence of poems, and felt I had to make the connection clear, so it has subsequently been retitled "On the fly-leaf of Goethe's *Venetian Epigrams*."

Third and Final Draft

On the fly-leaf of Goethe's *Venetian Epigrams*

The waitress brings me *un Americano.*
Bittersweet. Before me, its spine cracked,
the pages yellowing, your *Epigramme,*
read *in situ,* back in '86;

mercurially composed, creating a balance
in the rush of revolution and of love
as irresistible as the *acqua alta*
— the broken beds that were Christiane's gift —

the waitress moves her grace across the room,
could she turn water to wine? — remember
another, *there's a face you'd leave home for,* a friend

remarked, and remember Pound's grave, a chance find,
that day of the fireworks above Salute; later,
night filled with the benevolence of rain.

In my work, I'm interested in teasing out resonances and connections from a commonplace situation, in this case, reading in a café. Our everyday lives are connected with grand historical narratives; those from the past impact on the way we live today, and the way we live today will impact in larger and smaller ways on the future. We have a responsibility to the past and the future which, by making connections as in this poem, I try to point toward. Along with that sense of responsibility comes an awareness of the significance of our lives, in terms of the deeper cultural, spiritual, and political narratives we are living out, day after day.

Ken Cockburn was born in Kirkcaldy, Scotland, in 1960. He studied French and German at Aberdeen University, and Theatre Studies at University College Cardiff. He currently works as a freelance poet, editor, and writing tutor. His first collection of poems, *Souvenirs and Homelands*, was shortlisted for a Saltire Award in 1998. Poems have appeared subsequently in various anthologies, including *Dream State: the new Scottish poets* (2nd edition, 2002). The poem sequence, "On the fly-leaf of ... : a bookshelf" was shortlisted for the Deric Bolton Long Poem Award in 2003. His translations of German-language poets, including Goethe, Fontane, and Celan, as well as contemporary writers such as Arne Rautenberg, Christine Marendon, and Rudolf Bussman, have appeared in books and magazines, including *Chapman, Modern Poetry in Translation,* and *Days of Poetry and Wine: Medana 2005.*

Summer Dresses

BEVERLEY BIE BRAHIC

This poem started in response to an Andrew Motion poem in *The Times Literary Supplement*. It too looked out through a window and ended suggestively; beyond that the connection would not, I think, be evident. Maybe I was just feeling sexy and Motion's poem provided the spark I needed to start writing.

First Draft

Summer Dresses

I love to bring the summer dresses down
from the attic. A Sunday morning we lie
late in bed, your knees crooked into mine,
blackbirds rippling, a breeze

rustling maple, leaves grown thick enough
to block out the flint wall behind, still
small, though, and that bright green that still
betokens spring. No sign of mildew, should

I should have them sprayed? I dream.
You open shutters, sunlight floods in.
I'll take one armload of woollens up,
rummage for some cotton thing

to pull on, against my skin, light as a breeze.
You take a pee, come back to bed.

The first draft is pretty literal. Many of my first drafts are: I write down everything that comes to mind, letting line breaks fall where they fall; I'm on automatic pilot, trying to get all the way to the end of my thought before the inner censor kicks in. At this point, I try to leave whatever's on the page alone. I don't even reread it in case I drag it into the trash. Then, a day or two later, I sneak up on it, try to take it by surprise. If I still get that turned-on, prickly feeling, I redraft. Sometimes that prickly feeling is so strong — I think this poem was like that — that right away I start to play with it.

The first thing you notice about the draft is that it is in quatrains of something like pentameter, with a final couplet. Was Motion's poem a sonnet? I seem to recall it was. Second, the draft's logic is pretty straightforward: a narrative, in fact, not much left to the imagination. I wanted to jump around more, be disconnected, let things happen between the lines, create some mystery. I cut out a lot of the obvious connecting material and whittled the poem down to a single narrative moment from the three or four different moments — waking, dreaming, opening shutters, peeing, coming back to bed. I delayed introducing the second person until line 10. In the draft, the last line sounds like a statement: in the final version, it becomes an invitation, which creates more tension and lets the poem close on a note of uncertainty, or promise.

I played with diction, got rid of a real clunker, "betoken." "Bring down" becomes "fetch," whose e sound chimes with "dress"; "some cotton thing" becomes "some cotton stuff" — I love "stuff" because it sounds so conversational, yet is also an old Anglo-Saxon word for "material." Now the vowels and consonants of this line ("rummage for some cotton stuff") echo one another. I tweezed dull articles and pronouns. "A Sunday morning we lie late abed" becomes "Sunday a.m. late abed": more colloquial, snappier, staccato — livelier — in rhythm. I worked on sense-of-touch words — it's a love poem, after all — like "breezy fingers" (better than "a breeze rustling maple leaves"), and erotic imagery, such as "worms" and "spear tips," contrasts of hardness and softness, light and dark, eros and death, the little death and the big one: the worm that goes both ways.

Final Draft

Summer Dresses

I love to fetch my summer dresses
from the attic.
Sunday a.m. late abed
blackbirds praise worms, breezy fingers

stir the maple, whose leaves grow thick enough to hide
that flinty glint behind:

spear tips, arrowheads.
No trace of mildew yet.
Please, the earthworm says.

You open shutters, let light in. I'll
take a load of woolens up—
rummage for some cotton stuff

quick as a breeze, full of dark leaves.
Come back to bed.

I began "Summer Dresses" in May and finished it — still a fourteen-liner — in August, which is quick for me. I used it as the last poem in my collection *Against Gravity*, published in the UK by Worple Press. I still like it. I still think it is a good poem to end a collection with.

Oh yes, and when I wrote it I was working with Tom Lux in the Warren Wilson MFA program. Tom thought I should cut out the second-to-last line ("quick as a breeze, full of dark leaves") — I still don't know whether I agree with him.

Beverley Bie Brahic's collection *Against Gravity* was published in 2005. She lives in Paris where she teaches and translates. Her translations include Hélène Cixous' *Portrait of Jacques Derrida as a Young Jewish Saint* and *Dream I Tell You,* Jacques Derrida's *Geneses, Genealogies, Genre and Genius,* all from Columbia University Press, and works of modern and contemporary French poets. Her work has appeared in *Poetry, Fence, Colorado Review, Verse, The Times Literary Supplement, Poetry Review,* and elsewhere.

Confessional Self-Portrait: Liar

Ellen Peckham

Two or three years before "Liar," I drew the image for a print based upon my father's Alzheimer's, my despair for him, and the threat it posed to me. As I drew, I talked to myself and wrote the text.

So when later I launched a second critical biographical print in the same size and format — this based upon other fears and failings — I wanted a poem of similar linage to explicate but keep the design. And this time it was more difficult since the visuals were more diverse and the self-imposed requirements of a poem that "fit" dictated terseness.

It is impossible for me to write about the draft of the poem without writing about the visual content. They grew as one. The major themes I address are the threat of alcoholism, intellectual honesty, memory, and age. Each a towering issue not easily compressed into a few lines, a few square inches.

Of "Liar," the first draft was noted while in café Ferrara in New York. I had stopped after a meeting with a counselor and was feeling cynical and rather despaired of being able to change, so "If you believe her…" was written with one eyebrow up.

It soon became, first, "She draws in lies," which is, of course, technically impossible even given poetic license. "Portrait in light and lies" is less direct, a bit spooky, and explicates the light–dark mood.

The second version, "Showing what she'd have us see" strips the image, suggesting that the beautiful woman is façade. In the third and final version, "But in the mirror…" one is pointed to the surreal — is it a mirror or a pond uprighted with fish suggesting "fishy," and do you see the aged face in it?

Next, "veritas est" honors the wine's reputation as truth serum and its threat of addiction, and shows two homunculi imprisoned and trying to escape and the beast's jaws. The lines on wine were in the poem and in the drawing from the first, and the "veritas est" quote. I hope they elicit unease. They, too, are to be read cynically: Truth is … or is it?

With rewrites they moved through the text in relation to other glass — the mirror, the broken stemware.

12·17·96

believing here
~~If you believe too~~
you'll believing ~~it all~~.

~~Only~~ the mirror's reflection
and if the wine was—
meal to be — ~~double~~.
No more Veritas Est
now but threat

Looking for escape.
Wearing ~~a mask~~ disguises

The
ass's Beast mistress ~~if bear~~
weeping for the monkey
of memory.

~~The~~ Tears ~~are~~ hidden
by ~~believing~~ the mask.
And the blood's distraction

A. 26 ‡p1

in
Portrait of light and lies
Showing what she'd have
~~the~~ us see.

~~the~~ as much
In the mirror ~~there~~ veritas est
~~much the same~~ as ~~est~~
~~which~~ once was in the bottle

~~the~~ there's
Where ~~there~~ now ~~is~~ only threat.
The ~~tears~~ brainmischiev's
~~for~~ marked and ~~that~~ origins
~~tears a matter, tears~~
for the monkey of memory,
~~Would has been~~ Bloods ~~puts~~ for ~~the~~ tears
~~Bloods~~ ~~bloods~~ ~~the~~ distraction.

Portrait in light + lies
Showing what she'd have me see.
In the mirror as much veritas est
as once was in the bottle
Where now there's only threat.

In the canvas behind the main figure, the items referred to in "The beastmistress' mask …" shows a dancing bear, a leering monkey, and the bird from the Alzheimer's print.

Though well and happily married at the time, I was unable to let go of many painful and even destructive memories. And, having married late, I was unsure about how to function in the relationship. I feared being too demanding, too selfish still.

The woman is somewhat medieval — a figure from the past — and the mask hides her feelings, as I hid mine. She seeks to dominate her present and recognizes the monkeyshines of her past and the threat of her future. The beastmistress takes them all on in disguise.

And so, anxiety-ridden and despairing — she cuts herself. Many people do from frustration or hopelessness or as penance for what they can't forgive themselves. I do not. I simply write or draw, substituting ink for the blood others shed. The "… blood's …" distraction is on the page only — and so, going round, we end with another lie.

Final Version

Confessional Self-Portrait: Liar

Portrait in light and lies
Showing what she'd have us see.

But in the mirror as much veritas est
As once was in the bottle
Where now there's only threat.

The beastmistress' mask
Hides tears for monkey memory.

Only blood's a distraction.

Ellen Peckham (who until 2000 signed her prints E. Stoepel Peckham) was born in 1938 in Rochester, New York. She is a poet and a visual artist and has read, published, and exhibited across the United States and in Europe and Latin America. She frequently uses both art forms in a single work, the text decorating and explicating, the image illuminating. She is co-founder, with her husband, Anson, of Atelier A / E, the first gallery to open in the Chelsea arts area. Her poems have been published in many literary magazines, including *Rattapallax, Visions, The Literary Review,* and *The Amherst Review.*

Magnificent Frigatebird

Ernest Hilbert

For many years, I have enjoyed writing ekphrastic poetry. In ekphrasis, a poem is composed in response to a work of visual art, usually a sculpture or painting. The term derives from an ancient Greek descriptive rhetorical technique (the earliest example dates to 353 BC). Among the numerous opportunities afforded by my job at a large antiquarian bookseller is direct access to rare and exquisite examples of the bookmaker's art. Over the years, I have been fortunate to handle assorted editions of John James Audubon's iconic *Birds of America*. The plate that always struck me most keenly is that of the Magnificent Frigatebird (plate 271 of the elephant folio first edition, painted by Audubon in 1832, engraved, printed, and colored by R. Havell, 1835). Its nearly abstract structure recalled, for me, the imposing canvases of painters Robert Motherwell and Franz Kline. The Magnificent Frigatebird is one of the few birds posed by Audubon as if in motion rather than resting or grooming. Instead of perching on a log pecking its tail feathers, it dives and, in so doing, seems impossibly sleek and dangerous.

Image reproduced with the permission of Bauman Rare Books.

Many poets — I would venture to guess most — who choose to write on Audubon, and they are legion, tend to focus on the story behind the paintings. Audubon hunted a bird and then posed it with tethers and wire, like a taxidermist. He then hurriedly painted it in order to capture the freshness of the bird before rigor and decay set in. He also made notes regarding the culinary preparation and flavor of his birds. This is all quite interesting, but I wanted to join Audubon as he imagined the bird hurtling down on its prey, and so partake in the artist's fantasy. I believe that the Magnificent Frigatebird is one of his most successful creations, so I decided to charge my poem with purpose and energy, as he did.

After spending some time with the strangely captivating bird, I began to scratch preliminary notes in my Moleskine, which I use as a commonplace book. Those notes steeped for months, during which time I meditated about the subject's potential, though I could not bring myself to begin the poem. When I finally decided one summery Saturday morning to start, I flipped through my commonplace book and found these puzzling notes (when making notes, I underline words that approximate what I hope to say but that will be replaced at a later date):

Dark <u>message</u> falling
   [??̶?̶?̶] with
like a fighter jet or toy
           spacecraft
<u>Destroys</u> its [??̶?̶?̶] prey,
           Target
It strikes | feels no
    <u>assaults</u> | moment of
                         hesitation,   guilt
or remorse.   It is a black
beacon,   chevron of darkness
descending
so fast it makes
           no mistake

Sinister beside a
    <u>listening</u> sea

---

while a soft furred

life pisses the dust of
its <u>hidden</u> corner
helpless/powerless   *except to*
<u>lower</u> before <u>strength</u>
as absolute as <u>death</u>

Had I scribbled this mess? Needless to say, it did not seem like a great deal to work with, but the tone and central images were there.

I had devoted the previous year to my own breed of sonnet — what my friend Daniel Nester termed the "Hilbertian" sonnet — working toward a book to be titled *Sixty Sonnets*. Each is fourteen lines of iambic pentameter (though two examples in the sequence fall out of this meter: one is in octosyllabics, and the other, a string of epitaphs in trimeter), consisting of two sestets and a terminal couplet, rhymed ABCABC DEFDEF GG (I diverged from this scheme on one occasion to experiment with pararhyme, pairing fourteen high and low tones on a single rhyme). I find this modified brand of the classic sonnet serves me well in a variety of modes: satirical, elegiac, reflective, didactic, and absurdist. When writing in the ekphrastic mode, I tend to take my subjects seriously, and I endeavor to pack some gravity into the poems. I completed fifty-eight serviceable sonnets toward *Sixty Sonnets* (although I had more than sixty at one point, I discarded a number for their inferior quality). The final two required to complete the book eluded me. I chose The Magnificent Frigatebird to serve as muse for one of them (I have since completed the other, a Calavera).

After I baked my first draft, I let it sit on the windowsill to cool a while. I thought I had better look into the zoological end of things before I proceeded, since I was so preoccupied with the purely aesthetic qualities of the painting. When I did, I realized that my line about "small furred things, pissing in the dust" would have to be struck. The Magnificent Frigatebird's diet is pelagic, or "open sea," so that ruled out any furred thing known to man. It is the largest of the five species in the genus Fregata and known for its swiftness and maneuverability. Because of its size, brute force, and highly aggressive nature, the Magnificent Frigatebird has also been called the Man-of-War or Pirate Bird (you will see that my additional research paid off). It supplements its diet of fish by attacking other birds, often robbing them of their catches. So, right out of my first draft, a line was struck (the preceding line would be struck as well, but for different reasons).

Here is what I will term the first draft, constructed from my primary notes, with my first changes:

> The sharp dark ~~spike~~ [*thorn*] plummets like a dive bomber,
> Holding no moment of hesitation
> Or stalled human position such as guilt.
> ~~The small furred things, pissing in the dust~~, are
> Powerless beneath this black-light beacon,   5
> Long-beaked chevron of darkness, flashing, built
> To kill, nightmare ink ~~splatter~~ [*dash*] aiming down hard
> Like a stealth fighter, so ~~swift~~ [*fast*] it suffers
> No lapse of purpose. Balanced, sinister,
> Over a glittering sea, the lethal bird   10
> Lingers for new prey, swivels and hovers—
> Earth its vast ~~coliseum~~ [*arena*] and theater,
> Supreme as a blinding sun, terrible
> And perfect, death's own finished miracle.

Correcting for diet and habitat, I wound up with what I will call first draft (A):

> The sharp dark thorn plummets like a dive bomber,
> Holding no moment of hesitation
> Or stalled human position such as guilt.
> [*Fish, in their darting silvery clouds*], are
> Powerless beneath this black-light beacon,   5
> Long-beaked chevron of darkness, flashing, built
> To kill, nightmare ink dash aiming down hard
> Like a stealth fighter, so fast it suffers
> No lapse of purpose. Balanced, sinister,
> Over a glittering sea, the lethal bird   10
> Lingers for new prey, swivels and hovers—
> Earth its vast arena and theater,
> Supreme as a blinding sun, terrible
> And perfect, death's own finished miracle.

I was bothered by the weak use of the verb *are* as the fourth-line rhyme matching the all-important first line ending of the poem. The skittery verb was not up to the task I set it, but I decided to let it stand. I then packed up this modest first draft — I was quite pleased with it at the time — and sent it to a friend, David Yezzi, the executive editor of the *New Criterion*. A casual chat over a glass of Scotch with him is typically the equivalent of a master-class, and I trust him completely. He takes poetry very seriously and comments on the most meticulous aspects of rhythm and nuance as easily as the broadest of intention and symbolism. Upon reading my first draft, the one over which I still glowed with pride, he telephoned me and straightaway rebuked me on a startling number of points. My notion that the reader could somehow relate to the predatory bird was immediately dismissed as a naïve example of the sympathetic, or affective, fallacy. My evasive defense consisted of the argument that the bird could instead be viewed as majestically superhuman. This did not go over very well either. Yezzi pointed out that the grand, King James ending was not earned. The feeble poem could not support such weight, so the final couplet came to feel like a bit of sagging grandiosity. I asked him if he would let any living poet get away with it, and he answered no, though he provided a list of those who would be likely to do so anyway.

The poem also contained appalling redundancies, as one will observe in the third and ninth lines of the first draft. There was room only for one of these lines, so the third was struck altogether. Yezzi insisted I needed to be more tangible, abandon the unmerited grandiloquent abstractions, and draw the tone far down from its original altitude, which he referred to as being "nose-bleed" high. My replacement of the second, third, and fourth lines required a recalibration of all corresponding rhymes down the chain. "Swivels" was abolished as being too Hopkins-like, and the word *balanced* did not, itself, feel very balanced in the line. The fish did not need to be described as "powerless," so I gave them motion with a new verb placement (this also solved my problem of the flimsy "are" rhyme). The description of the bird as "lethal" was also judged superfluous and removed. I fought hard to keep "supreme," and it has survived right to the finished poem. I proceeded to apply these numerous and acute changes to the first draft:

> The sharp dark thorn plummets like a dive[-]bomber,
> ~~Holding no moment of hesitation~~ [*No human moment of hesitation*].
> ~~Or stalled human position such as guilt~~ [*It rushes through wind to unite with its goal*].
> ~~Fish, in their darting silvery clouds, are~~ [*Fish gather in quick silver clouds, swell, veer*].
> ~~Powerless~~ [*They swim*] beneath this black-light beacon,   5

Long-beaked chevron of darkness, ~~flashing, built~~ [*vivid coal*]
~~To kill, nightmare~~ [*Swiftly struck*] ink dash aiming down hard
Like a stealth fighter, so fast it suffers
No lapse of purpose. ~~Balanced,~~ [*Poised and*] sinister,
Over a ~~glittering~~ [glistening] sea, the ~~lethal bird~~ [*Pirate Bird*]   10
~~Lingers for new prey, swivels and~~ [*Studies the breakers for new kills,*]
hovers—
Earth its vast ~~arena~~ [*blank canvas*] and theater,
Supreme as ~~a blinding~~ [*midday*] sun, terrible
~~And perfect~~ [*Selected*], death's [*fond emissary*] ~~own finished miracle~~.

Once these modifications were in place, I needed to gain more control over the rhythm and pacing of the poem. At some points, the language had to speed forward, as if diving. At others it had to brake, as if hovering and observing. I used hyphenated words to drive the first sestet forward: "dive-bomber," "long-beaked," and "black-light," later "black-lit," which is more compressed. The "blinding" sun was deemed cliché and altered to "mid-day," which falls nicely midway through the penultimate line, forming a rhythmic fulcrum. Yezzi considered the presence of both "arena" and "the-ater" to be superfluous, since either can refer to both entertainment and war, thus introducing more texture than a single line will sustain. I elimi-nated "arena" (I originally attempted to wrench the impossible "coliseum" into the line) and replaced it with "blank canvas," which reinforced my original thought of the bird as an abstract artistic gesture.

I then recast the final line into something resembling its finished form. "Fond" struck us both as suitably ambiguous and mysterious. (I acted out a scenario: "look, mom, I made ambiguity," "that's nice, dear, just hold it over the sink.") What, exactly, was fond, and what was it fond of? I alighted on this line only after thirteen revisions. These fixes left me with a legiti-mate second draft, but I needed a new third line, something that could add to the sense of forward (or descending) motion. I moved "human" up to the second line and left the third line entirely vacant for several days. I tried five or six different lines and settled on "The world is wind. What goes below is prey." Although it scans beautifully, I was afraid that it would sound too much like Ted Hughes. Yezzi felt it sounded too much like David Jones, which amounts to more or less the same thing. Either way, it had to go (I admire both aforementioned poets for very different reasons, but this sort of weighty diction does not match my style). So I devised the line "it rushes through wind to unite with its goal," before deciding to enjamb and extend the second line into the third and altering it to "In its rush through raw wind to join its goal," which is made up entirely of rapid monosyllables that create the sensation of increasing velocity:

> The sharp dark thorn plummets like a dive-bomber,
> No human moment of hesitation.
> ~~The world is wind. What goes below is prey~~.
>
> [*It rushes through wind to unite with its goal.*]

Alternatively:

> [*In its rush through ~~warm~~ raw wind to join its goal*].
>
> Fish gather in quick[,] silver clouds, swell, veer.
> They swim beneath this black-lit beacon,   5
> Long-beaked chevron of darkness ~~in day~~ [*vivid coal*],
> Swiftly struck ink dash, aiming down hard
> Like a stealth fighter, so fast it suffers
> No lapse of purpose. Poised and sinister,
> Over a glistening sea, the Pirate Bird   10
> Studies the breakers for new kills, hovers [—]
> Earth its vast blank canvas and theater [—]
> Supreme as midday sun, brutal as the sea,
> ~~Selected~~ [*And chosen*], death's fond emissary.

The poem still needed to be polished. I aligned as many of the sounds and musical elements as I could without losing track of the sense of the poem, but the pace was not sufficiently defined. I added terminal em dashes in the eleventh and twelfth lines to slow that portion of the poem down, in order to provide the feel of hovering majestically over the sea, and to set off the thirteenth line, which refers to human artifice in "canvas" and "theater." I wanted to isolate it from the wild, authentic world of the bird. I then added "And chosen" to the last line and followed it with a comma. This final line is *acephalus*, or "headless," since the first foot has an assumed, or inaudible, syllable, which, constituting the first half of an iambic foot would have been unstressed. This trait adds to the experience of airy suspension followed by sharp attack. Moving back up the poem, I added a much needed comma between "quick" and "silver" to clarify that I was not using the word *quicksilver*, which is inappropriate in this environment. I changed "glittering" sea — which sounds a bit spangly and slows the line down with its unvoiced dental stop — and replaced it with the sibilant "glistening" sea.

This left me with a convincing third draft, which I took to be the final draft, with its newly installed lines and correlated later rhymes (some whole, some oblique; I tend to mingle both types in most poems unless I feel compelled to resort entirely to one or the other):

> The sharp dark thorn plummets like a dive-bomber,
> No human moment of hesitation
> In its rush through raw wind to join its goal.
> Fish gather in quick, silver clouds, swell, veer.
> They swim beneath this black-lit beacon,   5
> Long-beaked chevron of darkness, lance of coal,
> Swiftly struck ink dash, aiming down hard
> Like a stealth fighter, so fast it suffers
> No lapse of purpose. Poised and sinister,
> Over a glistening sea, the Pirate Bird   10
> Studies the breakers for new kills, hovers—
> Earth its vast blank canvas and theater—
> Supreme as midday sun, brutal as the sea,
> And chosen, death's fond emissary.

I then added the title, "Magnificent Frigatebird" (dropping the definite article) and the note *"Fregata magnificens,* John James Audubon, 1832." I showed the third draft to Yezzi and he charitably responded: "Wow. That's a knockout. Congrats." This is greater approval than I could have hoped for. The balm of praise quickly relieved the stings inflicted by earlier burrs of disapproval.

The terms *first* through *third* drafts are used for the sake of convenience and are hence reductive. They do not give full merit to the complexity and number of changes made to this poem, but they allow me a convenient frame in which to present my compositional process. Of course, many more small changes occurred right from the start, but endeavoring to record them all is a bit like trying to hold water in cupped hands. This is typical of my compositional technique. My changes usually number in the dozens or hundreds for a single sonnet. Moreover, wretched late changes will sometimes occur when, after months of living with a poem that seemed complete, I notice something I disapprove about the syntax, rhyme, or even philosophy of a poem, and the revision begins again. A change to any part of the poem will reverberate to other parts and necessitate additional changes until the synchronized whole settles again. Some poets, like Allen Ginsberg and Donald Hall, changed poems decades after they first appeared in print, but most of us are not permitted such luxury. Once a poem is published, the public may never see it again, so it is tremendously important to have all of one's prosodic ducks in a row right from the start. Brisk and therefore bracing criticism is an indispensable component of this process for me, and I rely heavily on the opinions of a small circle of exceptional readers, who offer no quarter and seek no prisoners. This level of exacting criticism and confidential exchange of ideas has led me to further assurance as a poet and, with hope, mastery of my chosen forms. And so, *voila*:

Magnificent Frigatebird

Fregata magnificens, John James Audubon, 1832

The sharp dark thorn plummets like a dive-bomber,
No human moment of hesitation
In its rush through raw wind to join its goal.
Fish gather in quick, silver clouds, swell, veer.
They swim beneath this black-lit beacon,
Long-beaked chevron of darkness, lance of coal,
Swiftly struck ink dash, aiming down hard
Like a stealth fighter, so fast it suffers
No lapse of purpose. Poised and sinister,
Over a glistening sea, the Pirate Bird
Studies the breakers for new kills, hovers—
Earth its vast blank canvas and theater—
Supreme as midday sun, brutal as the sea,
And chosen, death's fond emissary.

Ernest Hilbert is the editor of the *Contemporary Poetry Review*. His poetry has appeared in *The New Republic, American Poet, The Vocabula Review, The New Criterion, Boston Review, LIT, McSweeney's, American Scholar, Verse, Volt,* and *Fence*. He writes for a variety of publications, including *The New York Sun*, Scribner's *American Writers* series, and the Academy of American Poets. Hilbert received his doctorate in English Literature from Oxford University, where he earlier completed a master's degree and founded the *Oxford Quarterly*. He was the poetry editor for Random House's online magazine *Bold Type* for several years and later edited the magazine *now-Culture*. He works as an antiquarian book dealer and lives in Philadelphia with his fiancée, an archaeologist.

HIV Needs Assessment

Roy Jacobstein

First Draft

Needs Assessment, Malawi

Everywhere the faces, limbs and hair
are coal, obsidian, flawless black
sapphire, so the rare *mzungu**
stands out like those few white moths
did on industrial London's sooted trees.

A month of fluttering *The Warm Heart
of Africa*'s long length on this *Needs
Assessment*. The needs are many.
But let us not talk of that, as the people
do not. Focus instead on the purple

bougainvillea, golden light, pellucid
lapis sky that domes the volcanic hills,
its color mirrored in the crisp uniforms
of the single file of schoolgirls striding
the side of the road. And when the talk,

matter-of-fact, beyond resigned, bears left
at the corner, headed inevitably to the cousin's
funeral attended yesterday, to the two added
children your colleague is now raising,
to the funerals tomorrow, as the eight

of you ride together in the *Project Vehicle*
to the next clinic site, past the lone ads
for toothpaste and for study opportunities
abroad, and the many ads for caskets, fine
and rude, just sit there and say nothing.

Final Draft

HIV Needs Assessment

Everywhere the faces, hair, limbs
    are coal, obsidian, flawless black
        sapphire, thus the rare *mzungu**

like me stands out the way those
    remaining white moths once did
        on industrialized London's trees.

A month fluttering *The Warm Heart*
    of Africa's long length on this *Needs*
        Assessment. We've found the needs

many. But let us not talk of that,
    as the people do not. Focus instead
        on the vivid oleander & limpid sky

that domes the arid volcanic hills,
    its lapis mirrored in the uniforms
        of the file of schoolgirls who stride

the side of the road. And when the talk,
    matter-of-fact, beyond resigned, bears
        left at the roundabout, glances upon

a cousin's funeral attended yesterday,
    the two added children your colleague
        from Lilongwe is now raising alone,

funeral venues for this weekend, just

sit there as the *Project Vehicle* propels
you onward to the next *Site*, past

the lone ads for toothpaste
& for study opportunity abroad,
& the many for caskets ("lightweight,

can be carried by one"), & say nothing.

*Swahili for *white person*, literally "to travel around."

As can be seen from looking at the two versions of this poem, much has changed over the two-year period from its genesis to publication, although much has remained. To consider first what remains and why, let us consider the poem's structure, that is, its release of particulars to the reader and its movement in time. The poem remains a journey poem, one that takes us from "everywhere" to "nothing," even as we continue to "bear left at the roundabout." *Left*, we should note, not *right*: every word counts; there are no minutiae in our business, instructed Ezra Pound.

Some of the poem's black-and-white imagery is unchanged, too: "coal," "flawless black sapphire," "white moths," "caskets," "the lone ads for toothpaste." So, too, some of the jargony phrases of the narrator and of international development remain, to convey simultaneously meaning and distance, *"Needs Assessment"* and *"Project Vehicle,"* as does the employment of the Swahili term for the poem's speaker and his tribe, *"mzungu."*

The poem's basic arguments also remain: outsider-narrator, struggling to comprehend the incomprehensible, is rendered respectful, mute. Yet life and death — and the desire for personal advancement, as well as clean teeth — go on, notwithstanding. Commerce, too, goes on, from the days of the Industrial Revolution to our present age of the Information Revolution. And notwithstanding that public health may have eradicated some plagues that killed hundreds of millions — smallpox most notably — others remain in (that *Warm Heart* of) Africa: AIDS, the associated resurgence of tuberculosis, the persistence of malaria, major killers now and possibly in the future. And still the schoolgirls stride the side of the road.

But there are significant changes wrought in the revision process in this poem as well, changes that I had hoped would further elevate the poem out of ordinary reportage, that would, as Lucia Perillo put it in her introduc-

212

tion to my book that features this poem, distance it from "literary combat-tourism." So too the rather unimaginative and stolid blocks of five-line stanzas in the original version have been supplanted by skittering, stair-cased tercets, a form that I find lends a usefully unstable forward momentum to a poem. And in this case, that movement also enacts and thus reinforces our sense of journey, of the speaker and colleague, English-speaking *mzungu* and Malawian, riding together in that landscape of loss. Finally, the tercet form allows that strand of final tercet to carry a great deal of weight, weight equal to a full three lines, and ironically so, since it is about the lightening of the heavy burden (and also about the nothing).

Another significant change is that the poem has been augmented by subtraction, always a strategy for a writer to consider, and often a remarkably successful one. Gone from the final version are such words — and the images they convey — as "golden light," "pellucid," and "purple bougainvillea": a surfeit of nature imagery at odds with the currents of loss that suffuse the poem. And those lost words and images not particularly original or unusual either: one must always hear and heed another of Ezra Pound's useful dicta: "make it new!" Thus "lapis," with its Yeatsian echoes — I'm thinking of his well-known poems "Lapis Lazuli" and "Among School Children" — must suffice to carry the emotive load. An additional word-image that has departed the scene is "sooted." This adjective is at once unnecessary in context as well as unnecessarily, inadvertently, nonusefully loaded in a poem about blacks and whites and/or "us" and "them." Note in all these instances, the value of wielding one's "adjective lens," drawn from our doctor's black bag of tools for revision (by excision).

Some other changes borne on the revision process:

The use in the final version of the ampersand, which I find lends urgency and speed to a poem, strengthening the tensile strength of its connective tissue at the same time that it does away with the unsightly *ands* — my second least favorite word in any poem, after *of*. In addition, I cannot help thinking, whenever I deploy the ampersand, of the prematurely late poet, Larry Levis, whose long poems that dwell on loss, indeed on oblivion, are comprised of long lines usefully braided by, among other craft devices, the ampersand. Here I'm thinking particularly of, and strongly recommending to the reader, his posthumous book, *Elegy*.

The "funerals tomorrow" are gone, too, now only implied, and enlarged perhaps, by the revised "venues for this weekend"; but added is the burden of raising the surviving offspring.

The title has changed to immediately situate us — in the land of pandemic rather than the nation of Malawi — though those who know their African geography will still be better situated, via that euphonious capital that remains: Lilongwe, near-homonym, ironically so in this instance, of "the long way."

The final significant change brought about in the revision process involves the payoff. Not all American poets subscribe to Yeats's recommendation that a poem should "close with the click of a finely-made box," but I find that many of my poems seek after a kind of closure that is memorable, that rewards the reader's traversal down and across the lines. Thus the part of the poem that is still, for me, its most poignant aspect, is that lightening — and singularizing, individualizing — of the casket in the final two lines, via language plucked from the billboard. For now a single mourner — that may well be all who is left of the family — can carry the primary burden of burial and remembrance. No longer "fine and rude," the caskets, in the very language of impersonal commerce, of the billboard, of life that must go on, are now "lightweight."

"HIV Needs Assessment" appears in Roy Jacobstein's latest collection of poetry, *A Form of Optimism* (University Press of New England, 2006), which won the Samuel French Morse Prize, selected by Lucia Perillo, and was nominated for a Pulitzer Prize. His previous book of poetry, *Ripe*, won the Felix Pollak Prize, and was a finalist for The Academy of American Poets' Walt Whitman Award. His poetry appears in many literary venues, including *The Gettysburg Review, The Iowa Review, The Missouri Review, Parnassus, Poetry Daily, Shenandoah, The Threepenny Review,* and *TriQuarterly.* He has received several awards from *Prairie Schooner* and *Mid-American Review*'s James Wright Prize. His poetry is widely anthologized and is included in the textbook *LITERATURE: Reading Fiction, Poetry & Drama* (McGraw-Hill, 2006). He has an MD and MPH from the University of Michigan and an MFA from Warren Wilson College. A public health physician and former official of the U.S. Agency for International Development, he works in Africa and Asia on women's reproductive health programs and lives with his wife and daughter in Chapel Hill, North Carolina.

Anatomy of Disorder

PATTY SEYBURN

This is the first thorough draft of the poem:

12:19 a.m.

Open your primers to Shape, the fourth chapter
in the Anatomy of Disorder, writ yore,
and you'll find a daguerrotype of my eyelids —
beneath, fibers capable of exponential
reproduction, renegade begetting, vanishing

their trellis, as should good vines.
Don't get me wrong — I know the minions
of the Angel of Death crouch beneath my drapes,
eager to filch my soul from my animate
frame, should my breath hesitate. I know

that longing listens to the surf report:
("Don't bother. No waves. But there's hope
on the northwest horizon") and burrows its head
in Psyche's sand, emerging as a castle with turrets,
drawbridge and moat, subject to fits of mutability.

Remember: Capability Brown reshaped
the English Garden from contrivance
to the articulated wild. In his perfect hermitage,
he was overheard chiding a local child:
"You can't escape landscape."

I always loved the reiteration of lilac
and city block, pastel stock and power line,
thistle and used car lot with chrome hopes.
A triangle implies. Stairs have convictions;
the oval, qualities. When a trapezoid is present,

one can make predictions. The valentine has graciously
figured the human heart into a bi-valve container
with angles and curves for the furies
to tour with rhyming guidebooks, and there you are
on the back road to beauty and the sublime,

where the service is terrible — they have no
work ethic, those two, always Me Me Me.
We said: pipe down, you're nothing special
but they keep emerging — bedraggled, buoyant
with threat and decree. When Virginia Woolf

put stones like literature in her pockets
to weigh down her corpus, and took a constitutional
into the waves that broke and broke
and broke, each stone had its own shape,
its own responsibility — complicit,

along with the sea.

This poem began as a much longer poem — that's often the trajectory
of a poem, for me. I write an original draft that goes on expanding for a
while, at which time it hits critical mass and I realize that I've added one
too many appositions, one too many clauses, dragged out a sentence as
long as it can possibly go. In the case of this poem, it started as part of a series of poems with times for titles. I feel like these poems are obliquely
about parenting, mostly because I wrote them when I had insomnia during pregnancy, and odd images related to parturition and my physical condition would sneak into the poems. I also figured that I would not be
awake if I weren't pregnant, so there had to be some psychic connection between my child and the poem; of course, poems are children, I think, both
in that we parent them and they have the charm and indiscretion we wish
we could display as adults (and get away with).

So I was looking around my bedroom — I tended to think that if I actually got out of bed, I'd never get back to sleep, so I kept a pen and pad
on the dresser, and would reach up and scribble, nearly illegibly, in the
dark. Sometimes the accidents of my penmanship were fortuitous (such as
my student who wrote, "There is no escaping the inedible"). In this case, I

lie awake looking at the various shapes in my room, and so thought this poem would be a diatribe on those: the shape of things, of ideas, and how they shift.

What I came to realize was that the shapes were, to use Richard Hugo's idea of "the triggering town," triggers for the real subject of the poem, which would seem to be something about ... I'm really not sure. Perhaps about the tentative imposition of order on chaos, the impossibility of doing so, and/or the notion that we must take control of our own internal disorder, or else it will win out. Not to sound like a "cop-out," but I have gained some comfort with Keats's "Negative Capability," which is to say, I'm okay with not knowing everything about what I write. In any case, I found out that the first two stanzas of the poem were functioning as "warm-up," which makes them initially useful and ultimately dispensable — necessarily so, to make the poem "go." To find the "final" beginning of the poem, I looked for the line that I thought was most alive, and being a new Californian, originally a Detroiter, that would seem to be about surfing. I've glanced at the "Surf Reports" on the weather page of the *LA Times*, and they often use phrases that sound sort of existential, more about the human condition than the waves' condition.

So I cut the first two stanzas and pulled the middle stanzas of the poem almost verbatim from the earlier draft (I'll get back to the almost), and then I cut the fifth and sixth stanzas and I re-entered the older version at the very end of the sixth stanza. In other words: I started with an eight-stanza poem of five-line stanzas, and ended up with a poem of seven tercets: a poem of half the size. But poetry is about economy, right? When I said "almost" about keeping the middle of the poem, there's one notable word excision. In the old version, I had the word *Remember* between "mutability" and "Capability." For musical reasons, I wanted those two words together, so "remember" went under the redacting knife and did not emerge. Incidentally or not so, I encountered Capability Brown from two places: when I toured the English countryside with my husband, we learned about the wild English garden and their owners' penchant for the hermitage, complete with hermit. I also heard about this when seeing Tom Stoppard's play *Arcadia*, which is one of my favorite plays. I made up the phrase: "You can't escape landscape." Of course, that's the way a landscape architect would feel, I think.

I cut the fifth and sixth stanzas — enough, already, about shape. The word *buoyant* triggered the reference to Virginia Woolf that begins the conclusion of the poem — still in England, I suppose — and the notion of shape does emerge in the end — part of me still thinks of the final version of the poem as a study of shape, which everything has, even longing: giving a physical coherence to an idea. The poem begins and ends with the water, which, I suppose, is an obsession I've taken on as a converted Californian. The phrase "broke and broke / and broke" comes from Tennyson's poem, titled "Break, Break, Break," which I love. I keep trying to call a book by that title, but have not succeeded in writing that book, yet.

As far as the length and shape of the stanzas, I'll admit an affection for tercets: they don't seem as stodgy as quatrains (which I also love, but they do carry their history with them), and tercets are less "naked" than a couplet: I tend to feel that I should have something very important to say in a couplet, though contemporary poets often use couplets as exactly the opposite sort of container, a repository for the casual. I liked the two short lines beginning the tercet, and the longer third line — I get disappointed in poets who use a consistently short line; it seems like a cop-out to me: stretch out! I usually take my lineation cues from a couple of lines in the poem that seem to be working well. I didn't want "longing" and "listens" on the same line — too much alliteration — ending the line on longing seems a good invitation to keep reading, but together, the *l* sound would dominate and distract.

Looking back at the first draft, it's easy to see why I made certain decisions, generally favoring the internal music of the line. So "chide" and "child," "moat" and "mutability" (which also earned its keep due to Shelley's poem titled "Mutability" — with all the reference to landscape, for me "Anatomy" grounds itself in the Romantic tradition — I was probably reading Shelley when I wrote the first draft), "city block" and "pastel stock" (which did not survive the chopping block), "curves" and "furies" (sigh — will it find its way into another poem? Perhaps). What's more, I have a penchant for stretching out a line as long as it will go, and a little farther, not just for the sake of "information" or content, but to achieve a sort of breathlessness, as though the container of the poem will just barely hold; I want poems to do a great deal of work in relatively little space.

Here's where the poem ended up:

Anatomy of Disorder

I know that longing
listens to the surf report:
("Don't bother. No waves. Hope on the Northwest horizon")

and burrows its head
in Psyche's sand, emerging
a castle with turrets, drawbridge and moat, subject to fits

of mutability. Capability Brown
reshaped the English Garden
from contrivance to the articulated wild. In his perfect hermitage,

he was heard chiding a child:
"You can't escape landscape,"
and there you are on the back road to beauty and the sublime,

where the service is terrible —
they have no work ethic,
those two, always *Me Me Me*. We say: pipe down, you're nothing

special, but they keep
emerging — bedraggled,
buoyant with threat and decree. When Virginia Woolf put stones

like literature
in her pockets
to weigh down her corpus, and took a constitutional into the waves

that broke and broke
and broke, each stone
had its own shape, its own responsibility — complicit, along with the sea.

I like the sounds in a poem to intensify toward the end, so "sea" ideally echoes "decree" and "Me Me Me," though they are not too close together, so the poem doesn't get sing-songy. I don't use too many metaphors and similes: the only one in this poem is "stones like literature." Of course,

Woolf did put stones in her pockets, and I wanted them in the poem, as well, because they are part of Capability Brown's landscaping. But I also wanted the notion that literature, which I like to believe can save us, can also weigh us down. Ideally, it can do both, in moderation: provide us with gravitas, with substance, reasons to live, keep us from floating away.

Patty Seyburn has published two books of poems: *Mechanical Cluster* (Ohio State University Press, 2002) and *Diasporadic* (Helicon Nine Editions, 1998), which won the 1997 Marianne Moore Poetry Prize and the American Library Association's Notable Book Award for 2000. Her poems have appeared in numerous journals, including *The Paris Review, New England Review, Field, Slate, Crazyhorse, Cutbank, Quarterly West, Bellingham Review, Connecticut Review, Cimarron Review, Third Coast, Gulf Coast, Poetry East, Passages North, Seneca Review, Mudfish,* and *Western Humanities Review.* Her poems have been anthologized in *Legitimate Dangers: American Poets of the New Century* (Sarabande Books, 2005), *Chance of a Ghost* (Helicon Nine Editions, 2005), *American Poetry: The Next Generation* (Carnegie Mellon University Press, 2000), and *American Diaspora: Poetry of Exile* (University of Iowa Press, 2000). She earned an MFA from the University of California, Irvine, and a PhD from the University of Houston. She's written poetry reviews for *Slope* and *International Poetry Review,* and is co-editor of *POOL: A Journal of Poetry,* based in Los Angeles. She is assistant professor of English and Creative Writing at California State University, Long Beach.

Ants

Scott Wiggerman

Sometimes a sonnet is padded with words and phrases that exist in the poem only to satisfy its rhyme or rhythm. One obvious revision technique is to discard the form and rework the poem in free verse. However, sometimes a poem in free verse — especially a rambling, unwieldy one — is best served in revision by turning to the restraints and compression of a form. This was certainly the case with my poem "Ants," which in free verse digressed all over the map, but became a tight, controlled poem when revised as a sonnet.

Draft Version

Ants

These ants are schizzier than most:
swerving like race car drivers,
maneuvering through an invisible maze,
scurrying as if the bathroom were on fire.

Perhaps it's fear of the unknown.
Furious dots on white ceramic tiles—
how did they come to be here?
Are they hopelessly lost,
like shoppers foraging through
a ten-tiered puzzle of a parking garage?

I've never seen ants so two-toned,
like miniature saddle-shoes,
heads as red as New Mexico rocks,
but bodies of burnished brown.
Perhaps they're mutants
whose sense has been eaten away
by some noxious underground herbicide.

Or are these the ants who drew short sticks,
a scouting party determined by fate,
resigned to the dangerous mission
of exploring inner space?
I think of them as unlucky, not brave.

I knew a boy with a magnifying glass
who fried ants on pavement
till their frizzled bodies caved in like commas,
somehow crueler
than stomping a colony underfoot,
but we don't think about their agony.

I knew a girl who had an ant farm,
a kinetic frame of unbridled captives:
all show, energy going nowhere.

Even on my most wired days,
I couldn't hold a grain to such activity,
though I often display
a façade of purposefulness
as I meander through my life,
an odd little speck on a big blue planet.

"Ants" went through numerous revisions — none of which felt satisfactory — in the two years it took me to abandon it as a free verse poem and try it as a form poem. Originally thirty-seven lines that diverged in many directions, "Ants" was reduced to the sonnet's fourteen lines. I was forced to focus the poem on one central idea, which meant I had to cut, cut, cut. But how? The extended time between the original draft and the final one made it easier to cut anything that I had questioned or marked as a possible cut. Time can be a poet's best friend. A full five of the seven original stanzas were completely cut: stanzas of pure description (the first, third, and fourth) and those that forayed into other ant scenarios (the fifth and sixth). Some words (for example, "kinetic") or phrases ("scurrying as if the bathroom were on fire") from these stanzas eventually made their way back into the poem, but the drastic cuts helped me focus on the remaining two stanzas (the second and seventh), which seemed to be the core of the poem: the unanswered question of where these particular ants came from and the commonality of the ants to man himself, ant as metaphor for the "façade of purposefulness" (a line I chose to cut once I realized the images suggested it better than the phrase).

From these two stanzas, I pulled almost word for word what became the opening and closing lines of the sonnet, which are, in fact, analogous: "furious dots on white ceramic tiles" and "odd little speck on a big blue planet." These lines also provided two of the seven rhymes of the typical Shakespearian sonnet, not that the poem ended up being a typical sonnet, rather more of a deconstructed sonnet. I chose to vary the meter and the rhythm of the lines; to divide the sonnet into three unequal stanzas; to free the poem from the tyranny of the left margin; and to delay the "turn" until the final three lines of the poem. Writing about ants as "pyrotechnics of energy out of control," I wanted the poem to visually suggest the "kinetic movements" and aurally sound "erratic." This is not to suggest that I didn't want the poem to sound good. The poem not only has strong end-rhymes, but also several internal rhymes ("mission"/"ambition," "come"/"from," "kinetic"/"frenetic"); parallel syntax ("agitated or hopeless? frightened or playful?") and anaphora ("no single files / no mission to follow"); and plenty of what Pound called "melopoeia" — from assonance ("buzz of love") to alliteration ("big blue") to onomatopoeia ("dizzying buzz").

The word *I* does not appear in the finished sonnet. I moved the focus away from the "I" of the original draft ("as I meander through my life") into the more generic Everyman ("make me ponder ... / this sonnet, myself") so that the poem's epithet — "odd little speck on a big blue planet" — applies to every reader.

I never abandoned "Ants," for I knew there was something worth keeping in it. Time and distance helped, but it wasn't until I worked the poem into a form that the poem really came into a cohesive whole. While there are many form poems that should be abandoned in favor of free verse — no one wants a poem that sounds forced or artificial — the opposite is also true: some free verse poems need the focus and structure of form to succeed. Form is certainly a viable technique for revision.

Ants

Furious dots on white ceramic tiles
    scurry as if the bathroom were on fire.
Not your average ants—no single files,
    no mission to follow, nor ambition to admire—
just pyrotechnics of energy out of control.
Where did these erratic periods come from?
    Was it a pipe behind the sink, a secret keyhole?
Their paths are mutable, their emotions random—
    agitated or hopeless? frightened or playful?—
a case could be made for all of the above.

Their kinetic movements, frenetic but wistful,
    make me ponder the dizzying buzz of love,
this sonnet, myself, and a fitting epithet:
    odd little speck on a big blue planet.

"Ants" was published in the anthology *Celebrations* (July Literary Press, 2006).

Scott Wiggerman is author of *Vegetables and Other Relationships* (Plain View Press, 2000) and editor of the *Texas Poetry Calendar* (Dos Gatos Press), now in its ninth year. His work has appeared in numerous journals, including *Borderlands: Texas Poetry Review, Bay Windows, Gertrude, Midwest Poetry Review, Spillway*, and the *Paterson Literary Review*. In addition, his poems appear in several anthologies, including *Will Work for Peace* (Zeropanik Press, 1999), *The Cancer Poetry Project* (Fairview Press, 2001), *Affirming Flame* (Evelyn Street Press, 2002), *The Fairest of Them All* (Daniel & Daniel, 2003), and most recently, *This New Breed: Gents, Bad Boys and Barbarians 2* (Windstorm Creative, 2004) and *In the Arms of Words: Poems for Disaster Relief* (Sherman Asher, 2006).

A God not of *forces*, but *things*

MARTIN WALLS

In many ways, this poem was a "breakthrough" poem for me. Looking back over the drafts I can see — and indeed remember — struggles I was having.

I was, in this poem and others like it, struggling both to commit to writing detailed observations about the natural world and also to pare back those observations into tense, taut poems that say as much as they can in as few words.

Writing poetry often feels to me like making sculpture. Colleague Mairéad Byrne, who studied at Purdue with me, often reminds me that I used to say I was "chiseling away" at poems in my study. In fact, the other day she wrote to me asking about my latest work. "How's it going," she wrote, "got any good 'chiselers' out there?"

In terms of influences, when I wrote "A God not of *forces*, but *things*," I was reading American poets James Wright, Charles Wright, and Tom Andrews (my teacher), and Swedish poet Tomas Tranströmer.

Students would do well to study the exactitude of these poets' observations and how they commit them to language — using precise words; startling metaphor; a matter-of-fact voice (something of a tradition for "objectivist" poetry); and simple, sometimes long, end-stop lines.

Humbly, I present some examples from my poem:

• Exact observation and precise language: "Maple buds channel raindrops through their gargoyle shapes. / Light drips from a roof of branches. / / Half the vinca laid in."

• Startling metaphor: "Snail inches to the edge of the morning & lifts its head, a semi-liquid question mark."

• Matter-of-fact voice and end-stop lines: "If growth is the analogy of faith, then this kneeling's prayer, / And the simple act of gardening grounds a theology of the particular."

The first draft of this poem does well in the department of "exact observation and precise language," although any reader can see I poured in almost everything I saw, heard, and felt that morning. (One of my jobs as a graduate student was a gardener for my teacher Neil Myers. His wife's decision to put in ground cover led to this poem.)

225

Draft 1

Sub Rosa

Spring, Indiana—cardinals throw their blood tree to tree.
Crows ~~in the sycamore~~ following me with cosmic eyes.
Up there. Leaf buds ~~emerging~~ feathery & unsure as the first moths.

I set down the vinca, lay tools beside me—
~~Trowel, dibber, fork.~~

Light drips through ~~the leaking roof of~~ branches.
a   Permanent damp from the biblical rain.
Palmate leaves—sassafras, maple, dandelions—exalting, ~~giddily upwards.~~
Hard not to be swept away in this evangelism—

~~Ah well~~—this kneeling's praying of sorts, part focus, part turning away.
toward   ~~To~~ the doxology & hypostasis of soil—   _their_
toward   ~~To~~ pill bugs, militant ~~archangels, burdened~~ with articulate shields.
their   The thirteen-year Cicada curled in the ~~clay-streaked soil~~ like a sleeping buddah
    Snails raising ~~its~~ quidnunc head, a semi-liquid question mark,   like
    ~~its pouty mouth laughing.~~

From the wet shadows of violets, tiny white moths with Bible-~~brittle~~ wings.
~~Diabolical mosquitoes converge on my breath.~~   ~~I dare not touch them~~
~~Therefore, I stop breathing.~~

    ~~What did the priest say?~~   What the priest said abou
~~What was it the priest said?~~ Something about "a personal God."
Although the congregation wouldn't understand.

A millipede unwinds its clock-spring & time disappears—
The breeze extends liquid fingers, ~~tiny wavering buds like sea anemones~~
~~All over the sycamore—~~

                    what   flits + worms
~~I turn back—those unnerving things~~ one hears in childhood ~~flitting~~
    ~~& worming~~ inside the brain.

"A God not of *Forces*, but *Things*," he said—
    sycamore buds, the digital wind, light—

You'll recognize observations that made the final cut. That's not to say I didn't like or couldn't use some others. I notice, for instance, that the line about the millipede ("A millipede unwinds its clock-spring & time disappears—") went back into my journal, and was used again in a poem from my second book (*Commonwealth*) in a poem called "The Wonder Book of Autumn." Like a good gardener, I never throw anything away!

Another obvious change is in the title. I'm glad I cut the rather pretentious title "Sub Rosa." That phrase means "something hidden," literally, "beneath the roses."

Obviously, in a poem that combines gardening with a whispered, honest comment from a Catholic priest, it fits. But to have the priest's meaningful words up front fits better, is more intriguing, and is more accessible. That's an old revision trick, by the way, taking the last line and seeing if it does better leading the poem.

Even though this draft is a lot shorter, much work remains. Now I am attempting to raise the tension in the poem while keeping to a length and style that suits the subject.

Early in my career, I would often blatantly copy the style of other poets to see how their lines were constructed and what lesson I could draw. For instance, I notice in this draft how overtly I borrowed from Charles Wright.

Compare the crossed-out first line of my poem to a line from Wright's

Sub Rosa

snail inches out to the edge of the morning and lifts its head, a semi-liquid question mark
A snail lifts its head like a semi-liquid question mark. April. Contrary sky.
Maple buds channel the rain through their gargoyle shapes. Light drips from a
    roof of branches.
Half the vinca laid in.
    I descend towards the soil-paradise where archangel pill bugs stand guard
This kneeling's prayer, of sorts: I turn towards my paradise of soil, where pill
    bugs are the archangels.
And cicadas, white as cherubs, curl in the sound clay.
Moths ascend to our world on wings torn from the pages of a Bible.

And what's this I find, still flitting & worming? Something the priest once said
about "a personal God."
Although the congregation wouldn't understand.

*I remember something
the priest once said about
a personal God, in private
because the congregation
wouldn't understand.*

"A God not of Forces but Things," he said
    Maple leaf buds, the digital breeze, light—

227

poem "It's Turtles All the Way Down," a hand-typed draft of which he sent to Purdue's *Sycamore Review*, which I published as poetry editor, then framed! (The manuscript hangs above my desk to this day.)

- "I snap the book shut. February. Alternate Sky." — Charles Wright
- "A snail lifts its head like a semi-liquid question mark. April. Contrary sky." — MW

Obviously, I couldn't go with a line that was so close to Wright's, but it helped me get at the correct line, which appears above the draft line.

Another note about this line. To this day, I dislike similes. I find them too hesitant, with the tendency to dissipate energy. I'm glad I got rid of "like a semi-liquid question mark" and took the risk of the direct comparison.

At this stage, I'm struggling with how to get across the broad analogy between the old priest's private, pantheistic belief and my act of gardening.

Sub Rosa

April. Contrary sky. A snail lifts its head like a semi-liquid question mark.
Maple buds channel rain through gargoyle shapes. Light drips from a
    roof of branches.
                                        The old parable echoes
Half the vinca laid in: "The sower soweth the word," the gospel says.
~~Gardener,~~ If growth is the analogy of faith, then this kneeling's prayer, & a simple act of
    gardening grounds the theology of the particular:

Pill bugs are the archangels ~~in this~~, & cicadas, white as cherubs, curl in the
    paradisiacal clay.
Moths ascend to our world on wings torn from the pages of a Bible.

And what else, still flitting & worming?
Something the priest once said, about "a personal God." Though the
    congregation wouldn't understand.

"A God not of *forces* but *things*," he said
    Digital breeze, snails, corpuscles of light—   ...

("Pantheism" is the belief that God's being is found in every living thing, not "up there" in Heaven.)

You'll see that my attempts are clumsy. The metaphors comparing pill bugs to archangels and cicada grubs to cherubs are overwrought and melodramatic. I pared them back to say pill bugs are angels and grubs are saints. A slight change, but in the final draft the metaphors draw less attention to themselves and help the reader digest the poem.

Similarly, the try-out sentence "'The sower soweth the word,' the gospel says." can be faulted because it "tells" rather than "shows." Thankfully, I came to my senses and realized I did not have to work so hard to draw the analogy between gardening and faith.

This draft is from my book manuscript. A check mark suggests that I'm pretty pleased with it, although I think it actually means this poem is to remain in the manuscript as I go about "trimming the fat," so to speak. I cut several poems.

At this very late stage, I'm tinkering — thinking about typography and typesetting as much as about metaphors and line breaks.

It's true that you can "overthink" a poem. In this case, I'd done a silly thing, changing the phrase "theology of the particular" to "particular theology." The change was unnecessary and actually ruined the meaning of the phrase. I'm happy I caught that. Overthinking also can be seen in the last line, and I resisted the temptation to change "the brethren wouldn't" to "we'd never."

One last thought. Rarely these days do I keep so many drafts of a poem. My tendency now is to go straight from my journal to the computer, and for the most part erase drafts rather than print them and scribble on them.

This erasure is a shame. It's fascinating to look back at these drafts and understand what I was thinking and note my successes and failures.

I encourage you to make and keep handwritten drafts of your poems — they are powerful personal records, as intimate as a diary entry and as revealing as memoir.

Final Version

"A God not of *forces* but *things*."

Snail inches to edge of the morning & lifts its head, a semi-liquid
    question mark.

April. Maple buds channel raindrops through their gargoyle shapes.
Light drips from a roof of branches.

Half the vinca laid in—

If growth is the analogy of faith, then this kneeling's prayer,
And the simple act of gardening grounds a theology of the particular,

Where pillbugs are the angels, & cicadas, white as saints, curl in the
    paradisiacal clay.
Moths ascend the mortal world on wings torn from a Bible—

And what else is flitting & worming, in the mulch of memory?
Something a priest once said, in private, about "a personal God."

Something his brethren would never buy.

From *Small Human Detail in Care of National Trust* (Kalamazoo, MI: New Issues
Press, 2000)

Martin Walls is a Witter Bynner Poetry Fellow of the Library of Congress.
His latest book of poems is *Commonwealth* (March Street Press, 2005). His
poems have appeared in *FIELD, Epoch, The Gettysburg Review, Five Points,*
and elsewhere. He is assistant editor of *Making Music* and *International Mu-
sician* magazines, published in Syracuse, New York.

Above the River

Deena Linett

When I was first writing poetry, Donald Hall published my twenty-three-line poem, "The Power of Place." I should have realized — and did not — that place means everything to me, that it both nourishes and compels poetry. If I were a different person, I could perhaps have predicted "Above the River," when I went to Hawthornden Castle, Scotland, in 2002, because the poem is almost entirely a response to the particularities of that place filtered through my personality and history.

My first fellowship to Hawthornden Castle International Retreat for Writers in 1996 changed my life, but I wasn't able to say how. I had fallen in love with the varieties of Scottish accents, had learned a bit about the country and something of its history, but I wasn't aware that I'd begun a group of poems that would become my first collection, *Rare Earths* (BOA Editions, Ltd., 2001), fictive letters in the voices of women who lived in the islands off northwest Scotland from 1727 to 1994.

I returned to Hawthornden in 2002 with a novel I would work on, and though I completed it, my response to that place seems to have required poems. My 2006 book, *Woman Crossing a Field*, which includes "Above the River," was made possible by my residency there.

Hawthornden, parts of which date from the fifteenth century, stands on a triangular slice of land, a pink stone rampart visible as you approach, and deep glen on two sides.* At the back of the Castle just outside a pair of French doors is a small terrace bordered by a low stone wall that looks out over the glen, which just there is a semi-circular enclosing bowl. Below, the silver thread of the Water of Esk (as one Fellow put it, double water: Esk means "water" in old Gaelic) and everywhere you look, trees.

On the Castle's second floor, immediately above the pink-and-cream colored stone wall where I — and sometimes other Fellows — would sit, gazing into the trees beneath the moody Scottish sky, there's a study and library. In that very quiet space one day, as we looked into the trees through heavy rain, George Messo, editor of the *Near East Review*, told me the names of the trees we could see. He had worked for the Scottish Wildlife Trust, and we had often talked about the spectacular beauty of Scotland. Eight miles from Edinburgh, we could see yew, rowan, birch, cedar, sycamore, oak, elder, maple, Scots pine, beech, ash, and hawthorne. That bird I pointed to, the one with the red back, was a kestrel, he said.

As I put together the pages that constitute this essay, I am astonished at how much of the poem was present from the beginning. And I hadn't realized how many people are part of my making process. As I gathered the pages with the early drafts, I see that some of what made the poem possible is what George Messo told me, and much of the finished poem was first expressed in letters to friends before — or during — the drafting, as if I were readying the language for the poem.

Here is the final poem. Following, some of the thinking that contributed to its present shape.

Above the River
Hawthornden Castle, Scotland

Light moves down the bowl of trees and fills it
with detail. Sounds of the river rise. Everywhere
this interpenetration of event: in the small room

just beyond, the serving women take their tea
and when I walk inside, domestic smells —
of laundry being done, and cooking, clean

and reassuring — the world is very close:
the Water of Esk cuts scarps into the stone
ancient trees move in and out of shadow

and now the gift of one desire: to sit and watch
all day as light moves over the glen. Birds
at altitude inhabit all of it, skies awash with weather

which like a petulant child cries and whines,
slurs soft Scots and pocks the lochs
with Gaelic in the four, the six, the endless

directions, lays hands on leafed and firred and dead
stripped trees and the ten thousand greens; beams.
As if King Midas, repenting of the stillness

but unwilling or unable to desist from his enchantment,
here and there dabbed gold on sweeps of leaves
and gilded the great trees. I want to see

what birds see as they angle down into the glen
along the river or circle north toward town
with clear untutored eye, and without longing.

It appears there's not much personality in this poem; it looks outward and doesn't focus on the speaker. Though it doesn't tell you much about her, there's a great deal of me in it, as letters to friends show.

Letter to A: "I go to Glasgow on Saturday (have mixed feelings about leaving here, as you might imagine — it's not often a poor Jewish girl from south Florida gets to live in a castle)." I think "poor Jewish girl" [though it's been decades since I was a girl — or poor] goes quite a way to explaining the "serving women" in line 4. The serving women might well have been invisible to someone privileged, but I had talked with the women who worked at the Castle doing the cooking and laundry and cleaning. Jean said the weather had been "diabolical," pretty extreme language, for a Scot.

Letter to B: "Weather is perfect for me: cool, crispy when it's not raining. It whines, cries — hard — then it's sunny and brilliant, all within a few minutes. Literally. This AM during breakfast, before I went to E'burgh, the sun came out and brightly lit the breakfast room. Then someone said Look: in brilliant sun, heavy pouring rain. And, to quote one of my poems, *you can see the weather coming on for miles*, so there are glorious skies constantly changing, and you can see dark areas with very black clouds and blue and white clouds, all in the same vast sky. I do love it here."

Letter to C: "It's gloriously beautiful here. There's a lovely low stone wall overlooking the Water of Esk about 60 feet down in a deep tree-rich glen (steep valley) or brae (steep valley near river) and I love sitting (rain or shine) and looking at it. If rain, indoors
:)

Letter to D: "I've heard *wonderful* music — or it was just what I needed — and Scottish folk on BBC Radio na Gael." The reference to Gaelic probably explains "slurs soft Scots and pocks the lochs / with Gaelic" as well as demonstrating an immersion in, and sensitivity to, language.

Letter to E: "The woods are extraordinarily beautiful here. There's a guy who's worked in forests and even he says they're remarkable. We all talk about it; all of us writers, nobody has the right language for *these glorious woods*."

This letter is to my most urban friend, a New Yorker, with whom I share a need for cities, so it remains significant to me how passionate my responses to Scotland were — and remain. To the same friend, more about the land:

"Sunday we walked to Rosslyn Chapel, which is near Rosslyn Castle's ruins — in the days when it was whole it looked exactly like the pictures in our children's books of King Arthur's castle — with round turrets and of course the crenelated walls and slots instead of windows. So we walked. People said, You just turn right at the rhododendron bush (as if there were only one) and walk along the path till you get to the sign and then turn right. There were four of us, a Canadian, a Dutch woman, a Pole with a surfeit of z's in his name, and me. We walked for an hour & ten minutes and then we got to steps cut into the steep hill. How steep? A book on Rosslyn (just as often spelled Roslin) & Hawthornden (1897) I've been reading today says 'the tourist must be prepared to 'Set a stout heart to a stae brae.' We climbed and climbed and climbed about 4,000 steps cut into the brae, and when the steps stopped at little earthen landings and I couldn't breathe, G kept saying, 'It's not much farther,' but it was."

Letter to F: "The weather here's like a petulant child: it cries horribly, absolutely DUMPING water (even in brilliant sun — so if there are no clouds, where does this rain come from?) and then beaming happily and warmly in a few minutes. I like its changeableness and the rain hasn't bothered me. T. doesn't like it and complains goodnaturedly, with a kind of self-mocking amusement."

Reading the letters now, I can see they were drafts of the poem, but of course at the time I wasn't aware of that — all the assertions I set out so neatly here were inchoate, were fog, and when conscious, turbulent inside my head. During the four years between 2002, when I was in Scotland, and the 2006 submission of this poem to a contest at the New England Poetry Club, I had no idea of the connections, though I knew there were dozens of drafts.

Some of the drafts:

> A red bird crosses the wide top of the bowl of trees
> rooted sixty, eighty? feet below [and high up here
> in the six-sided study at the windows,
> the wild untroubled Scottish sky over all of us]
> and Water of Esk pounding noisily over stones, the rain
> slurring soft Scots and pocking the lochs with Gaelic,
> all the textures and all the colors of green
> in the four, the six, the endless directions, the leafed
> and firred, the dead stripped trees haven't, like God,
> asked us to admire them. Why then do we want to
> throw ourselves onto them as onto mercy?

The six-sided study meant a lot to me, but the poem didn't need it once I got "the four, the six, the endless directions" and I think it's possible to ascribe those lines to my conversations with George Messo; we had agreed that the world's endlessness is more available in Scotland than perhaps in other places. Since then, Messo has lived in the vast deserts of Saudi Arabia and Oman, so I suppose he would say they are also places one can sense the finite infinity of the world.

I think I lifted the fourth line "the wild untroubled Scottish sky" from another poem, one that had appeared in the first book, but slightly altered. In "Giacometti in Edinburgh" one line records "the wild high Scottish sky," and there too King Midas makes an appearance. In some way I haven't yet got hold of, they are linked in me: Midas and the forests of Scotland, and the skies. Perhaps it would be useful to set out the lines of the earlier poem:

. . . .   You will have to give it up, all this,
light tangled in the branches and beneath the trees

in little coins, surprise and hope and grief
and error, and for one brief moment all of it

is glorious. As if King Midas had been waiting
in the woods, stepped out onto the green,

struck everything to polished stillness —
even you, fixed by light, unable to breathe.

"Giacometti in Edinburgh," *Rare Earths*, 2001

But it's unacceptable to repeat oneself. Other drafts of "Above the River" show twelve or fourteen blocky stanzas very like the one above beginning "A red bird" — which Messo told me was a kestrel. There are lines about "the ten thousand greens" from the beginning of the drafts, and a frequent end — one I couldn't get past for a long time was

I want to see what birds see as they angle down
into the glen along the river or circle north toward town,
their calls not beautiful, not song, ringing in the distance.

I think these lines — including "toward town" and "not beautiful, not song" were my attempt to unbeautify what I'd made as beautiful as I could, the light filling "bowl of trees," which was there from the beginning. The final version of the poem does that: the birds "circle north toward town"; that and "clear untutored eye," are not a poetic language. Perhaps I thought after all that music, which I worried was overmuch ("slurs soft Scots and pocks the lochs") and King Midas, after wishing to "sit and watch / all day as light moves" the poem needed to come down to earth, to the daily, to a "clear untutored eye, and without longing." *Longing* is perhaps too "poetic" and "pretty." In the twenty-first century, we don't want pretty.

So my esthetic determines my choices. Perhaps it's truer to say my esthetic is the ground beneath all my words and all my choices.

Another draft says "birds / are the only creatures capable of being just

236

the right distance above to see it / in the breadth and detail that might go some way toward satisfying."

Terrible lines. Awful. I wrote them with the line breaks shown here, but even as I typed the words — I write by hand only when I haven't access to a keyboard — I knew they were awful. You have to be willing to waste a great deal of paper and spend a lot of time. I don't know how conscious I was then of feeling my way forward to "Birds / at altitude inhabit all of it" and "clear untutored eye" but they were where I was going, and when I found them, I was confident that they represented what I wanted, what — in an ugly phrase I avoid — I was "trying to do."

I do think that's when a poem is finished. When the thing made approximates the thing attempted — or imagined — when the thing made, laid over the drafts, follows the same floor-plan, so to speak, it is finished. Another way to say this is a corruption of a book I read in graduate school more than twenty years ago whose title and author I've (alas) forgotten: when you look through a screened window, you're not aware of the screen. You're looking at the trees beyond, or the life out on the street. But if there are two screens and they don't line up, you'll see only the grids not overlaid properly on one another. When the poem's finished, the little squares line up, so you can see the poem without interference.

"Those are terrible lines," I said earlier and, wincing, again here: how bad they are. But I have learned over the years that you have to be willing to write them. You don't have to show them to anybody, but you have to be willing to put them down, and the reason for that seems to me extraordinarily important.

You don't know what they're going *toward*; you can't know what they'll yield, until you write it. Imagine the line as a branch growing on a flowering tree — an apple tree, a pear tree — if you cut the branch off near the trunk, you can't know what the end of the branch with its new little green leaves and buds and eventual flowers and fruit would look like because you'd never get to it. You won't know whether it would be fertile or sterile. You won't know if its curve into the blue air would be beautiful or twisted. Or dead. You have to get out of the way and let it be what it is, even when it's ugly or terrible.

I believe this absolutely. So I'm a bit embarrassed by the really crummy choice of words here but I'm doing them anyway: I have to because I don't know where they're going.

I don't know why King Midas appears to me in Scottish woods, and no place else. We need *somebody* responsible for dabbing light on trees, so out of the woods steps King Midas again, who, perhaps with Demeter, is the only myth I bring into the present from my childhood. My notes say things like, "Because you can see the cloud bank that soon will cover you, and beyond the white clear-weather billows, blue here and there, you can believe it's possible that things will change, despair blow past and over." So weather would always be part of this poem, and weather is easy, Joan Didion says, so if you do weather, you have to do something worthwhile with it. Since weather's so much a part of my experience of Scotland, I needed to find ways to make it interesting.

"Interesting" means a lot here: it means not what I might *like*, or *want to say* (see running for office, below) but what the poem requires, what the *art* of poetry, not just my one little poem, requires. The art of poetry requires that the work be new: if it's going to be familiar, if anybody could make it, if it isn't my uniquely made object, if it's going to be greeting-card verse, why bother: it's not going to be a poem. A poem is an art form, like a quartet or a trio, played by people who know something of the tradition and history and — in their own time — reach of that particular endeavor.

What happened to the idea of throwing ourselves onto the trees as onto mercy? you might fairly ask. I don't know. The poem didn't need it. This is huge.

Poems aren't about what I want to write; they're about what they're about. This sounds mysterious, but it's not: I am trying to describe — briefly — the work of more than a quarter century of submission to a process.

If you want to write poems, you have to let the poem tell you what it wants.† You're there to provide it. If you want to make a speech, run for office; if you want to tell people how to live, get a pulpit. If you want to write poems, you have to understand that your subconscious is smarter than you are — smarter, that is, than your conscious mind, and if you listen to it, it will surprise and delight you — and sometimes your readers. Poems aren't about what you have decided you would write, or what you want to say.

So finally my poem wasn't about God and admiration. It's about the mindlessness of birds (closer to cold-blooded animals than to us) and plenitude and beauty and trees; trees don't need our admiration; it's we who need to admire them. Finally, it was about the daily — cooking and laundry — and the "interpenetration of event" — how everything in some sense leans on everything else. Indoors you're aware of the world outside, you're aware of how the "serving women" are present and enable certain comforts, how the light makes everything possible.

I have twenty-one pages of drafts, undated. Originally, the previous sentence read "There are twenty-one pages ...." "There are" is less interesting than "I have." This is the sort of thing I'm aware of now, working at writing for more than twenty years; I learned it from Donald Hall. Care with every word: that's what poems require. I'm aware that I keep using the word *require*, but nothing else says quite what I mean with the firm exactitude that word does: it brooks no opposition. One of the many draft pages says

THE WALLS: OUR LIMITS, THE WORLD'S;
PERSONALITY / INCAPACITY: AND TIME

In one draft on that page, "domestic scents" would rhyme with "event" but I was so busy with other parts of the poem — as with "dabbed" and "daubed" (below) — I lost track of it immediately, writing:

and when I walk inside, the domestic scents
smells of laundry being done and cooking
                    clean familiar

seagreen
lightgreen
blackgreen
yellowgreen
bluegreen
brightgreen
limegreen.

birch and oak; see trees file. LISTS of both in one poem??? The Glen hawthorne, pink and purple, creamy yellowy off-white, red and blue and

bird-call diminishing as the bird flies down the glen and north toward Edinburgh.
And the light (SEE FOG?) comes from so far away

to illumine (pool on the?) leaves it's not possible —
not accurate

Note "not accurate." A poem must be accurate. It must be true to the world it renders, the world in which it lives. This is not negotiable. Of course it doesn't mean you can't write about dragons. If about them, however, it must be true to dragons.

As if we have been slung into a bowl of light.

And the shadow of the house falls
and a yellow-white brown branch declares itself

What IF ALL DAY I WATCHED LIGHT MOVE OVER THE
    GLEN?
And the great trees move as if underwater
slowly, as if dreaming, curtseying; first north
then south as the wind trembles them.

rivers and cuts of scarps and stone.
Sitting and watching the light all day

What I want to do is what lies beneath the daily
the cauldron of heaving rocking swaying slashing melted stone

While I felt parts of the poem represented me well — that is, spoke my feelings or attempts truly — I was worried about the whole. I never felt that *ah*, that satisfied feeling of closure or certainty I have with some poems; I wasn't sure this one was good enough — for anybody else's eyes, for a contest I sent it to, for the book. When it won special recognition (from the New England Poetry Club, which Amy Lowell and Robert Frost among others, had founded), I knew I could include it in the new book, *Woman Crossing a Field* (BOA Editions, Ltd., 2006). The many files in which the poem appears, the dozens upon dozens of pages, demonstrate my feeling for the materials the poem addresses, though it is now a mere twenty-four lines. Revision goes on forever. Typing this essay, I see the lost opportunity to rhyme "scent" with "event" and I wish I'd used "daubed" instead of "dabbed" in the penultimate stanza. "Daubed" is more interesting because less common, and probably more precise.

I never know what will work its way into a poem, so in Edinburgh, at the Royal Museum of Scotland, on Independence Day in the United States, I scrawled in my notebook:

> Statue of St Andrew, 9th C., says Celtic influence came from Ireland but the Andrew cult came from Europe to the *east* of Scotland.
>
> The Carnyx (pl: carnyces) found at Deskford, which is on the sea, east of the Moray Firth, is the pike with dragon-head; used in battle 100 BCE–200 AD (approx).

Writing demands attention: everything pertains, whether it's finally in the poem or not. Everything contributes to the weight of the made object in the world. So I wrote down the plural of "carnyx" — a word I'll likely never use. But though neither the word nor anything about St Andrew appears in the poem, they constitute the *field*, the *surround*, the embrace or environment, of the particular place that made this poem necessary. They're part of what I know, or needed to know, for the particular poem to emerge.

Particularity is critical. Attempts to write a "universal" poem are usually dreadful because the universal is located *in* the particular: if you are true to one particular, you've said something about the world. The right word — *not the approximately right word*‡ — makes the poem, which can have no vague generalities, no slack lines, no foggy passages: it must show, with glittering clarity, the thing it renders.

During the drafting of this essay, I happened on an interview with Jim Harrison in *The Writer's Chronicle*. Harrison says something marvelous to do with writing what the poem needs, particularlity and "the universal." He's been reading a lot of "Dogen, who's the classic from fourteenth century Japan. He said this alarming but painfully true thing: 'To study the self is to forget the self; to forget the self is to be one with ten thousand things.' "§

Finally, the awareness of language, the sensitivity to the new word, in this case *carnyces*, is part of the apparatus you carry around with you if you're a poet. Before digital photography, people — Ansel Adams, for example — used huge cameras that were cumbersome and hard to carry over rough terrain, but they were the necessary apparatus. For us it is language.

We're lucky: language weighs nothing, and we bring it with us everywhere.

Deena Linett has published prize-winning novels and short fiction. Her second collection of poems from BOA Editions, Ltd., *Woman Crossing a Field*, appeared in June 2006. In summer 2004, she was resident at The Centre for Writers & Translators on Gotland, in the Baltic Sea. She has twice had fellowships to Hawthornden Castle, Scotland, and to Yaddo, and is professor of English at Montclair State University.

* *The Concise Scots Dictionary* defines *glen* as "a valley or hollow, *chf* one traversed by a stream or river, and *freq* narrow and steep-sided; a mountain valley ...." Glen: from Scots and Irish Gaelic *gleann*; early Irish Gaelic *glenn*. Brae: the (steep or sloping) bank of a river or lake or shore of the sea ... a bank or stretch of ground rising fairly steeply... an upland, mountainous district.

† See Joan Didion, "Why I Write," 1979.

‡ Ursula K. LeGuin, *The Wave in the Mind*, 233.

§ "An Interview with Jim Harrison," by Nancy Bunge, *The Writer's Chronicle*, May/Summer 2006; quoted material appears on 24.

Through the Plots

JEANNE M. LESINSKI

No one could escape the images associated with Hurricane Katrina. They were everywhere — TV, radio, print media. One image caught my attention while driving and listening to NPR. The Disaster Mortuary Rescue Team was retrieving coffins and remains that had gone astray in the hurricane floodwaters. I immediately thought, "There's a poem in that." There was.

Some days later, I looked online for photos of New Orleans cemeteries. I made some notes and, as I often do, drew some sketches. I put this material aside for eight months, until I happened upon the book *Hurricane Katrina: The Storm That Changed America* (Time, 2006). In it, I found three particularly striking photos: a marble statue foregrounding open crypts; a silver coffin sitting on a desolate roadside; and in Southern Memorial Gardens, open mausoleums with urns and debris on the ground.

I knew right away that I wanted to begin the poem with an image of wind and water in a cemetery because I thought of how coffins are like boats (and dead ancient warriors were sent off in boats as a form of burial). I found it both ironic and disquieting to think that the dead might, like the

Katrina
Hurricane winds roared through,
prying open heavy doors, snapping
moorings, setting afloat in leaves, shingles,
rushing water soiled with the coffins
of parish ancestors

the body of feline,
an unfortunate

living, be displaced by the storm. I also knew I wanted to end the poem with the image of a casket on the shoulder of a road, which reminded me of photos I had seen of people trying to leave the area. In my poem, I wanted to express the hopelessness some people must have felt because of their losses.

Upon looking at my first draft of sentence 1, I decided to omit "Katrina" so that the narrative could apply to any hurricane. I decided not to break up the action by having the description of the water precede "coffins of parish ancestors," a phrase that I condensed to "parishioners," which also has a religious connotation. Likewise, "the body of an unfortunate feline" became the more suggestive and less wordy "lives of a tabby." Because "shredded leaves" and "shingles" signal the destruction of nature and the destruction of man-made things, respectively, I wanted a term that would indicate loss of life. I chose "a tabby" to be both specific (a particular kind of cat) and nonspecific (in the association of cats with "nine lives" and the many lives — animal and human — lost). I used "moorings" and "afloat," terms that have nautical meanings, to create the metaphor of coffins as boats.

After I typed sentence 1, I added in longhand the line "urns, toppled from mausoleums, / opened, scattered remains." I realized when I typed it that "toppled" should be "toppling" and "scattered" should be "scattering" to maintain the parallelism of the verbs. I also realized that the second "opened" was unnecessary because, for the remains to be scattered, the urns would have to be open.

The words ending in *–ing* make a string of trochees and create a continuous rhythm, like flowing water. The verbs are active, and "roared," "rushing," and "snapping" are onomatopoetic. This sentence contains many hard consonant sounds (*b, p, d, r, h, t, k*), which create a biting tone. Yet the various *o* sounds throughout and the softer sounds of *v* and *sh* ("shredded leaves, shingles, / the lives") near the end suggest wind and water, respectively.

I soon realized that the arrangement of words on the page could also suggest water. To do this, I dispensed with a title and began with the phrase "Through the plots" set toward the right margin. That the segments are short further suggests the patterns water makes when it flows around obstacles. I tried to make the caesuras such that a word I particularly wanted to emphasize would be positioned immediately before the break of white space or nearest the right margin. In the case of "prying open stone doors, / lids," I put the caesura between "doors" and "lids," to suggest an opening. Likewise, the final phrase of the poem, with the white space flowing downward diagonally from left to right, mimics a road.

With sentence 2, the narrative moves from the broad sweep to focus specifically on the dead. I had read in *Hurricane Katrina* that some southern Louisianians scare their children with stories of caskets floating off during floods, much as other people might tell scary stories about the Bogeyman. So I referenced this practice in the first phrase, which acted like a topic sentence, then created a sense of suspense with "unknown destinations." The alliteration ("tales told") and consonance using *t* give the sentence a brittle character, which contrasts with the soft sounds ending sentence 1.

My early drafts did not contain sentence 3, but after writing sentence 4, the poem seemed unfinished. Then I remembered the photo with the angel statue, whose broken wing tip seemed to signify the hopelessness of the situation. By having the statue witness the exodus of the dead, I would continue the narrative and create a transition to the last sentence in which one casket is seen at its destination.

Again, hard consonant sounds (*ch, cl, cr, pr, h, tch, w, t, k*) predominate, continuing the edgy tone. The pace remains quick due to the majority of short vowel sounds and trochees, yet the most important words — "prayer," "broken," and "go" — contain long vowel sounds that are accentuated. I particularly chose "lichen" over the alternative "moss" to continue the consonance between "lichen," "encrusted," "clasped," and "broken."

Each sentence of the poem begins with a subordinate clause, a pattern that acts as a unifying device. "Winds," "water," "with," "wing," and "waiting" and the various long and short *o* sounds evenly spaced throughout also unify the poem. The open *a* sounds of sentence 3 lead into sentence 4 with "After the water" forming a bridge. The hard consonant sounds of sentence 3 also give way to the alliterative *s* ("single, silver") and consonance between "receded" and "rested" of sentence 4.

I chose "coffin" over "casket" in order to link with *f* the key words in the sentence ("after," "coffin," and "lift"). I ended the poem with the only simile in the work ("a single silver coffin rested / on the shoulder, / like a hitchhiker / waiting / for a lift.") because it seemed to sum up all that had preceded it. The predominant meter, the trochee, creates a sense of urgency, until the very end of the poem. With "like a hitchhiker / waiting / for a lift" the poem's cascading rhythm finds a resolution in the mirrored pattern of trochee, bacchic and then trochee, anapest.

Here is the finished poem:

<pre>
                                      Through the plots
                         hurricane winds roared,
         prying open stone doors,   lids,
                    toppling urns,
                                   scattering remains,
         snapping moorings,
                   setting afloat parishioners' coffins
                              in rushing water—soiled
         with shredded leaves, shingles,   the lives of a tabby.

         As in tales told   to frighten children,
                         the dead left   for unknown destinations.

                   Marble hands clasped in prayer,
         a lichen-encrusted angel,   one wingtip broken,
                   watched them go.
                                   After the water receded,
                         a single silver coffin rested
             on the shoulder,   like a hitchhiker
                   waiting
                      for a lift.
</pre>

Jeanne M. Lesinski has published four children's books, including *Bill Gates* (Lerner), as well as numerous articles for magazines and reference books. Her poems have appeared or are forthcoming in *Pennsylvania English*, *The Binnacle*, *Cardinal Sins*, *Lynx*, *Main Channel Voices*, and *The Dunes Review*. She writes from Bay City, Michigan.

Monument

GARY J. WHITEHEAD

I drafted this poem two days after the experience it describes — my parents meeting me in Mount Saint Mary's cemetery in Pawtucket, Rhode Island, where I'd gone to walk my dog, and their showing me their names on the family gravestone. It was a shock, a grim reminder of their age and mortality, and I couldn't get the moment out of my mind.

Granite

Pink granite of the moment
    I'd take back
from the rows of the dead,
solid slab of the future these days erase.

The poem began with the image of the stone: "Pink granite of the moment." I liked the sound of this line as an opener. The consonance of the *n* and *m* sounds seemed to convey the heaviness I felt without giving away too much in the image. Next came: "I'd take back / from the rows of the dead, / solid slab of the future these days erase." These lines made for a solid first stanza, setting the graveyard scene and the idea of unstoppable time. I appreciated the sibilance of "solid slab" and the assonance of "days erase." The sentence ended there, making a quatrain, so I started a new stanza:

We'd gone to chase sticks
    on a sleep-over stay, a Sunday
    already yesterday, July,
and we'd stuck to the south road of Mt. St. Mary's
so as not to desecrate,
so as to stay in shade.

This, too, seemed to work, echoing the sibilance and assonance that ended the first stanza. Moreover, it provided the exposition of when ("Sunday … yesterday" and "July") and where ("the south road of Mt. St. Mary's").

In the second draft, however, I decided that the metaphors "granite of the moment" and "solid slab of the future" in such proximity seemed gra- 247 tuitous. I also realized that I hadn't mentioned my dog; thus, the line "We'd gone to chase sticks" might be confusing. In revision, I considered the blocky feeling of these two end-stopped stanzas and the complete lack of caesuras in the first stanza; I wanted to create the effect of a series of cinematic fade-outs or wipes instead of two long takes, and I wanted to use enjambment to suggest the meandering action of walking:

> Pink granite moment—what
>   we went to,
> my dog, my God and me
>
> yesterday, yes, not today,
>   chasing sticks, sticking
>   to the road, the south, and where it went
>   through Mount Saint Mary's
>   so as not to desecrate
>   so as to stay
>
> in shade.

Back to the first draft, in stanza three, perhaps realizing I hadn't mentioned my dog, I elaborated a bit. Then I made an abrupt transition to seeing the chapel where three years prior I'd said my last goodbyes to my maternal grandmother. Here I felt the need to get back to that time, a cold autumn day with snow flurries, a day that contrasted dramatically with the hot July day of the walk. The flashback would also provide motivation for the next action of the poem, my desire to see my grandmother's gravestone (which in reality I hadn't ever seen), and my phone call to my parents to ask where the grave was located in the cemetery. Immediately after writing the stanza, I crossed out nearly four lines, again because the metaphor seemed forced:

> A graveyard's got no leash laws.
> And I carry bags.
> But then the chapel was a calendar
> blown back and my eyes snow globes
> because it was snowing a few years ago
> and I was saying goodbye

to my Voa Voa who~~'d died~~ in her casket
had already blown back to her beginning.
Now I wanted to see the stone,
and on the phone my father
said they'd drive over to show me.

The climax of the poem, I knew, would be my parents showing me their
own names on the stone, and in the last two stanzas I described the scene
as I remembered it:

On the face the name FERNANDES,
(my mother's name). And my mother
there beside me on her bad knees
and looking old. And my father
with his bad posture.

"But where's her first name?
Where's Voo Voo?" I said.
They took me around the stone,
and there were their names
already chiseled in
with just the dates
waiting.

Writing the second draft, I knew I'd said too much, that I'd overwritten.
Did the reader really need to know I'd made a cell phone call to my parents? Or that I walked past the chapel where we'd had the final service
after my grandmother's funeral? Were either of these details crucial to the
drama of the poem? I didn't think so. I merely needed to get the reader to
the stone. Instead of the flashback, I expanded on the start of the third
stanza with irony and wordplay: "Graveyards have lease laws, not leash /
laws, and besides / I carry the little body / / bags." I liked the comedic nature of this sentence, especially since it would come just before the serious
punch, a punch I knew I wanted to make even more serious. In the actual
experience, it was a shock to see my parents' names on the gravestone, but
in retrospect it was even more shocking to me because my mother has
twice survived cancer. In my own mind I've imagined her death, her funeral, many times. And so, to the punch:

... But hold it, the moment—
    granite, pink,
when I saw my grandparents' stone, my dog
and me no longer alone
because my mother had driven there—
the survivor, breast and bladder, rather
    not talk about that—
to check on the flowers, to
touch the last name, to—
    I don't know?—show

me the other names—hers
    and my father's—
        chiseled
in with just the dates
                            waiting.

The easiest way to the punch seemed obvious, not through flashback, but by returning to the moment with which I'd begun, the "Pink granite moment" of the first line, now reversed. There's also the pun, the segue from comedy to tragedy, from the "little body / / bags" (doggy waste bags) to "hold it, the moment." Here, again, I wanted the sounds to convey the shift in tone, and so the assonant finality of "granite, pink" and the sonorousness of "stone" and "alone." Rather than go into detail about my mother's cancer, I intuited that it seemed enough to do it obliquely and at the same time to continue skipping the stone of the *er* sound across the stanza ("longer ... mother ... there ... survivor ... bladder, rather ... flowers"), the same sound that culminates in the climactic lines, "the other names—hers / and my father's." I was satisfied with the same ending as in the first draft, "dates / waiting," since these two words seemed to say it all: my parents will die soon, and the dates of their deaths will be "chiseled" (connoting my feeling of being "cheated") on the gravestone.

My first title of the poem, composed after the first draft, was "Mount Saint Mary's." It can be seen as an erasure under the second title, "Granite," on the first draft. On the second draft, I changed the title to "Monument(al)." I wanted a title that suggested the *monumental* significance of the experience while naming the key object, the *monument*. The parenthetical "al" seemed too contrived, though. In writing the third draft, I looked up the word *monument*:

1. A structure, such as a building or sculpture, erected as a memorial.
2. An inscribed marker placed at a grave; a tombstone.
3. Something venerated for its enduring historic significance or association with a notable past person or thing.
4. An outstanding enduring achievement.
5. An exceptional example.
6. An object, such as a post or stone, fixed in the ground so as to mark a boundary or position.
7. A written document, especially a legal one.

The single word denoted all I wanted it to. Moreover, with its stressed/unstressed/stressed trisyllabic balance, it seemed to serve as a microcosm for the poem itself.

I wrote the first two drafts in a blank journal with a mechanical pencil, and the third draft on my laptop. I attribute some of the indentation and line breaks of the first two drafts to the size of the page in the journal. The second draft shows a movement toward tercets, toward threes. I love the tercet form, and this poem kept pulling toward this stanza shape. The third draft suggests this pull, but, perhaps like the speaker and his notions of parental mortality, it resists its full realization. Making final edits on the computer, I read the poem aloud to myself, seeking satisfying rhythms and sounds (for instance, changing "yesterday, yes, not today," to "yesterday, yes, today, too"), as well as interesting line breaks (in the sixth stanza, offsetting the tercet with a beginning and ending em dash; in the seventh stanza, beginning each line with the preposition "to"; and in the final stanza, letting the lines diminish in length to the final word, "waiting").

A final word on reversals. In the first stanza, there's the reversal of "dog" and "God," the one all too there and the other all too not there. When this line repeats later, "my God" has been intentionally omitted. "Pink granite" in the first line of the poem is also reversed into "granite, pink." And, of course, there is the reverse side of the stone itself. Though I did find myself wishing the experience never happened, I didn't set out to use the device of reversal. It was fortuitous or intuitive. Happily so.

Monument

Pink granite moment—
what we went to,
my dog, my God and me

yesterday, yes, today, too,
chasing sticks, sticking
to the road, the south,
and where it went

through Mount Saint Mary's
so as not to desecrate
so as to stay in shade.

Graveyards have
lease laws, not
leash laws,
and besides
I carry a little body bag.

But hold it, the moment—
granite, pink,
when I saw my grandparents' stone,
my dog and me
no longer alone
because my mother
had driven there

—my mother, the survivor,
breast and bladder,
rather not talk about that—

to check on the flowers she'd left,
to touch the last name,
to—I don't know?—show me

the names on the slab's other side,

hers and my father's,
chiseled already,
just the dates
waiting.

Gary J. Whitehead's work appears or is forthcoming in *Poetry, Crab Orchard Review, The Christian Science Monitor,* and *Alimentum.* His first full-length collection of poems was published in 2005 by Salmon Publishing / Dufour Editions, and he has also published three chapbooks, two of which were winners of national competitions (Sow's Ear Press and White Eagle Coffee Store Press). His third chapbook was published in 2006 by Finishing Line Press. Other awards include a New York Foundation for the Arts Fellowship in Poetry, the Pearl Hogrefe Fellowship in Poetry at Iowa State University, and two Galway Kinnell Poetry Prizes. His most recent award was the PEN Northwest Margery Davis Boyden Wilderness Writing Residency, which offered him seven months of writing and solitude in a backwoods cabin in Oregon.

Middletown

KATHLEEN KIRK

First Draft

Middletown

When we arrive, I am wavering
in my belief in myself as a woman
who will know enough to say no to a man
with real leather seats. We pass a house
with too many dogs. I feel them
at my throat, clamoring for the slag

of my bitten heart. He could ruin
me, I could ruin him.
I know when we kiss how soft my lips
will seem to him, how sharp the shadow
on his chin. I'm sure I've been here before,
maybe in a dream…the road curves

around a tavern, eyeless and bored,
a red brick church, a pile of rock
where once a little house surprised
its own foundation by burning to the ground
after a woman shot her husband
in the chest, his palm prints on the barrel.

When I first wrote the poem "Middletown," I had given myself an interesting task: an exercise by Richard Hugo, explained in the essay "Stray Thoughts on Roethke and Teaching" in his book *The Triggering Town: Lectures and Essays on Poetry and Writing* (W.W. Norton, 1979). Hugo bases his exercise on a final exam given by his own teacher, the poet Theodore Roethke, a man particularly in love with the musicality of poetry. In Hugo's variation, I had to incorporate five nouns, verbs, and adjectives from three lists and follow a sort of invented form. This is it: three six-line stanzas of four beats per line, internal slant rhymes (at least two per stanza), external slant rhymes (one per stanza), no more than two end stops per stanza, and standard and correct sentences throughout.

Hugo's final rule is this: "The poem must be meaningless," which he calls a "sadistic invention of [his] own." With that "rule," Hugo encourages poets to distract themselves from trying to mean something significant and instead to enjoy the formal and musical challenges of the writing process, discovering a more authentic meaning or content along the way. Since that is something I have discovered on my own as a writer, I particularly enjoy that "rule" and I trust utterly to the seeming "distractions" of formal challenges. Like many other writers, of prose as well as poetry, I tend to discover what I have to say by writing it down. Concentrating on the formal challenges frees me from an internal censor or critic, and I can discover what's *really* lurking inside.

It's easy to see on the page, even in the first draft, the structure of this invented form. I even refer to the form in a companion poem, "Apology," shared later in this essay. Of interest now is my use of those slant rhymes, both internal — arrive/waver and/or wavering/clamoring (for the *v* sound in one set and the *ing* sound in the other set), belief/myself, bitten/ruin, him/chin, kiss/lips (very slant), brick/rock — and external — woman/man, ruin/him, ground/husband (all so slant as to seem suspect). Hugo also allows but discourages true rhyme, which I have interspersed, including some exact rhyme, internally and externally: ruin/ruin (exact), around/ground, and know/no (also an exact rhyme of the homophone sort). These rhyming and diction choices get honed later, but they first emerged here in the genesis of the poem.

Also of interest in the first draft are the words I used from Hugo's three lists:

Nouns: throat, belief, rock, dog, slag, eye (in "eyeless," used as an adjective instead, giving me six and not just the required five from this list)

Verbs: to kiss, to curve, to ruin, to surprise ("to bite," from Hugo's list of infinitives, is there as an allusion provided by the dogs and in the adjective "bitten," and "to say" is to come in draft two)

Adjectives: wavering (which I used instead in a verb phrase as a state of being), soft, sharp, leather, red

The content I discovered by immersing myself in the formal challenges was that of a dangerous landscape in midlife. The title, "Middletown," the name of an actual small town in central Illinois, encouraged that content. In this poem, the speaker is a woman contemplating an affair. So many people do crazy things during their midlife crisis that the content risks cliché, but I think the poem avoids it with the choice of concrete images ("a tavern, eyeless and bored") and the inclusion of a story I heard about a murder in this actual town. In this draft, the speaker thinks of herself "as a woman / who will know enough to say no to a man," but she isn't quite sure.

In the next draft, in fact, the woman says yes.

Second Draft (responding to comments and suggestions from an editor, John Bellinger, of *Comstock Review*, which eventually published the poem in the Fall/Winter 2005 issue)

Middletown

When we arrive, I am wavering
in my belief in myself as a woman
who knows enough to say no to a man
with real leather seats. I say yes.
We pass a house with too many dogs.
I feel them at my throat clamoring

for the gristle of my bitten heart.
This man could ruin me, I could
ruin him. I know when we kiss
how soft my lips will seem to him,
how sharp the shadow on his chin.
I'm sure I've been here before: the road

curves around a tavern, eyeless
and bored, a red brick church, rubble
where once a house surprised its own
foundation, burning to the ground
after a woman shot her husband
in the chest, his palms on the barrel.

This draft emerged from email conversations with John Bellinger of *Comstock Review*. Seeking some streamlining and clarifications, but unaware of my chosen invented form, John made some wonderful suggestions that I retained in the final draft eventually published in the magazine. The word *slag* troubled him, for instance, and I changed it to something dogs might actually enjoy chewing — gristle. The discrepancy between saying no and the later kissing troubled John, too, so a very obvious change in line 4 is a content change — "I say yes" — in which the speaker makes a clear choice. Missing from the second draft, then, is the big white space after the second line of the second stanza, where in the first draft the speaker is left to contemplate the blank future, and potential huge loss if she makes this mistake, risking her emotional vulnerability to a man who might not be prepared to respect or protect her. Adding the word *yes* builds up the s sounds of "kiss" and "gristle," a dangerous snaky sibilance. Revising this poem did indeed let me enjoy the pure music of the sounds, something Theodore Roethke would have appreciated. Later changes kept me honest. I made sure I didn't swirl away into the musical sounds without honoring discovered content and preserving emotional honesty.

John suggested a last line leaving the man's palms on the gun barrel, and I tried it for a while, though it told a slightly different story from the historical truth. I do feel free to "lie" in a poem to tell an emotional truth, but in this particular draft I wasn't yet sure how things would turn out in the poem.

In this draft, I liked how "bitten" not only reminded me of "smitten," as when a person is struck by love, but was also a slant rhyme with "gristle," the new word that replaced "slag."

But it didn't stay!

Third Draft (now in further discussion with *Comstock*'s Peggy Flanders)

Middletown

When we arrive, I am wavering
in my belief in myself as a woman
who knows enough to say no to a man
with real leather seats. Turning,
we pass a house with too many dogs.

I feel them at my throat clamor
for the gristle of my risen heart.
This man could ruin me, I could
ruin him. I know when we kiss
how soft my lips will seem to him,
how sharp the shadow on his chin.
I'm sure I've been here before: the road

curves around a tavern, eyeless
and bored, a red brick church, rubble
where once a house surprised its own
foundation, burning to the ground
after a woman shot her husband
in the chest, his palms on the barrel.

In the third draft, "bitten" is replaced by "risen," which now combines the uplift of being struck by love with the actual fear of both love and multiple, clamorous dogs. We say, "My heart was in my throat" when we are really scared. Here, the dogs go after "the gristle of my risen heart" in a new and better internal slant rhyme: gristle/risen.

There is still no big blank space for the contemplated ruin. Both revisions changed the line breaks dramatically. The content is also dramatically changed again. No decision is made. The speaker does not say yes; she stays in the car, describing the ride she's on with this guy. Line 3 includes a pointed caesura that recalls past deleted blank space, and turns on the word *Turning*, which reinforces a meandering enjambment throughout the poem, where the poem's lines turn frequently, as the car turns frequently on the streets of the small town. The word *clamor* loses its *ing*, which is fine, since poems don't need too many *ing* words, but a (very) slant rhyme is maintained: wavering/turning.

Somewhere in the revision process, I had actually lost track of which Hugo words I was using. In conversation with John and later with editor Peggy Flanders, I double-checked and reported to them by email:

Turns out I *did* use 15 words from the 3 Hugo lists in this poem: throat, belief, rock (now rubble), slag (now gristle), eye (as eyeless), dog, kiss, curve, ruin, surprised, soft, wavering, sharp, leather, red.

Changes in diction (word choice) gave me a new slant rhyme: rubble/barrel. Line break changes gave me: could/road (with a nice, hard feel, reminiscent of something I'd liked in the original draft, when "bored" was a line break). The line breaks and adjustments also continued to reinforce a persistent but subtle (non-metrical) four-beat line.

Subtle changes continued in the final draft.

Fourth and Final Draft, Published Version

Middletown

When we arrive, I am wavering
in my belief in myself as a woman
who knows enough to say no to a man
with real leather seats. Turning,
we pass a house with too many dogs.
I feel them at my throat clamor

for the gristle of my risen heart.
This man could ruin me, I could
ruin him. I know when we kiss
how soft my lips will seem to him,
how sharp the shadow on his chin.
I'm sure I've been here before: the road

curves around a tavern, eyeless
and bored, a red brick church, rubble
where once a house surprised its own
foundation, burning to the ground
after a woman shot her husband
in the chest, *his* palm prints on the barrel.

Everything came together in the final draft, where the most obvious change is the restoration of a content point: palm *prints* on the gun barrel, which is a subtler visual image implying a later criminal investigation and the need for evidence in a murder case where there is a troubled husband–wife relationship. Bold use of italics on "his" in the last line creates a spondee (*his* palm) in a different place than before, and, so close to the caesura, emphasizes the odd fact that they are his prints, not hers. He evidently pulled the gun toward himself, though she aimed the gun, making him strangely complicit in the homicide. There are still four beats in this line, but they are erratic and hard to scan. I want the ending to be disturbing on all levels.

This draft retains some other subtle changes that emerged during the revision process, such as the loss of "little," which had troubled John, and the subsequent line break on "own," a nice mournful-sounding word that puts a content emphasis on the phrase "surprised its own," as if the house surprised its own inhabitants, which it did, the idea transforming into something more concrete (pardon the pun) with the word *foundation* in the next line. Another subtle content change retains an impulse from the original draft, which often happens in the long revision process. Ever since the speaker stopped saying "yes" in revision, her intuitive sense that they *will* kiss someday, the danger will *not* be avoided, underscores the overall risk-taking of the poem and retains the mystery; there is still something unsaid, something undone, something unsolved. This works well with the "palm prints," I think.

The final draft still follows the basic rules laid out by Hugo, even with the diction changes, as I pointed out to Peggy in comparing it to another poem taken by *Comstock* for the same issue, "Apology," and printed on the page facing "Middletown."

Apology

I'm going to open the same little box
again, the same three stanzas of six
lines each, with subtle internal rhymes
and at least one obvious external
slant rhyme, and see what I find this time.
You'll see it, too, the unexpected

gift, all unwrapped on the table
between us, like a direct question,
the one you evaded, after a short
silence. You won't see it. You don't
like poetry. That's all I want
you to see, how we have nothing

in common. See? That wasn't so hard,
was it? You could read my poem
and not see yourself there, across
the table from me, my hands around
a paper cup of coffee, its thin steam
offering this invisible apology.

"Apology" was revised, too, the "thin steam" image appearing in revision. Its similarity to "Middletown" in shape and structure is obvious, as are such slant rhymes as box/six, rhymes/time, poem/steam. I don't use the Hugo lists of words, but I do explain the form as a way of trying to apologize. In the end, the steam has to do it alone.

As a companion piece, "Apology" suggests the mistake of the affair, and the danger of it all was avoided, and the woman is now apologizing to the potential lover for not going through with it. By itself, "Middletown" leaves all dangerous possibilities open. One is in third person, the speaker working it out in her head, perhaps exaggerating the danger. The other is a direct address, but it is a poem, and seems to be about an unspoken apology, one delivered in a self-referential poem that the addressed "listener" won't be able to understand, and so, ultimately, the mystery remains. Indeed, what if the speaker in "Apology" is addressing her husband, "apologizing" without admitting anything? In either case, the listener has evaded a direct question, there is little communication, and the poor woman is stuck with someone who doesn't like poetry. Taken separately, the poems needn't suggest a linked narrative at all. Taken together or separately, the evidence must be closely examined to get at any authentic truth.

Both poems use Standard American English and syntax, with "no tricks," as demanded by Hugo in his exercise. Any "tricks" are of the subtle sort mentioned earlier. Yes, in "Middletown," the lines "This man could ruin me, I could / ruin him" might, in the strictest sense, require a semicolon instead of a comma, but, in addition to poetic license, contemporary handbooks do allow a comma sometimes to link very short, related phrases, so that's how I look at it here. You can follow each sentence across lines or even across a stanza, and it is essentially grammatically correct.

What I like about "Middletown" is its peculiar mix of mystery and emotional honesty. The woman, at midlife in a small Midwestern town, really doesn't know what to do. She is ambivalent, and ambivalence is a good emotional root system for a poem. The poem also has a dreamlike quality, even though the overt reference in the first draft — "maybe in a dream" — was revised out (to avoid both ellipses and cliché). The "been here before" aspect and the twists and turns still evoke a recurring dream with danger in the background. In real life, I used to have a recurring dream of traveling as a passenger in a car, with a male driver, potentially dangerous, a dream that went away after I escaped a truly dangerous man later in life. I have dealt with it in other writings, and, as a content issue, any overt reference to the dream is unnecessary here in "Middletown." As a mood thing, or a tonal thing, the eerie dreamlike quality is enough for me.

I love that this poem is about a town, and titled for it, since it emerged from Hugo's book, *The Triggering Town*, in which he urges poets to let a town trigger a poem. It can be a town you know well or one you don't know at all, preferably the latter, leaving you open to discover your content. I did a series of these town poems that are also invented form poems. I have one called "Towanda," about a town near me, also about midlife. I did find my emotional triggers, then, in this exercise. Somehow, though, I think I might not write a poem called "Normal," after the town I live in now.

I do think the poem *means* something, despite Hugo's "sadistic" rule that the poem be "meaningless." I wouldn't be able to restate its meaning in clear prose; if I could, there would have been no need for the poem. Its authentic emotional content is still about midlife ambivalence, risk taking, and potentially dangerous mistakes, and it discovers an interesting truth: that, even if the wife commits a crime of betrayal, the husband was somehow complicit in it. Yes, she has aimed at his heart, but he has pulled the gun toward himself, inviting the fatal wound. You could argue this interpretation, which is all to the good. I *want* mystery; I *want* to provoke interpretation in this poem.

I still find the most exciting meanings of poems in the inextricable connection of form and content, here enhanced by my revision process. I was lucky in this case — in that two editors wished to join me as I revised, offering encouragement and concrete suggestions. As a poetry editor myself, I am glad when I can offer such help, but the publishing and literary editing conditions of today make that a pretty rare occurrence. Fortunately, what replaces the editor–writer relationship of the past is the close teacher–writer relationship of the present, with so many creative writing programs thriving in the United States.

Ultimately, though, the writer must become her own best and trusted critic and take on responsibility for revising until the poem becomes what it wants to be. Compose freely, I suggest to both myself and others, without concern for the internal critic/censor, and revise carefully, calling on the internal critic/editor for aid. The poem needs to *be*. As Emily Dickinson said, "The poet lights the lamp and then goes out himself. But the light goes on — and on." So you must let the light shine as brightly as it can.

Kathleen Kirk is an editor of *RHINO*, a literary annual, and the author of *Selected Roles* (Moon Journal Press, 2006), a chapbook of theater/persona poems. Her poems, stories, and essays have appeared in a variety of journals and anthologies, including *ACM, Common Review, Comstock Review, Ekphrasis, Folio, Fourth River, Midnight Mind, Poetry East, Puerto del Sol, Quarter After Eight, Seeding the Snow, Spoon River Poetry Review, E: The 2002 Emily Dickinson Awards Anthology* (Universities West Press, 2003), *In A Fine Frenzy: Poets Respond to Shakespeare* (University of Iowa Press, 2005), *Sacred Fire* (Adams Media, 2006), and *Regrets Only* (Little Pear Press, 2006).

Skating on Lake Monona

CATHERINE WILEY

S kating on Lake Monona" echoes my apprenticeship as a poet. In 1992, I sent an early draft to a writer kind enough to read and comment on my efforts; the poem was accepted for publication by two journals in 2005. I am relieved to say that most of my poems no longer require over a decade to revise, but the slow growth of this particular work taught me something, so I cannot begrudge the years of germination, hibernation, and festering. Pulling this one from the "abandoned" folder, I had to ask myself what every writer should consider: why bother? Why do we write at all, and why do we commit ourselves to perfecting what we write?

This is not the only poem that took me over a decade to revise, but it is one whose drafts I saved with a second reader's comments. "Skating on Lake Monona" illustrates how crucial that second reader, second pair of eyes, second heart and brain, is to my writing. We write alone, yes, but I now know that it is impossible to revise — to re-see — by myself. Second readers lead to second, and multiple, readings by the writer. A second look is the source for revision.

Here is the early version, not the first draft, but nearly:

Silence Sometimes Cracks

Silence sometimes cracks into hope
Shards of color in a lake
Frozen thick and black
A leaf
Suspended en route to earth
Stuck glittering
Imperfection holds
Our attention
To mistakes
Excess more interesting than enough.

The effort not to use words
But to find them

Small as bubbles
Disfiguring the glass
We skated over
The weight of expectation
Holds
Presses hard
On the tiny expirations
Drops of wet breath
We hang meaning upon.

We speak like skaters
Trusting the lake not to break
No thaw to surprise our bound feet
And mittened tongues
Knowing that
Silence no heavier than air
Becomes with words attached
The crush of history's
Unbearable hope
Holding
Us up.

As a beginner, I took many years to discover what works and what doesn't, and to recognize my own bad habits. Like many novice poets, I tended to overexplain and assume my reader would not get it (that is, recognize my brilliance) unless I spelled out The Point in big, fancy abstractions. My initial second reader was Christiane Jacox-Kyle, whose first collection, *Bears Dancing in the Northern Air* (Yale, 1991), I had loved and whom I invited to read at my campus in 1992. Upon receiving this version, she generously did not tell me to just start over, but wrote, "I like the metaphor but want to see [you] clearly establishing [a] real situation before leaning on metaphor." I am groping to communicate something here, but because I have not considered why I've bothered, communication is less important than self-expression, and the poem fails to communicate much of anything.

I present a lake, vaguely, but before I have created a decent image of it, I force it into metaphor. And exactly what the metaphor stands for is far too ambiguous, open to "interpretation" and thus useless as a tool for communicating. I am too concerned with abstractions like "silence," "hope," "imperfection," "attention," "mistakes," "excess" all in only the first stanza. I'm trying to write a poem about increasing silence in a relationship, two people who are having a difficult time talking to each other and thus relating at all. Using the lake was a good instinct — it was real and was really frozen a dramatic black — but the poem gets stymied by its own cleverness about language, speech, even post-structuralism. The ideas take precedence over the stuff (I did not yet know the famous William Carlos Williams adage, "No ideas but in things"). It took me a few years to learn that literary theory does not belong in a poem except, possibly, as a joke. In this draft, I ask the reader to consider that history is nothing but language, language is nothing but air ... how clever. And boring for readers who are not graduate students in literary studies.

Here's a revision of that version, with essentially cosmetic changes (in other words not a revision at all but a polishing). The only true, and telling, change is the title:

Skating on Lake Monona

Silence sometimes cracks into hope:
shards of color in the lake, frozen
thick and black. A leaf suspended
en route to earth, stuck glittering,
an interruption in the ice grown
perfect one winter, steeled before
the snow. We skated alone on ice
and books, noting each excess, each mistake.

The effort not to use words but
to find them, small as bubbles
disfiguring the glass
we skated over. The weight
of expectation holds, presses
hard on the tiny expirations,
drops of wet breath
where we hang meaning.

We speak like skaters, trusting
the lake not to break.

No thaw to surprise our bound feet
and mittened tongues, knowing that
silence no heavier than air
becomes with words attached the crush
of history's unbearable
hope, holding us up.

Amazingly, in retrospect, I sent this version to Chris, and she scribbled even more notes on it. She noted the sentence fragment beginning the second stanza, and wisely asked who the speaker is in the first stanza. I knew the speaker was a younger version of me, but why should my reader know this, or care? There are still no people in this poem (despite the weird skating on books at the end of the first stanza, to which no one but a graduate student could possibly relate), just ideas floating in the lake. Chris wrote, "dramatic situation not clear" and "clarify persona early on (you don't have to say specifically who, but right now the first 6–7 lines are disembodied and poems need to be embodied in a specific voice)." What she gently points to is the utter absence of voice, the speaker's coy disappearance into a disembodied "we," and the naive assumption that readers will automatically insert themselves into what remains a nearly invisible situation.

As I learned, and as I now recite to my creative writing students, the range of human emotions is limited, but human experience is not, so write about experience and the things that fill it, not emotion. I had yet to learn that truism with this poem, so I put it away for several years. When I returned to it, to that black lake and long-dead love, I managed a substantial revision:

Skating on Lake Monona

Our last December the lake froze
thick and black before snow fell.
While you read I sped over shards
in dark ice: read and green leaves
suspended, white bubbles, a fish
caught a few inches from the top.

The window in the living room
(the room you'd taken over, cornered
in that broken chair propped with books)

faced the lake. Did you ever see me
twirling with red cheeks and nose,
dizzy in the rush of speed and cold?

At the house I could not get used
to your piles of paper and books;
after three years needing such ginger steps
that I gave up the living room,
the lake view, and went outside
for air too cold to inhale.

Knowing the lake could be crossed on skates
pushed me away, crouched, arms slicing
the chill. Turning where I pleased,
my blades rasped white calligraphy
on the ice as the sun's cold lens
lit up the snow-dust dazzling my eyes.

Snow and wind soon scalloped the lake
into ridges, jags, dangerous
depressions. December thawed gaunt and raw;
Monona lost its luminous, hard hope
and I quietly passed what remained
of winter planning my spring.

Now there are real people and a place in time. This version is more literally true — I skated, my boyfriend did not; his piles of paper and chair
did command the lake view from the front window; he could have seen
me on the lake (but whether he ever looked I'll never know). Finally, the
lake is used not as an end in itself, but to carry the human story. Even a
reader who has never skated on a lake has experienced a failed love, and
this failure, not the lake, is the point of emotional contact. Readers are invited in to the poem, the situation, the two real lives, through the image of
the frozen lake. Here, the lake is allowed to stay a lake without the unwieldy metaphorical impositions of my early drafts. Indeed, the ice now
implies freedom more than anything else, an idea that comes, appropri-
ately, from the literal truth of skating across it.

I was fond of this version for a long time, unwilling to discard the smart double meaning of "spring," the literal truth of the snow dust shining in the sun, the big idea of "hope" in the last stanza. But there is too much information, and I have yet to sift what is needed from what is mere adornment. With several more drafts plus my regular writers' group feedback come the final polish and a surprise.

Here's the poem as it appears in the Summer/Fall 2005 issue of *Tar Wolf Review*, and the Summer 2006 issue of *Calyx*:

Skating on Lake Monona

Our last December the lake froze
thick and black before snow fell,
a thing that almost never
happened, water flat as stone.
The window in the living room
faced the lake, and while you read
I sped over mottled leaves stuck
in the ice, white bubbles, a fish
inches from the top. Did you see
me spin, red and dizzy with cold?

At home I could not wind around
your paper piles, your books.
I gave up the living room,
went out for air too stiff to sigh,
pushed off from the bank, crouched,
arms slicing chill. Turning where
they pleased, my blades wrote
codes of white calligraphy.

In just one week the lake thawed
into ridges, jags, dangerous
depressions; winter settled in
and we could not warm the living room
despite the windows hung
with blankets, the ragged quilt.

We never did hang blankets over the windows to warm the place, but we did sleep under his grandmother's quilt. This quilt, as the closing word and picture of the poem, provides a wonderful gesture of a last-ditch effort from the couple, even though the skater, the speaker, has learned over the course of the poem that the relationship cannot be salvaged (a truth implied in the first line). There is real sadness at the end despite the liberation illustrated in the second stanza. He did look up from his books to see her skate, though perhaps never saw her at all; she knows this and can accept that the relationship is over. The poem is still "about" all kinds of things, except, interestingly, the big things it began with: silence and hope. Lake Monona now dominates as a force controlled by nature, like the relationship that has run its course and cannot be brought back to life.

In the long process of revision, and in my reliance on second readers, I answered my unvoiced question about why I write. I write, as I believe most of us do, out of loneliness coupled with a desire to connect to other people. Poetry may be a paradoxically impersonal method of reaching out, but the poem that elicits an "oh yes, me, too" from its auditor or reader is the one that does its job of communicating. And to bring a poem to the point of communicating, to work it as close to perfection as I can, I require and celebrate my second readers.

Catherine Wiley published a chapbook in 2003 that was a finalist for the 2004 Colorado Book Award. She has published poems here and there, and has nearly completed her personal metamorphosis from academic writer to creative writer.

Meditation on My Name

PHEBUS ETIENNE

I wanted to write a poem about a name — a familiar exercise for emerging poets since names can be burdens or blessings connected as they are to who we are or hope to become. Since I am not American born, but a member of the Haitian Diaspora, I travel with questions about identity. My name was something I whispered at introductions because it was destined to be mispronounced or shortened. Teachers and classmates of my adopted country always pronounced the first syllable with a long *e*, an imprecision that bothered, and still bothers, me because I used the French accent, which was closer to a long *a* sound. There was also the incessant teasing: "Fayva," a shoe store, now defunct; "Fallabus," "Mavis," "Peebus," and the self-righteous American shortening that came with the insistence to assimilate and left me with "Faye."

Many times my father told me how, why he named me, and although I came across my name in literature, I had not examined what it represents to me. Now, I questioned: What was the origin of my name? Am I in any way a reflection of that name? Was the name a gift to me, or did it represent something else for my father? My attempt at the answers resulted in the poem "Meditation on My Name."

The First Making

I did not want to include my name in any stanza, but I did want to provide many details about its origins. The hope was that the intelligent, reasonably literate audience I long for would have enough definitive information to decipher the name without needing it revealed. An epigraph or footnote could be included so that readers who didn't remember or didn't know the myth would be satisfied with some degree of clarity after reading or hearing the poem.

Draft 1

Meditation on a Name

I was concept swimming in the ocean

271

beneath my mother's lungs when Esmeralda voiced
the name of a soldier on screen. *You* christened me
after that son, claiming this your mortal plea,
summons for endurance, a necessary trait in all Haitians.

Watching you with your mother, I saw her rancor
for your unplanned existence, your needs
becoming mists in her periphery as she gave
extravagant love to two other sons. In your reel,
one woman could ever be enough. How could you
not envy a man so idolized by a gypsy girl?

Father, I am nothing like that soldier, the object slick as a villanelle.
I will not purse lovers, premeditate to discard or betray.
If I am to mirror this sobriquet, I appropriate
lineage to myth of the ancient who first carried it.
I want to slay whatever dragon and pilot my chariot
across foreign states, orchestrate a samba
which resonates happy under your sixty-seven-year-old feet.
You will come this way again as a child, mended, whole,
your guardians proud as Zeus and Leto
when they welcomed Artemis and his twin.

Phebus Etienne
March 1, 2006
Phebus – Variation of Phoebus Apollo – Greek god of light; god of poetry,
music, prophecy, and healing; son of Zeus and Leto; twin brother of Artemis.

The initial draft had several problems:
Stanza One: The narrative was stilted, closer to prose, nonlinear, and
half done. There was an "I" voice and a "you" along with a vague reference
to a particular Haitian trait. This portion was trying to do too much. But a
draft, after all, is warm-up for the bigger event. The intent might be clear
in the mind, but most times, it does not reveal itself on the page until several attempts have been made.
Stanza Two: In terms of tone, "you" in this poem seemed accusatory
and at the same time turned the speaker into a victim. Although I was aiming for allusion to a particular movie, the word *reel* seemed to be just floating by itself. Readers would also wonder about this gypsy girl.

Stanza Three: Reference to the soldier begged for more exposition. There wasn't enough explanation here on the origin of the speaker's name — at least in terms of where the father retrieved it. There was too much telling here and not enough showing.

Simple reference to the myth of Phoebus Apollo, I thought, may not clarify connection to the speaker. The note, "Phebus — Variation of Phoebus Apollo — Greek god of light; god of poetry, music, prophecy and healing; son of Zeus and Leto; twin brother of Artemis," needed lengthening if it was to remain. More details were required to cork cracks in the narrative.

Crafting the Version I Live with for Now

Getting the Whole Story

Research and careful reading became useful tools of control over material available. If this were a historical poem about an event recognizable to a wider audience, for example, it would be necessary to learn as much as possible in order to detail with accuracy. More knowledge of a topic will always result in more choice. Abundant resources made it easier to filter, to find what was necessary for the narrative.

Even while working with myth as a back story, it was important to be accurate. There were various versions of the myth, but once I chose a version, I was obligated to be true to it. After learning about the life and feats of Phoebus Apollo, I defined him as "Greek god of light; god of poetry, music, prophecy and healing; slayer of the dragon Python; son of Zeus and Leto; object of love for Clytie, a sprite, who watched his chariot cross the sky for nine days and became a sunflower; and twin brother of Artemis, the goddess of the wilderness, wild animals, the hunt, and fertility."

Research revealed an error in how I presented the myth. The first draft mentioned, "Artemis and his twin." Artemis was female.

What to Keep and What to Store in the 'Usable Stuff for Later' File

With information at hand, I decided which portions to include and what to leave out of the narrative. It was interesting to me that my name was misspelled on my birth certificate, that Clytie had watched the sky for nine days, and that I was born in the ninth month of the year. However, I wasn't sure if these details would be "Ah-hah moments" or minutiae to readers. Those details have been stored in case a poem about numerology or coincidence emerges down the line.

Characters within the poem — the daughter, the father, a soldier, Esmeralda, Hugo, Phoebus Apollo, Zeus, Leto, and Artemis — seemed overwhelming for a one-page poem, but somehow necessary to my vision of the piece. How could I use these figures to convey emotion, give them relevancy while avoiding confusion?

I had a similar question concerning the order of poems in a manuscript about memory and the present day. In paraphrase, Sharon Olds said, "Show it as it happened." Keeping that in mind, I shifted details to shape the story, to make it linear. Drafts following the first were similar versions with words shifted and stanzas shuffled. Here is the second draft, better in narrative and clarity than the first:

Meditation on My Name

Designated a catacomb for rancor
because of his unwanted birth,
my father's boyhood hungers were
opaque in his mother's eyes as she gave
extravagant love to his brothers.
In his reel, wifely acquiescence,
a medley of mistresses, my loyalty
as daughter could not fill the crater.
How could he not envy the altarpiece

of a gypsy beauty? So Esmeralda
christened me from the screen
with a son/god's name and I became
oracle for past iniquity. My usher
would never admit mortal conceit,
defending his choice of sobriquet as summons
for the endurance necessary in all Haitians.

I am nothing like Hugo's soldier,
that object slick as a villanelle,
pursuing lovers, premeditating
to discard or betray. No would-be suitor
will transform to heliotrope in my light.
I want valor for slaying dragons

scorching the gate to sanctuary of marigolds
and copious tables of tropical ambrosias.
I mask laments as devotionals
to chariot my fate across foreign sands,
to compose boleros, epics
which resonate for centuries.

If galaxies divine what is virtuous,
then my father will begin again
elsewhere, as a child, mended, whole,
with guardians proud as Zeus and Leto
when they welcomed Artemis and her twin.

Phebus Etienne
March 16, 2006

Stanza One: The readers learn of an unwanted son who fathered a daughter and named her, while she was in the womb, with a moniker from a movie.

Stanza Two: Identity of the gypsy girl was made more concrete because she was given a name, Esmeralda. Her own name, the speaker believed, was given for reasons other than that it would strengthen her resolve because she was destined for a difficult life.

Stanza Three: I didn't assume that readers would be familiar with Victor Hugo's *The Hunchback of Notre Dame,* which gave life to Esmeralda and the cunning, not-so-kind soldier, Phoebus. So, the author was mentioned without including the novel's or movie's title.

Stanza Four: Final stanza aimed for resolution. The error concerning Artemis' gender was corrected.

Finishing and Refinishing

Evoking Ideas

What artist has not dreamed of forging ideas to be read and analyzed long after bones become dust? In a workshop with Philip Levine, he said, "Go for the biggest poem that you can write." Aiming to be relevant, to be notable at any vocation is a worthwhile pursuit, but this desire can obstruct clarity and contribute to overwritten pieces. I have been guilty of overloading poems with images or words in an attempt to create metaphysical weight. Since multiple interpretations don't insult me, I keep trying for density and emotional complexity.

Here, the first stanza began the reference to the movie from which the name emerged, with "reel" serving as a metaphor, or at least an indication of the father's vision of his life. I also liked hinting at the idea of cinema, its connection to reality and myth.

The third stanza attempted to link speaker to myth by examining commonalities with the god. The speaker mentions Apollo's attributes saying, "No would-be suitor will transform to heliotrope," and that valor would be welcomed to "slay any dragon," since this Greek god's light turned a sprite to sunflower and he slew the first dragon.

Language

A classmate once commented that he wrote for his grandmother to comprehend every word, and he felt my vocabulary, which was sometimes unfamiliar to him and would be foreign to his grandmother, was unnecessary for my poems, or as he put it, "He didn't need it." Being diplomatic, I didn't suggest that he was lazy and that perhaps he and his grandmother should consider using a dictionary.

To me the fun in writing is in the play and interplay of words. I could shift phrases for hours to find the best original composition. Why write, "The wide streets were cold," when more work can yield "The avenues sprawled like rivers bitter with ice"? I admire wordsmiths able to convey wisdom and ideas with sparse language and elegance. But not everyone can be Lucille Clifton or Stanley Kunitz.

With this poem, my quest for innovative language continued and "father" was substituted for "usher" and "name" became "sobriquet." "Rancor" worked better than "bitterness or resentment," and "catacomb" was more evocative and imagistic than "urn" or "burial ground." Dictionary and thesaurus searches provided "heliotrope" instead of "sunflower" and "altarpiece" instead of "a man so idolized by a gypsy girl."

Grammar and Syntax

When it came to grammar, I focused on verb tenses and tried to make sure that the voice and time placement remained consistent. I also questioned syntax and searched for errors in usage. If certain words were imperfect fits as defined, I examined ways in which I used them versus ways they were used traditionally.

"Sobriquet," for example, was defined primarily as a "humorous nickname," with "name" and "term of endearment" as secondary definitions. I chose to use it because I wasn't given and didn't want a nickname, so my one name serves as formal label and "tag." Sobriquet with its French roots emphasized, too, the origin of the name.

Sound and Line Breaks

One of the challenges in finalizing a poem or writing a "version I can live with" is finding ways to incorporate sound. In stanza one, there are hard *c* sounds in the alliteration of "catacomb" and "crater." End rhymes have been difficult for me, so I have not attempted them often. But I like working with internal rhymes, and in stanza two, we have "name" and "became," and in stanza three, "compose" followed by "boleros."

Line breaks or what is considered a line can become a philosophical puzzle. I operate more on instinct and seek to have something happen, some action, in each line. If a line was not a complete thought, there was opportunity for enjambment, to create anticipation for the next line; better still, if the following line was a surprise and took the reader in unexpected directions.

Sound was useful in line breaks, too, because ultimately, the poem will be spoken. I tended to write metrically although I did not count syllables or stresses in this free-verse work. It seemed to be more of an internal meter for my voice. I read my poem aloud and broke lines in a manner that came close to the rhythm of my natural speech.

Finished! Is It Really?

I would not be the first to suggest that poems are never truly finished since I have revised poems after publication. But like children, they must eventually be let go, to find their own way in the universe.

Before writing this poem, as I stated earlier, I wanted to answer the following questions:

• What was the origin of the name?
• Is the person who carries the name in any way a reflection of that name?
• Was the name a gift to me, or did it represent something else for the one who did the naming?

The most recent version of the poem answered the question of origin in stanzas one and two. Stanza three responded to the question concerning whether the speaker was like the god, and the answer is no, but the aspiration existed. The poem tried to answer the question of what the name represented. I learned that the name was not about the person carrying it all, but about the father. It represented to him a sort of redemption, a wish for some recognition, a love that he never received.

Born in Port-au-Prince, Haiti, Phebus Etienne grew up in East Orange, New Jersey. She completed writing programs at Rider University and New York University. Her work has appeared in *Making Callaloo: 25 Years of Black Literature, Gathering Ground: A Reader Celebrating Cave Canem's First Decade, Paterson Literary Review, Lips, Poet Lore, Mudfish,* and *The Caribbean Writer.* She received a Poetry Fellowship from the New Jersey State Council on the Arts and a Grant-in-Aid from The Whiting Foundation.

Phebus Etienne died unexpectedly in 2007.

Brown Tree, Yellow Bird

NATE PRITTS

First Version

Brown Tree, Yellow Bird

Once calculated & proven, any equation can have its name
preserved forever in the vast & meaty heavens, the empty quadrants
of empty space. So saith the benevolent Abacus,
whom we little empty-headed ones can always always count on.
If only everybody knew where the sweetest bliss was to be found!
Imagine the raucous dogpile that would ensue, making it impossible
to get a table near the window without a long wait. The exact duration
of such penance remains unknown & unknowable to us mortals.
Most things are out of our hands & luckily too for, oh,
the many zany & pointless things we'd do to ourselves if we could.
Bananas in the bowl on the kitchen counter turn slowly brown
& nothing I can do will stop that. I'm helpless in the face of so many things.
My big hands grasp & grasp. The house I left
because I thought it was sapping my strength has a brown tree, leafless
in November, with one yellow bird, nesting.
During certain times of the year, the ratio of bird to tree is higher
but these are the days of proud sole ownership. I list my many failings
with examples as I drive my car through the stop sign
at the beginning of my neighborhood, the stop sign that never works.
I've thought seriously about changing my name
to make it more complicated & ambiguous, harder to pronounce;
long into the inky night, I've wondered about dyeing my hair yellow
& learning to live with what I can't live with. My fears can save me
is something I wrote on a leaf, then stuck to the bottom of my shoe
so I could walk it off. Tuesdays I pretend I'm that lonely yellow bird,
scared that I might decide to fly away & scared that the opposite might
    happen,
that I might stay & sing beautifully while I slowly rot away.

I was lying on the floor of my daughter's bedroom reading her a Sesame Street book, a book that had been my son's before hers and my wife's before either of them were ever around. One of the covers (there were two covers since it was a flipbook) showed a father and son staring up into the branches of a gigantic tree. Sitting there on one of the branches, presumably singing something shockingly lovely, was a little yellow bird.

So I had a title and that's typically how a poem of mine starts — there's an image, or a specific idea or emotion with an image attached, a riff — and I start collecting language to go with that. In a way, my writing process is one of constraint. I could start with anything anywhere. But as soon as I lay down some words, as soon as those words snake their way from thought to thought, I close off possibilities, I add constraints, and I'm forced to work within those new considerations. These are generative; one line leads to the next just as one thought or impression leads to the next. The discursive logic of the poem tries to lay these associative connections bare.

Juan Ramon Jimenez was said to rip the cover off his copy of any new edition of his poems so that he wouldn't feel as if they were finished, so that he could open up his head to the process of going back in, pen in hand, to make things better. I certainly feel this way about my own work, that it is always in process, and that I am always trying to "make it better." Of course, that's a problematic word, "better," and I think what I mean is closer and more responsive to the intellectual, linguistic, and emotional contours intended and available.

In talking about the revisions of "Brown Tree, Yellow Bird," I suppose I should start with the most immediately obvious change. In its first incarnation, this poem was cast in one long stanza; the revised version is in couplets. The poem has always had a sort of back-and-forth feel to me, first this then that. Initially, I felt that presenting the poem as one unified utterance was the way to go, to force the reader to deal with the onslaught of considerations and thoughts the speaker has. However, I settled on the couplet for the way it enforces the sense of the speaker speaking to himself, working things through, and being of two minds about some of the intellectual and emotional stakes of the poem. The revised version also chops off the first four lines:

Once calculated & proven, any equation can have its name
preserved forever in the vast & meaty heavens, the empty quadrants
of empty space. So saith the benevolent Abacus,
whom we little empty-headed ones can always always count on.

I had to get rid of my abacus joke, but ultimately it felt like the consciousness in this poem was just circling here, looking for a place to land. I wanted to cut right to it. I was in a workshop where the late great Aga Shahid Ali said that you should always try chopping off the first few lines (and/or the last few lines) of your poem to see what develops. Even if I ultimately put the lines back, this act of starting from somewhere different, or ending somewhere new, often provides many helpful ideas.

The last line of the poem I changed from:

that I might stay & sing beautifully while I slowly rot away.

to:

that I might stay & sing beautifully.

This was a much harder call for me. I liked the rhythm of the first version but started to question what it was actually saying. My wife was never happy with it, telling me that it was a negative thread in what she knew was an ultimately positive web. I kept putting her off but finally realized she was right. I didn't think this was a negative poem, and I didn't want it to end on a negative note. At the end of the new version, the speaker seems to have learned something about persistence and its ability to make us feel valued in life. The speaker in the initial version seems to hedge his bets a little, to not be so resolved in his decisions, and that just didn't ring true.

Through all its riffs — the colors I kept using and reusing, the sense of helplessness coupled with a desire to be more active, the mysterious moments and the constant determination to push through it all — this poem is one of my favorites, one that seems to really be capturing a moment, enacting that moment, throwing me back into the moment again and again.

Revised Version

Brown Tree, Yellow Bird

If only everybody knew where the sweetest bliss was to be found!
Imagine the raucous dogpile that would ensue, making it impossible

to get a table near the window without a long wait
or reservations made months in advance. I have reservations

281

about all of this. Luckily, most things are out of our hands because, oh,
the many zany & pointless things we'd do to ourselves if we could.

Bananas in the bowl on the kitchen counter turn slowly brown
& nothing I can do will stop that. I'm helpless in the face of so many things:

flat tire, spoiling fruit, the color yellow. The idea of wood, so solid,
terrifies me. My big hands grasp & grasp. The house I left

because I thought it was sapping my strength has a big brown tree, leafless
in November, with one small yellow bird, nesting.

During certain times of the year, the ratio of bird to tree is higher
but these are the days of proud sole ownership. I list my many failings

with examples as I drive my car through the stop sign
at the beginning of my neighborhood, the stop sign that never works.

I've thought seriously about changing my name
to make it more complicated & ambiguous, harder to pronounce;

long into the inky night, I've wondered about dyeing my hair yellow
& learning to live with what I can't live with. My fears can save me

is something I wrote on a leaf, then stuck to the bottom of my shoe
so I could walk it off. Tuesdays I pretend I'm that lonely yellow bird,

scared that I might decide to fly away & scared that the opposite might
    happen,
that I might stay & sing beautifully.

Nate Pritts has published poems and criticism in many journals, both on-line and print, as well as three chapbooks, the most recent of which is *Big Crisis*. The editor and sole shareholder of *H_NGM_N*, an online journal of poetry and poetics, Nate lives in Natchitoches, Louisiana, where he is an assistant professor at Northwestern State University.

Lottery

Rasma Haidri

William Wordsworth's famous definition of poetry as the "spontaneous overflow of powerful feelings from emotions recollected in tranquility" appears at first to argue against revision. Something in the word *spontaneous* seems antithetical to revision, or so I thought when I first learned about Wordsworth back in college. At that time, I imagined he meant he lounged dreamily on a divan until, with a gold nib quill, he set about drafting the lines of a poem.

I believe part of this may have been right. Not the part about lounging dreamily, but the part about drafting. In this essay, I want to explore how through the hard work of revision over a long time, I was able to recollect the "spontaneous overflow of powerful feelings" that were central to my poem "Lottery."

The incident that spurred my poem was a time I took my mother grocery shopping, and she unexpectedly asked me to help her buy a lottery ticket. I was moved by the event and felt a need to tell about it. Now, I could have gone home and told my spouse about what happened and how it made me feel, but this retelling wouldn't have been a poem. In order to get at the poem, I needed to grasp the deepest feelings the incident aroused in me. In other words, I needed to get to what Wordsworth meant by recollecting a "spontaneous overflow of powerful feelings."

The problem with words about feelings or emotions is that they are abstract. Any word I might insert into the phrase "It made me feel ____" is going to be theoretical, as if we are talking about the emotion. In poetry, we need to recollect the emotion itself. In doing so, we come up with a rendering of an ordinary event that is somehow bigger than the sum of its parts.

Sometimes beginning writers feel that to take a poem through many drafts is to apply some sort of censorship to it, to tame its spirited individuality and make it conform. They resist revision because they fear editing away the poem's essence. Experience has taught me that revision can be the very means by which I recollect in tranquility. Each revision removes hindrances until the poem's "spontaneous overflow of powerful feelings" is released.

Let us see how this worked in the poem "Lottery." The situation was that my mother depended on me for grocery shopping. During one routine outing, she surprised me by saying she wanted to buy a lottery ticket. I found the experience disquieting and wrote about it afterwards in my journal.

Many elements of what will be the final poem are already here, the beginning line in particular. "That's 6 and a half million a year ..." is at the heart of the poem. Had my mother not said these words, I probably would have experienced the entire lottery ticket incident differently. I didn't think about this as I scribbled hurriedly in my journal, but intuitively I must have known it, which is why it's the first thing I wrote. The line remains intact in all the revisions, and by the final version is positioned as a hinge that widens the poem's perspective, essentially dividing it in two parts: what happened and what I felt about what happened.

The point of view of the journal entry switches between speaking to the mother using the second-person pronoun (you) to speaking about her in the third person (she). Here already the emerging poem hints at the need to try out different wordings before it settles on a final perspective and answers the core questions that must be asked about all poems. Just who is being addressed? Who is being asked to identify with the speaker of the poem? How does changing the relationship between the poem's speaker and audience affect the poem's impact?

The journal entry strives for verisimilitude in its use of descriptive details such as swaying, weaving, rummaging, digging; the color of the cardboard and wallet; the almost slow motion observation of the contents of the purse flowing out. There is also attention to what we might call plot-detail: I also bought a ticket, it was computer generated, the purchase happened two weeks before my departure on a trip and now we're back in the store to check the winning numbers, and so on. I'm all for authentic description and concrete sensory detail. They typically lend credibility and vitality to a poem, and steer one away from the pitfall of abstractions. However, the journal entry shows the tedium of excessive details that don't know why they are there. We can say these details are not "organic" to the poem, meaning they are not a natural expression of the poem's bigger idea. It took me many drafts to realize that removing inorganic details was my main task in revising "Lottery." At this journal stage of writing, I didn't know the poem's bigger idea. In fact, I had only the vaguest inkling of why I was compelled to write about the event at all.

Draft 1 of the poem is essentially identical to the journal entry. It appears that as soon as I had a hard copy in my hand, I attacked it with a pencil. Note the hard black lines indicating my confidence that, for example, removing the line break at "a year" was going to improve the poem. I am glad that I work through my drafts like this with a pencil instead of

That's 6 million and a half a year after taxes
you tell me, of the man who won
$111 million. That's more than trump!
I have our lottery tickets in here you
pt to your black billfold in the brown
ribbing. Rummage further for into
your handbag. Kleenex, and bent envelopes,
a crumpled single dollars rising
over your wrists as you dig.
The lottery tickets are two weeks old.
Bought on the eve of my departure
for California when I took her to
Woodman's to buy everything she
needed while I was gone. Two
Cartons of cigarettes, 3 gal. of
milk, bot Rice cakes and
black bellied bottles of diet rite -
I want to buy a lottery ticket
you said, and weaved your way,
half blind, exhausted, sore knee

Handwritten journal entry, page 1, June 1993

from side to side pushed the
weight of your body to the far end
of the stove, by videos and ice cream
and packaged liquor.
You had your numbers picked out.
Written large and clear on a tear
of scrap cardboard, bright yellow.

Neither of us knew how to go
about it. Mother could not teach
daughter. Daughter could not get it
done - I rubbed in the dots for you.
Bought a computer generated one
for me - only lingering slightly
over your numbers. Trying to
register their significance -
and not seeing any immediately
didn't dare intrude into their
origin - not on what
you are basing your luck. Just
as now I don't not your

how they figure if you know how
they figured decided how many fans
to divide $111 million by to
make this man rich for the rest
of his life, or what
(I don't want to ask) you would do
if our tickets had one
with the money - buying back your
teeth, your eye sight, your light
strong bones and lean flesh -

You didn't check our numbers
that night it was on vacation.
But no one else has planned it
you tell me as if that's all
it takes to mean everything,
all of it, is out there
waiting for us to win, to call
Claim, start celebrating.

Handwritten journal entry, pages 2–3, June 1993

obliterating text on a word processor, because inevitably my revision of the first draft overcompensates. For example, isn't the line break at "half a million / a year for life" much better than the more pedestrian "... million a year / for life"?

At this stage in the revision, I am fiddling very much with words, not having yet grasped the poem's central idea. Much of this is trivial. I seem to think in line 4 that "winter" instead of "summer" will bring the poem more alive, as will substituting "deeper" for "further" two lines down. In some ways, I am only making the poem more wordy, such as adding "though" (an abstract word and therefore best avoided) in the first line of the fourth stanza. What was I thinking? Presumably I was looking for some kind of fluidity, having found the full stops jarring.

I am somewhat aware in this draft of needing to cut down on plot-detail. In the second stanza, "the eve of my trip" is meant to supplant the entire first two and a half lines. "That week" instead of "while I was gone" is an attempt at succinctness. Neither of these really accomplishes much. A more significant change is that I have removed my own lottery ticket from the narrative. In the poem's penultimate line "for us to claim our winnings" gives way to "just waiting / for you," which brings the poem's focus more onto the "you" who is my mother. A small word change in the final line may on first glance seem trivial. However, replacing "a" with "this" works toward bringing the poem more in touch with itself. The indefinite article ("a") makes the celebration generic, belonging to anyone, and limits it to a celebration of the winnings referred to in the preceding line. The demonstrative pronoun ("this") brings the celebration closer to the "you" and opens up the possibility that the celebration is potentially of much more than the winnings. Along with the insertion of "this," the word "winnings" has been decisively crossed out. Here I am instinctively getting closer to the poem's central idea, the essence that will show the event to be bigger than the sum of its parts.

Two other alterations in Draft 1 significantly aid the poem's evolution. First of all, with the parentheses around the first stanza and arrow pointing down I am aware of the need to move the section starting with "That's six and a half million ..." to its pivotal position farther on in the poem. I have also added *"for life,"* which I remembered my mother had said, even though it was not written in the original journal entry. Compared to word fiddling, this is a major insight. The other marked change from the journal entry is at the end of the fifth stanza where I have added a long line. This

Rasma Haidri
6422 Hubbard Ave.
Middleton, WI 5356

First Draft

Lottery Ticket

That's six and a half million *a year*
~~a year~~ *for life*
you tell me of the man
who won. *last* ~~summer~~ *winter,*
~~I have our lottery tickets in here,~~
~~you point to your black billfold,~~
as you rumage further into your purse, *deeper*
all kleenex, bent envelopes, a crumpled dollar bill
rising over your wrists as you dig.
~~for our two week~~
~~The lottery tickets are two weeks old.~~
~~Bought on the eve of my departure~~
~~for California, when~~ I took you to Woodmans *the eve of my trip*
to buy everything you would need ~~while I was gone:~~
Two cartons of cigarettes, *that week*
Three gallons of milk,
Rice cakes and black bottles of diet cola.
I want to buy a lottery ticket, you ~~had said,~~ *added*
and weaved your way, half-blind, worn out,
on stiff knees, to the far end of the store
by the videos, ice cream and packaged liquor.

You already had your numbers picked out,
written in large clear cursive on a scrap of yellow cardboard.

Neither of us knew how to go about it, *though*
I fumbled, rubbing in the dots for you.
Lingering ~~only~~ slightly over your numbers,
trying to register their significance. ~~and~~ *factory nos., and found none*
~~Not seeing any I didn't pry into their origin, ask~~ *ask their origin,*
on what you were banking your luck.
now, as you search for the ticket,
Just as ~~know~~ I don't ask ~~you~~ how they figured
the number of years in "the rest of his life"
~~for the last $100 million~~ winner, or what
you would do with the money.
~~Could you~~ buy back your teeth,
your eyesight, your light strong bones
and lean flesh? *The long southern evenings* ~~tattoos~~
~~your~~ ~~tattoos~~ *4 children yes & the children playing a squirt guns & netting fir*
You didn't check ~~our numbers~~ *the ticket number.*
that night I was on vacation.
But no one else has claimed it...
You say, as if that alone
means that everything, all of it,
is still out there ~~for us,~~ just waiting
for ~~us to claim our winnings~~ *for you* ~~to claim~~
and strike up ~~a~~ celebration.
this

Draft 1 of "Lottery," undated

addition is not plot-detail, but rather what we might call story:

> The long southern evenings
> ~~when you and four~~ 4 children   you + the children playing (with)
> squirt guns + netting fireflies

These lines are evidence of recollection in tranquility, to return to Wordsworth a moment. They were not part of what happened on the grocery outing, but as I worked with this first draft they came to me, a childhood memory connected to the idea of what the lottery money could buy back. They had been in my subconscious all along, subliminally feeding the pathos I felt for my mother during this whole lottery ticket episode. While working with the first draft, and feeling some frustration at the ineffectiveness of my word fiddling, they came as Wordsworth says: "a spontaneous overflow of powerful feeling recollected in tranquility." They are at the heart of the poem that is trying to emerge from this overly detailed and heavily narrative first draft.

My process is always the same when writing poems: handwritten journal entry becomes a typed first draft. Then the printed first draft gets marked up with handwritten notes, and the whole thing gets typed into a second draft, which is then printed and marked up and so on. Until I am able to read a typed and properly set up version of the poem, the way it would appear in print, I cannot see (or hear) where changes need to be made. The subsequent drafts of "Lottery" each achieve a significant alteration, as well as word substitutions and line breaks.

In Draft 2, I have typed in the lines about the fireflies and elaborated further: we caught them because in my hometown of Oak Ridge, Tennessee, researchers would pay us thirty cents for a hundred bugs. The fact that we had to freeze the fireflies doesn't get added until the final draft of the poem, but the importance of being paid for them is clear to me. The handwritten comment to the right of the penultimate stanza confirms this. I jotted it down as a woman in my poetry group said it: "Big expectations of Big money."

This was not the first time that someone in my poetry group pointed out the essence of my own poem to me. That is the value of a good poetry critique group. "Big expectations of Big money" is an overt statement of the theme implicit in the lines I had chosen to add. This was encouraging. It meant I had started to feel the pulse of the poem.

One of my changes in Draft 2 is of paramount importance, and remained unaltered through the remaining drafts: switching from the second- to third-person pronoun. The seemingly simple changes in the first two lines of Draft 2 actually represent leaps of development. I can recreate them like this:

> Everything you would need
> the week of my vacation
> could be found at Woodman's:

> Everything you would need
> during the week of my vacation
> could be found at Woodman's:

> Everything my mother needed
> during the week of my vacation
> could be found at Woodman's:

> Everything my mother needed
> could be found at Woodman's:

The fourth set of lines does two things that appear nearly counterintuitive. First, it says much more than the previous ones, even though it has fewer words. Why? Because it is not watered down by superfluous information. My going on vacation had *nothing* to do with the poem, yet it was hard for me to let go of talking about it. We sometimes refer to lines like this as scaffolding. They were a necessary structure to get into the poem, but once the actual poem emerges, much like a house under construction, more and more of the scaffolding must be done away with. Writers are averse to doing this. Often we don't recognize scaffolding for what it is. We feel emotionally attached to it because it was in the poem from the onset. From this we get the well-known adage: Kill your babies.

Second, the reduction in the fourth set of lines brings the reader more closely into the poem. This is done, oddly enough, by removing the rather intimate personal pronoun "you" and referring to the mother in the third person. This distancing of the mother works to draw the reader in because the poem's first-person narrator is now confiding her observations in the reader. When the "I" was engaged directly with the mother, we, the read-

The Lottery Ticket

Everything ~~you would~~ my mother needed
~~during the week of~~ my vacation
could be found at Woodman's:
two cartons of ciggarettes
three gallons of milk
unsalted rice cakes and
six black bottles of diet cola.

I want to
buy a lottery ticket,
she ~~you~~ added and weaved worn-out,
stiff-kneed, half-blind,
to the far end of the store
near the videos, ice cream,
and packaged liquor.

Neither of us knew how to go about it.

She ~~You~~ had already chosen the ~~your~~ numbers,
written ~~them~~ in large cursive
on a tear of yellow cardboard.

I fumbled, rubbing in the dots ~~for you~~.
Lingered slightly over her ~~your~~ numbers
to register their significance, but found none.

You did not check the ticket while I was gone,
and look for it now in ~~the depths of~~ your purse,
kleenex, envelopes, a dollar bill
rising over your wrists as you dig.

That's six and a half million a year for life!
~~you tell me~~ of the man who won last winter,
and I do not ask/how they figured
the number of years in his life, nor do I ask
what you would do with the money:
Buy back your teeth?! Your eyesight,
light bones and lean flesh?
Buy back the Tennessee summers
she ~~you~~ played squirt guns with us sold
and caught fireflies we ~~could sell~~ to science
for thirty cents a hundred?

No one else has claimed it!
~~you~~ say, as if that alone
makes everything possible, out there
and all of it is ~~just~~ still waiting for you
to start up this celebration.

She kept the ticket
I have our ticket in here
she said, rumaging in her
kleenex, envelopes, a love d
rising over her wrists

Big expectations of Big m

Draft 2 of "Lottery," undated

ers, were observing the scene from a distance and didn't really feel involved with these two people huddled over their lottery ticket. With "you" gone from the poem, the reader observes the scene shoulder to shoulder with the narrator. Now the "I" is telling the reader *about* the mother, allowing the reader to share observations and know thoughts the mother is not privy to. These thoughts, the ones about fireflies and squirt guns and a long ago youthful mother, contain the poem's soul. They are the thoughts overflowing with powerful feeling. They are the ones that were recollected in tranquility while fiddling with revisions.

In Draft 3, the contents of the purse, stanza six, are wisely removed. Not much else happens. The first stanza remains in past tense, and I still can't decide on the indefinite or demonstrative pronoun for the celebration in the last line. I have unwisely turned the fireflies into wedding rings, a true fact from childhood, but I seem to have decided "Big expectations of Big money" was not the theme after all.

With Draft 3, I thought maybe the poem was as good as it was going to get. Unfortunately, these drafts are not dated, but they cover the course of a year. The original journal entry was in June 1993. Draft 4 has a handwritten note I know was from summer 1994.

In Draft 4, things pick up. I return to the idea of selling the fireflies to science. I spot prosaic language in the fifth stanza and realize that "lingering over her numbers trying to register their significance" is depicted more clearly if I don't actually say it. Two other very significant changes are made, ones that shake the poem fully loose of its scaffolding: I put the poem into present tense and cut the last two lines. The switch to present tense, tried out methodically from verb to verb, releases the poem from its anchor in the past. This immediacy brings the reader even closer to the narrator's shoulder, right into the moment itself. The speaker is no longer relating something that once happened but delivering a blow-by-blow account of the poignant event as it unfolds.

By cutting the two last lines of the poem, I do away with the troublesome "celebration." Often when a word or line is a source of recurring doubt and consternation, it is really identifying itself as part of the scaffolding. Take these lines away, and lo and behold, the poem has found its true ending. "As if / everything is still possible" made my breath stop. Note the emphatically solid period I drew at the end. Still possible. Full

Lottery

Everything my mother needed
could be found at Woodman's:
two cartons of ciggarettes
three gallons of milk
unsalted rice cakes and
six black bottles of diet cola.

I want to buy a lottery ticket,
she added and weaved stiff-kneed,
half-blind, to the far end of the store
near the videos and packaged liquor.

She had already chosen numbers,
written them in large cursive
on a tear of yellow cardboard.

Neither of us knew how to go about it.

I fumbled, rubbing in the dots,
lingering slightly over her numbers
to register their significance, but found none.

I have our ticket in here, she says,
kleenex, envelopes, a lone dollar
rising over her wrists as she digs.

That's six and a half million a year for life!
she says of the man who won last winter.
and I do not ask
how one figured the years left in his life,
nor do I ask
if we could buy back   *she will*
her teeth and eyesight,   *her mouth full of teeth,*
her light bones and lean flesh.
Buy back the Tennessee summers
she played squirt guns with us
and caught fireflies we made into wedding rings.

No one else has claimed it!   *that means*
she says, as if everything is still possible,
just waiting for her
to start up this celebration.
                    a

all fit

Draft 3 of "Lottery," undated

293

stop. By Draft 4, I have begun to grasp the poem. Superfluous portions of the original poem are removed, and essential memories that concretize my feelings are added. The poem's relationship to the reader is enhanced by two grammatical changes: the third-person point of view and present verb tense. The poem is there.

Still I keep fiddling. Subsequent drafts show I still believe there really is a right and wrong choice between "filling" and "rubbing" in the dots. There is a revision dated April 1995 in which I am changing line breaks to beat the band. Still, no more significant changes happen or are needed. About three years after I initially wrote the poem, I type up a draft that I start sending out for publication.

A final episode in the evolution of this poem is worth sharing. Sometime in 1996, I sent a batch of about five poems to the literary journal *Prairie Schooner*, and in January 1997, I was delighted to receive an acceptance contract for a poem called "Books." I shared this news with my mother, as I did all news regarding my poetry, so long as it wasn't about her. I would never, for example, have shown her the poem "Lottery." In fact, had a poem such as "Lottery" come into publication, I would have made very certain it was in a journal my mother had not heard of or would never come across. If, for example, *Prairie Schooner* had accepted "Lottery," I would never have mentioned the journal's name to my mother, and certainly not boasted about my publication contract with them.

Ten months later, on a Saturday in November, my mother awoke early, sat up in bed, and died instantly of a heart attack. This shock had me still reverberating in some zone of incredulity and disbelief when three days later, along with the very first sympathy cards to arrive in my mailbox, were proofs from *Prairie Schooner* for my poem "Books" *and* the poem "Lottery." I stared dumbfounded at the papers in my hand, and when I had recovered somewhat went searching for the magazine contract. Sure enough, it was for one poem only. For "Books."

There are two versions of the world we can choose to live in. In one, we are constantly struggling against the fact that things go wrong, mistakes are made, bad things happen, and people die. In the other world, there are no mistakes. Everything just happens and is perfect. I didn't know about that second world until the poem "Lottery" managed to get itself published in what seemed to be cahoots with my dead mother. Posted in Nebraska on the last day of her life, the poem came into my hands as a gift, a mistake, or a miracle. It was labeled "proof."

Rasma Haidri
6422 Hubbard
Middleton, WI

Lottery

Everything my mother needed
could be found at Woodman's:
two cartons of ciggarettes
three gallons of milk
unsalted rice cakes and
six black bottles of diet cola.

I want to buy a lottery ticket,
she added and weaved stiff-kneed,
half-blind, to the far end of the store
near the videos and packaged liquor.

She had already chosen numbers,
written them in large cursive
on a tear of yellow cardboard.

Neither of us knew how to go about it.

I fumbled, rubbing in the dots,
lingering slightly over her numbers
to register their significance, but found none.

That's six and a half million a year for life!
she says of the man who won last winter
and I do not ask
how one figured the years left in his life.
Nor do I ask
if she will buy back
her teeth, eyesight,
light bones and lean flesh.
Buy back the summers
we played squirt guns
and caught fireflies to make
into wedding rings.

No one has claimed it!
she whispers, as if
everything is still possible,
just waiting for her
to start up a celebration.

Draft 4 of "Lottery," Summer 1994

Lottery

Everything my mother needs
can be found at Woodman's:
two cartons of ciggarettes
a gallon of milk,
unsalted rice cakes and
six black bottles of diet cola.

I want to buy a lottery ticket,
she adds and weaves stiff-kneed,
half-blind, to the far end of the store
near the videos and packaged liquor.

She has already chosen the numbers,
written them in large cursive
on a scrap of yellow cardboard.

Neither of us knows how to go about it.

I fumble, rubbing in the dots,
lingering slightly over her numbers
but find no significance.

That's six and a half million a year for life!
she says of the man who won last winter
and I do not ask how one figures
the number of years left in his life.
Nor do I ask if she will buy back
her teeth, eyes, strong bones and lean flesh.
Buy back the summers
she played squirt guns with us
and caught fireflies I could sell to science
for thirty cents a hundred.

No one has claimed it!
she whispers, as if everything
is still possible.

Final draft of "Lottery," 1996

In the spring of 1998, "Lottery" was printed in a special poetry issue of *Prairie Schooner*. I had spent nearly five years with that poem, revisiting it, trying to get it to breathe and speak. My work in revising the poem was to remove verbiage and supply the words and grammar it asked for. In other words, I worked to get to know it. I worked to hear what it had to say. When you revise a poem, think of yourself as listening to it. Strain your ears and screw off your own chatter. For the longest time, I thought I knew that "Lottery" was about despair. Then the poem showed up on my doorstep of its own accord, and I glimpsed something bigger. Perhaps *everything is still possible.*

Rasma Haidri grew up in Tennessee and currently makes her home on the Arctic coast of Norway, where she teaches English. Her fiction, poems, and essays have been granted awards by The Wisconsin Academy of Sciences, Western Michigan University, The Southern Women Writers' Association, *Passages North,* and *Mindfire Renewed.* Her writing has appeared in *Nimrod, Prairie Schooner, Fourth Genre, Fine Madness, Kalliope,* and many other literary journals. Anthologies featuring her work include *The Pocket Parenting Guide* (Puddinghouse Press), *The Writing Group Book* (Chicago Review Press), *Proposing on the Brooklyn Bridge* (Grayson Books), *Waking up American* (Seal Press), *Only the Sea Keeps* (Bayeux Arts), and *Fresh Water* (Michigan State University Press).

A Bedroom Community

KATHLEEN FLENNIKEN

A Bedroom Community" was the first of many poems I've written about the town where I grew up — Richland, Washington. Richland, built by the government during World War II, was adjacent to the Hanford Nuclear Reservation, where for several decades plutonium was produced for U.S. national defense.

I didn't realize this poem would be the start of a series. All I knew, as I conceived the first draft, was my impulse to describe my town and its unusual circumstances, and to mark especially the death of my friend Carolyn's father, which resulted from his years of radiation exposure at Hanford. Here is the first draft:

A Bedroom Community

What a good way to describe our town, as though
behind our drawn curtains we reclined in our nightcaps

while swamp coolers churned and sprinklers hissed
every daylight hour to fend off desert brown, while the fog
of DDT from the mosquito truck settled finer than ash,

while bitter cold hardened the sagebrush landscape,
or dust storms packed the air with grit in fall and spring,

while our fathers rose and dressed and boarded
the fleet of blue buses that took them away

and other men came to our doorsteps
collecting bottles of household urine like anti-milkmen,

while beyond the shelter belt of Russian Olive trees,
trains with their secret cargo blew their horns
at 8:00 and 8:00 and shuffled past,

298

while the wide Columbia rolled by,
entraining its secrets, carrying secrets downstream
that no walleye or steelhead could repeat.

Our fathers came home and drank
and emptied their pockets of badges and keys
and didn't speak of what they'd seen or done,
left and came home, day upon year

while the rest of us slept.

for C. D. F.

This first draft contained nearly all the ideas I eventually included in the final draft. The title (which is a phrase used often to describe Richland to outsiders) worked as a point of departure for my first line/idea, and the line length, tone, movement through the seasons, the way the poem shadowed the fathers, the strange absence of the rest of the townspeople all felt right. But the poem wasn't "there." It didn't have the power I hoped for and seemed too abbreviated. I put it aside and turned my attention to other projects.

When I returned to "A Bedroom Community" eight months later, I decided to put it entirely in couplets. The new short stanzas lent the piece visual regularity, and I appreciated the additional white space they introduced, which strengthened the ghost town effect. I also felt compelled to bring Carolyn and her father more decidedly into the poem, so I abandoned the dedication "for C. D. F." and took the riskier step of addressing Carolyn directly toward the end of the piece. This was the most important edit I made. It raised my personal stake in the poem and forced the reader to face up to a named victim, no longer an anonymous "they." Once I embedded Carolyn's name in the poem, the poem no longer felt insufficient. It had the gravity I wanted.

I also worked extensively on the sound of lines. Note the change in the milk truck/bottled urine phrasing in stanza five (couplet four in the next draft). The revised version is more iambic and also subtler. In general, the couplet form draws attention to flabby phrasing because it isolates each line — there's nowhere to hide. In the second draft, the poem's lines become shorter, tighter.

Second Draft

A Bedroom Community

What a good description of our town.
Bedded down in our nightcaps, curtains drawn

as swamp coolers and sprinklers hissed
every brown summer hour, or sagebrush

hardened in the cold. It was still dark
as our fathers rose, dressed, and boarded

blue buses that whisked them away, and men
in milk trucks came collecting bottled urine

from our doorsteps. Beyond the shelter belt
of Russian olive trees, cargo trains shuffled past

at 8:00 and 8:00, and the wide Columbia
rolled by, silent with walleye and steelhead.

We pulled our covers up
and our fathers never spoke a word

though some of them grew sick—
Carolyn, your father's blood and marrow

witnessed it. Whistles from the train.
The buses came. Our fathers left.

Oh Carolyn—while the rest of us slept.

At this point, I felt the poem was close, and I could no longer put it
away. It went into heavy rotation with a couple of other works in progress.
I showed it to my few close readers — mentors, more precisely — who
gave me some excellent suggestions to help smooth the clunky spots, like
removing the unnecessary first line. This excision set the poem down a lit-

tle more gracefully, and on quicker feet. I changed the buses' movement from "whisking" to "pulling away" for its sober, wrenching connotation, and introduced the phrase *overburdened fathers* to suggest "body burden," a measure of radionuclide exposure.

One of my readers urged me to turn the casual near and slant rhymes that are peppered throughout (men-urine, wide-walleye, train-came, left-slept) into something more intentional, especially since some of the couplets already hinted at a consistent rhyme scheme. Mostly this entailed revising line breaks in order to locate rhymes at the end of lines. I didn't attempt end rhyme in every couplet — such a drastic shift would have impacted the poem's language too deeply, and I didn't want it to become stilted — but the final draft echoes with repeating sounds that sharpen the poem's edges and give the conclusion more finality.

The last revision has been the most problematic. More than one reader resisted the line "your father's blood and marrow / witnessed it." The word *witnessed* is too melodramatic, I was advised; it's overused and has unwanted religious and pseudo-religious overtones. I played with it over several months, unsuccessfully, always returning to "witnessed it" for its sound. I've revised it again, I hope for the last time. The line is critical because the poem hinges here, transforms from detached recollection into testimony.

Final Version

A Bedroom Community

We were all bedded down
in our nightcaps, curtains drawn

as swamp coolers and sprinklers
hissed every brown summer hour, or in winter

sagebrush hardened in the cold. It was still dark
as our fathers rose, dressed, and boarded

blue buses that pulled away, and men
in milk trucks came collecting bottled urine

from our doorsteps. Beyond the shelter belt
of Russian olive trees, cargo trains shuffled past

at 8:00 and 8:00, and the wide
Columbia rolled by, silent with walleye

and steelhead. We pulled up our covers
while our overburdened fathers

dragged home to fix a drink,
and some of them grew sick—

Carolyn, your father's marrow
testified. Whistles from the train,

the buses came, our fathers left.
Oh Carolyn—while the rest of us slept.

Kathleen Flenniken's first collection, *Famous*, winner of the Prairie
Schooner Book Prize in Poetry, was published in 2006 by University of Nebraska Press. Her poems have appeared in *Poetry, The Southern Review, Poetry Daily,* and *The Iowa Review.* She is the recipient of fellowships from the
NEA and Artist Trust.

On Reading *Descartes' Error*

JUDITH STRASSER

O n Reading *Descartes' Error*" was published in *Poetry* in June 1995. The story behind the poem is one that I have often told to my students because it illustrates how a poet must listen carefully to others' comments and criticism, and then do what feels right, even if it means disregarding those comments.

First Draft

On Reading *Descartes' Error*
> "I see feelings as having a truly privileged status."
> — Dr. Antonio Damasio

Emotion's essential to reason. The eminent doctor's
words made me want to send his book to you. I thought
of a plain brown envelope, protective plastic bubbles,
a friend who'd write the address and mail the package
from foreign territory. Anonymous.

Death notices:
that's all we expect to get from each other now. Once,
I opened one from you: my first oncologist, moved (like
you) to California, a brain tumor, 49. You liked
the guy well enough, but I sensed quiet satisfaction
in the way you penned my name: you used to say I was tough,
I'd outlive all my doctors, outlive everyone, even you.

This summer I sent word that your high school English teacher
died. She used to gather favorite students to drink coffee
and smoke and talk at the counter at Rennebohm's drugstore;
you told me that just after we met. Left behind in your
home town, I came to be friends with her. We shared poetry.
I wrote on the Post-It stuck to the clipping, "I thought
you would want to know."

                              Once I told you I believed
I'd caused my own Hodgkin's Disease. *I thought I'd have to*
die. Not die, exactly, but get so sick I couldn't take care
of everything anymore. You'd have to do the housework,
cook for the children, drive the carpool to nursery school.
That made you mad. You bullied me with reason: science
proves no such connection between the body and the brain.
You mourned the loss of my clear thinking. You were convinced
I was insane, or the chemo had fried my mind.
                                        What died
that year was never marked by formal newsprint notice.
You could not make me stay by force of your pure reason.
No more could you grasp the meaning of my poetry.

As you can see, the poem came to me almost whole, in a rush, prompted by my reading of Antonio Damasio's book, *Descartes' Error* and my wish that I could get my ex-husband, a very rational scientist, to read it. We had argued endlessly, especially in the last year of our marriage, about the relationship of feelings and reason, and it seemed to me that Damasio's book used scientific explanations that my ex-husband would understand to clinch my side of the argument. I knew from the beginning that I needed to use Damasio's words as an epigraph; in a revision, I decided that I needed more than just a single sentence, so I could get into the poem faster, and also needed to identify him as a neurologist, not simply as "Dr."

My style — especially in the early '90s — was very narrative, and the first revisions I made were intended to tighten the language and make it somewhat more poetic. Thus, in lines 1 and 2, "The eminent doctor's / words made me want to send his book to you" became "The words / make me want to continue our argument, send you his book." And in the second stanza, "Once, / I opened one [a death notice] from you: my first oncologist" became "You / sent me the first: my oncologist." And then, in a further revision, "You started it. I slit open / the envelope: my oncologist."

I had difficulty with the ending of the poem. In the first version, the last line said what I meant: "No more could you grasp the meaning of my poetry." But it was not until I wrote more about Mrs. S. (who was actually Miss H. at the time she taught my ex-husband) that I realized I could bring her in to the ending, giving her (rather than me) the hopeless task of trying to teach this guy to understand feeling, poetry, me.

Second Draft

On Reading *Descartes' Error*

"I see feelings as having a truly privileged status...
[F]eelings have a say on how the rest of the brain and cognition
go about their business. Their influence is immense."
                    — Neurologist Antonio R. Damasio

The words make me want to send you his book, continue
our fight, prove I was right. I think of a plain brown
envelope, protective bubble-wrap, a friend who'd write
the address and mail the package from some foreign place.

Anonymous.
            Death notices: that's all we expect to get
from each other these days. You started it. I slit open
the envelope: my first oncologist, moved west (like you), dead
of a brain tumor, 49. You liked the guy well enough, but

I sensed some satisfaction in the way you penned my name.
You used to say I was tough, I'd outlive all my doctors,
outlive everyone, even you. This summer I sent word that
your 12th-grade teacher had died. She was the first part

of your childhood you ever told me about. She used to
gather favorite students to drink coffee and smoke and talk
about life and literature at Rennebohm's after school; you
had a crush on her. We came to be friends. She showed me

her poetry. I wrote on the Post-It I stuck to the obit,
"I thought you would want to know."
                    Once I told you I believed
I'd caused my own Hodgkin's Disease. *I felt I'd have to die.*
Not die, exactly, but get so sick I couldn't take care
of everything anymore. You'd have to do the housework, cook
for the children, drive the carpool to nursery school.
That made you mad. You ranted, spouted statistics, cited

Descartes, bullied with reason: science proves nothing

about connections between the body and the mind. You mourned
the loss of my clear thinking. You were convinced I'd gone
insane. Maybe the chemo had fried my brain. What died
that year was never marked by formal notice. It's taking ages

to decompose. But we have all moved on: you, me, neuroscience.
What I know now: you could not make me stay
by the force of your pure reason, anymore than Mrs. S. was able
to teach you the meaning of poetry.

The second draft of the poem felt right to me, in terms of language. I
had tightened the narrative, eliminating the prosaicness in the third stanza
by removing "you told me that just after we met," for example, and adding
specifics in the last stanza: "You ranted, spouted statistics, cited /
Descartes" that connected our argument with Damasio. I also changed
some words to highlight rhyme: "obit" instead of "clipping" to rhyme with
"Post-It" and "brain" instead of "mind" after "gone insane." I brought it to
my writing group. They said it wasn't a poem. In the margin of this draft,
I wrote their comments: "short prose piece?" "Creative nonfiction rap?"
They also questioned the line, "Maybe the chemo had fried my brain." I
thought they were wrong about all of that. I really *believed* in this poem,
and I thought that line — which was exactly what my ex-husband thought
— was, however saucy and "unpoetic," absolutely right on. I did agree
that the stanza breaks weren't working, and that somehow the first eight-
een lines should be one stanza, and the rest of the poem, a second stanza.

I decided, without telling my poet friends, that I would send the revised poem to *Poetry*, which at the time was edited by Joseph Parisi. If he
accepted it, it would prove that however much of a story I was telling, this
was truly a poem. At the time, I'd had just a few poems published anywhere, and I knew this was more than audacious — ridiculous, really. But
to my astonishment Parisi accepted the poem, and suggested the stanza
break after line 5. He said, "it's a logical place ... and would be congruent
with what you do below:

Anonymous.
        Death notices: that's all we expect...

and

I thought you would want to know.
                    Once I told...."

Final Version, as published in *Poetry*, June 1995

On Reading *Descartes' Error*

> "I see feelings as having a truly privileged
> status.... [F]eelings have a say on how the rest of the
> brain and cognition go about their business. Their
> influence is immense."
> — Neurologist Antonio R. Damasio

The words make me want to send you his book, continue
our fight, prove I was right. I think of a plain brown
envelope, protective bubble-wrap, a friend who'd write
the address and mail the package from some foreign place.
Anonymous.

          Death notices: that's all we expect
from each other these days. You started it. I slit open
the envelope: my oncologist, moved west (like you), dead
of a brain tumor, 49. You liked the guy well enough, but
I sensed some satisfaction in the way you penned my name.
You used to say I was tough, I'd outlive all my doctors,
outlive everyone, even you. This summer I sent word that
your 12th-grade teacher had died. She was the first part
of your childhood you ever told me about. She used to
gather favorite students to drink coffee and smoke and talk
about life and literature at Rennebohm's after school; you
had a crush on her. We came to be friends. She showed me
her poetry. I wrote on the Post-It I stuck to the obit,
"I thought you would want to know."

          Once I told you I believed
I'd caused my own Hodgkin's Disease. *I felt I'd have to die.*

Not die, exactly, but get so sick I couldn't take care
of everything anymore. You'd have to do the housework, cook
for the children, drive the carpool to nursery school.
That made you mad. You ranted, spouted statistics, cited
Descartes, bullied with reason: science proves nothing
about connections between the body and the mind. You mourned
the loss of my clear thinking. You were convinced I'd gone
insane. Maybe the chemo had fried my brain. What died
that year was never marked by formal notice. It's taking ages
to decompose. But we have all moved on: you, me, neuroscience.
What I know now: you could not make me stay
by the force of your pure reason, anymore than Miss H. was able
to teach you the meaning of poetry.

Judith Strasser is the author of a memoir, *Black Eye: Escaping a Marriage, Writing a Life* (University of Wisconsin Press, 2004), and the co-editor, with Robin Chapman, of an anthology, *On Retirement: 75 Poems* (University of Iowa Press, 2007). "On Reading *Descartes' Error*" is reprinted in *The Reason/Unreason Project*, her full-length collection, which won the Lewis-Clark Expedition Award and was published in 2006.

Given

SARAH PEMBERTON STRONG

When I sat down to write a poem on a Saturday morning at the end of November, what came to mind was an image I'd witnessed a few days earlier: my mother carefully labeling each of four pies she had just baked for Thanksgiving. At the time, I was struck by the illogic of her action: Why was she labeling them? We weren't going anywhere. And why had she baked four pies in the first place when there would only be five of us at dinner? I was mystified and slightly exasperated: she had done a lot of extra, unnecessary work.

It was this reaction of mine that dictated the wry tone of the poem's first stanza, written in the style of a word problem from a math textbook: from a mathematical standpoint, the numbers made no sense. I was not sure where the poem would go from there.

Early Draft

Giving Thanks

If one child leaves home at seventeen
and the other still lives there at twenty-five, how
many pounds of turkey are needed if
two-fifths of the guests are vegetarian?
My mother baked four pies for five people.
She covers the leftovers, writes on the foil
Pecan. Apple. Pumpkin. Lime Pie—which
tells me she couldn't find
key limes, used instead the dark green ones
the dog was carrying across the kitchen floor
like a brace of felled doves.
If the third child calls during dessert, weeping
in California, who
gets to take home the leftovers?
When my brother lifted the knife, sluiced open
the browned skin over the sternum, juice

burst forth like milk from a new mother's
breasts. The sweetness wants out, the
nourishment aches to be given,
like the plums in summer that split their
skin while still on the branches, their dark
juice falling to the pavement like
rain, the sticky scent begging take me, take me.

As the poem developed, I began to understand how to work this odd
equation. In exploring what gave rise to those four pies, occasioned by a
holiday whose emotional origins I'd thought I had little connection to, I
discovered the urge to be generous presenting itself over and over in different forms.

I am fortunate to have among my friends a fellow writer to trade work
with. Once a month, I have lunch with the poet Suzanne Heyd, and the
two of us review, critique, and generally midwife each other's poems into
being. As usual, she had a number of wise suggestions about a middle draft
of this poem, now called "The Mathematics of Giving." (I say "middle" because there were eight or nine drafts in all; the draft I showed her occurred
somewhere around the halfway point.)

Middle Draft

The Mathematics of Giving

For a dinner with five people, my mother has baked
four pies. If one child leaves home at seventeen
and the other still lives there at twenty-six, how
many pounds of turkey are needed if
two-fifths of the guests are vegetarian? She
covers the pie plates, writes on the foil
Pecan. Apple. Pumpkin. Lime Pie—she couldn't
find Key limes in November, used instead
the dark green ones the dog got hold of and gummed
like a newly-shot dove. He dropped
the slobbered Persians at her feet and looked up
hoping. Quivering with the gift. Even the dead
bird—when my brother lifts the knife

and slices the glistening body, juice
bursts forth like milk from a new mother's
breasts. The plum tree in the front yard sets its buds
for the day the indigo skins split themselves with the weight
of their longing to fall. We'd come home in summer
to dark hearts drumming the pavement like rain, the
sticky fragrance chalking the air with its proof: Take
me. This is what I'm for.

The mother not finding Key limes, Suzanne remarked, is taking up too much of the poem's time. She was right: in real life, *my* mother couldn't find Key limes and had to buy regular green ones, but in the poem, who cared? I'd been confusing the inspiration for the poem with the poem itself, and this real-life detail was not advancing the narrative, the theme, or the imagery in any meaningful way. I refocused, cut two lines and made the pie Key lime. This also got rid of the obscure reference to the kind of lime the dog offers the mother in the poem — common, dark green limes are indeed a variety known as Persian, but who knows this without looking it up? Nobody, including me — it had been a distracting choice, not an illuminating one.

Suzanne suggested that the line "milk from a new mother's breasts" might be too much — too literal, overdone. This felt true to me — I had already excised "the sweetness wants out ... aches to be given" for the same reason. As I had learned from writing a novel, *showing* the reader something is almost always a stronger choice than *telling* it. (In the final draft, the breast imagery reappears, reassigned as a descriptor of the turkey. The word feels natural here, and is a far more subtle spot from which to provide overtones of meaning.) Suzanne also suggested I rethink the relationship between the plum tree and the rest of the scene I was describing: why jump away from the present to the vague "in summer"? I took her advice and rewrote those lines to keep the tree directly relevant to the action at hand.

Though mathematics had a prominent place in the poem's imagery, "The Mathematics of Giving" didn't feel right as a title — it seemed too vague. I pondered the vocabulary of math, its forms. If the poem was a mathematical formula, what did that mean? The poem ended with a proof, so what preceded the ending must be what was being proved. In geometry, all proofs start out with a given — and there it was: "Given," the perfect title.

I wasn't satisfied with the visual shape of the poem as it looked in the middle draft either. Written without stanzas, the poem on the page looked squished to me, as though it couldn't breathe. After much trial and error, I separated the poem into five stanzas. The first four each contain one dominant action or image: excessive baking, the dog's hopeful gift, the slicing of the turkey, the fruiting tree. The final stanza, with its metaphor of plums as hearts, both concludes the narrative and is a culmination of the poem's theme, or project: that the desire to give is intrinsic to who we are.

Final Version

Given

For a dinner with five people, my mother
has baked four pies. If one child
leaves home at seventeen and the other
still lives there at twenty-six, how many
pounds of turkey are needed
if two-fifths of the guests
are vegetarian? She writes on the foil

Pecan. Apple. Pumpkin. Key
Lime—the limes the dog got hold of and
gummed over like newly-shot
doves. He dropped the slobbered
citrus at her feet and looked up
hoping. Quivering with the gift.

Even the dead bird—when
my brother lifts the knife
and slices the glistening body, juice
bursts forth in a flood over his hand.

She's glazed the breast with
plums from the tree outside, where
the indigo skins split themselves
with the weight of their longing
to fall: I came home

to dark hearts drumming the
pavement like rain, their purple fragrance
chalking the air with a proof:
Take me. This is what I'm for.

First published in *The Southern Review*, Spring 2007

Sarah Pemberton Strong's poetry has appeared in *Atlanta Review, The Cream City Review, Seattle Review, The Southern Review, The Sun*, and elsewhere. She is also the author of a novel, *Burning the Sea* (Alyson, 2002). She lives in New Haven, Connecticut, where she divides her time between writing, teaching poetry workshops, and working as a plumber.

Lacuna

Robin E. Sampson

Which word I found first, *lacuna* or *ma*, I don't remember. Even the original seed poem, the one that was just in my head, is gone. This is ironic considering the theme of what finally became the poem. I had stumbled upon some art terms while searching for something that meant "not there." I was looking for a word that captured the dichotomy of negative and positive aspects of loss. I used both print and online dictionaries and thesauruses. I kept finding words, but never what I was looking for. I was starting to get very frustrated, almost at the point of giving up, when I came across two words in fairly rapid succession that were almost perfect, the definition of one leading to the other.

Lacuna was defined as "an empty space or a missing part; a gap, a void." As a term used most by art historians and art conservators, it describes a missing chunk of fresco or a missing part of a manuscript. You know something was there, and can maybe approximate what it was, but can never reconstruct it with any certainty. The word *ma* means "negative space" and is used in the Japanese art tradition to describe the blank area of a painting or drawing or the space separating the stems of an ikebana arrangement. The theory is that what isn't there is as important as what is. I'd never heard either of these terms before (or didn't remember them), though I was familiar with what they represented from a college art history class I'd taken almost thirty years earlier. So instead of writing down the seed poem, I started working with these two words.

"Lacuna" became the title right away. The poem started to be about a search, in vain, for something to fill in the holes that pockmarked certain memories from my childhood. I tried to stay focused on the meanings of the two words I'd found as I wrote.

First Draft

Lacuna

Self-defined by what is
not there, she traces edges,

sees only minus, holds
her life up to the bare bulb,
examines the void.
Negative is equal to bad.
Space is empty, a lack,
a shortage of something.
Certain what is missing
cannot be replaced, still
she struggles
to first stabilize,
then repair the damage.
She gathers shards,
collects pigments,
always seeking to fill.
What remains will still
be only a reconstruction,
a museum replica. Instead,
she must learn the value of *ma*,
the space between.

This started as a very personal poem, and I was not too happy with what I had on the page. I knew I needed feedback to get to the core of what I was trying to say. Sometimes a poet is too close to the poem to see it, to hear it. Though I was describing my situation, I knew that somewhere in there was the universal. I printed ten copies to take to workshop, then I changed a line and had to cross out the old one and write in the new on all of them. "What remains will still" became "The resulting canvas is," though this line was dropped in the next revision. I had the definitions of the words *lacuna* and *ma* as footnotes.

The workshop was well attended the night I went, and I got back nine copies marked with various suggestions. Lines were crossed out, others circled or underlined. Comments to change words or move line breaks were numerous. The general comments were positive, so I knew this was not a throw-away. One person wrote "I love this poem!!!" and I kept that copy on top as I worked as positive reinforcement. Afterwards, I sat at my computer with the suggested revisions and started working.

Several people had suggested I start with "she traces edges," and so I tried that as the first line and liked how it sounded. I dropped the original first line and the lines "her life up to the bare bulb" and "a museum replica." I moved other words and phrases around according to the suggestions I'd received. I came up with a couple of new lines while pondering the concept of *ma*. The connect-the-dots of constellations and even chaos theory found their way into the poem. I rearranged and rearranged. Then something interesting happened.

As I was cutting and pasting lines on the computer screen, not paying as much attention to line breaks as to the words themselves, the poem started taking on a shape. It looked as if a bite had been taken out of the poem. Since the visual image of a disintegrating fresco was in my mind while writing the poem, I noticed the synchronicity of the shape of the poem to its meaning and started working consciously with that. By keeping the short line breaks in the middle and lengthening the lines at the end to form the tumbled down debris at the base, I could illustrate *lacuna*. I found that the last line had to be a bit shorter because nothing I did to make the last line the longest worked, and I wanted to end with the word *ma*. When I finished this revision, I saw more than a collection of words; I saw a picture. It could be a partial silhouette with head, neck, and shoulders or an overhanging rock formation, or a wave beginning to break.

At this point, I was keeping the definitions as footnotes. Even though I was pleased with this new version, I decided to take it to another writing group with some of the same people I work-shopped it with originally. Of course, after I emailed this and the other poems to the members of this group, I made a couple of changes. I made the definition of *lacuna* an epigraph and kept that of *ma* as a footnote since this term had been confusing to some people in the previous workshop, thinking I was referring to "mother." I read it through, aloud, several times. It felt "done" to me. In fact, it felt so done that the next day, along with two other poems, I submitted it to *The Bitter Oleander*. Several days later, at the critique group, I listened to various suggestions and actually considered some, even though I'd already sent it out.

When I opened the letter accepting "Lacuna" for publication, the comments made by the editor confirmed for me that I'd been able to accomplish what I had set out to do with this poem. Sometimes shape poems seem contrived to me, and I was worried that this work would seem that way. But because of the way the words tumble on the page, the poem works. Even though originally a page poem, this was also chosen for the first set of a poetry performance group and worked quite well as a spoken word piece. This poem is one I worked hard on, though I wouldn't say I struggled with it. It is probably the one poem I am most proud of (waits for lightning to strike) because it is to me a perfect mélange of art and craft.

Lacuna
> — *an empty space or a missing part; a gap, a void*

She traces edges, sees only minus.
Examines the negative space where
she resides, self-defined by lack.
Weathered fragments peel away
from her wall, litter the ground.
She struggles
to stabilize,
then repair
the damage.
Gathers shards,
collects pigments,
attempts reconstruction.
What is missing cannot be
replaced or even reproduced.
Separation forms the patterns, the
constellations are shaped as much from
blackness as from stars. Chaos creates order.
She will learn to value *ma*[*]

First published in *The Bitter Oleander*, Volume 10, Number 2

* Negative space, from the Japanese art tradition.

Robin E. Sampson took the long road home to poetry and other persuasions of the written word after swearing off it as a teenager. Along the way, she got a degree in geology, was a bass player in a bar band, became a wife and mother to three kids, counseled breastfeeding mothers for twelve years, worked various odd jobs, and took up more hobbies than should be legal. A member of the Connecticut-based six-woman poetry performance troupe Shijin, she has published work in their chapbook *We Shijin, Book 1*, as well as in *The Bitter Oleander*, *Wicked Alice*, *The New Verse News*, and the anthologies *The Book of Hope* and *The Company We Keep*.

Habit

MARY-SHERMAN WILLIS

I began the poem in 2003. I wanted to write about my sister's drug addiction and set it in Washington D.C., our home town. Certain lines floated into my head, and I wanted them in the poem — "the air silk with his perfume," and "his voice a web of ribbons around her head." Some lines were taken from her stories about this period in her life. And I wanted the title to be "Felo-de-Se," about the self-immolation of addiction. So here is the first draft, from January 2003:

Felo-de-Se

1.
It was so fifteen to be drawn from the playground to the contents
of his pockets, to his car, and to his need to show her the things
he could give her. But it was OK: her girlfriends were with her.
He hummed, "Good morning little schoolgirl" to her
through the chain link fence, his hands rattling keys. She knew
that song. It was about an Italian boy
who didn't say much, eyes illegible, a half-smile.
She looked in his face, the wind in her clean hair,
and talked tough, which amused him.

He gave her dope and hot jewelry. To her friends he gave
trinkets and baubles and gold chains. He gave them rides
and fed them pastries and coffee at Avignon Frères
after school. They held their cigarettes for him to light,
and he passed them joints and pills and packets of powder.
Then he'd vanish, leaving them with their fathers
who were not at home, and their mothers, who were busy.
When she went to school, she would be waiting for him,
listening for his car, looking for his shadow.

Her friends told her things they knew
she didn't know about him—that he'd called,

stopped by. She said she didn't care.
What did she need to know anyway?
He'd say he was a student at Georgetown, or GW,
that he lived on 15ᵗʰ Street, or in Bethesda, or in Arlington.
Yet she knew by that time that the air was silk
with his perfume, that his voice was a web of ribbons
around her head, that nothing felt real without him.
That he could go where she couldn't.

2.
Now there is an alien who occupies her to the limits of her skin,
who works her jaws and her tongue
and the cords of her throat to speak

with that charm, that junkie charm
to soothe, cajole, to massage
like an accountant the sums and totals
of pain management

and leaves nothing: no marker,
no map, nothing to remember
what is true about her
except what was true before.

    I put the poem away for a month or so, and when I took it out again, I realized that a straight-up free-verse narrative with a few lyrical bits tossed in had failed to convey the general power or mechanism of addiction or the personal stake I had in the poem. It lacked tension. And part 2, its resolution, was pat and abstract (my typical strategy in the face of difficult emotion), and tonally inconsistent with part 1.

    Meanwhile, I'd been thinking about the word *habit*, my sister's word for her condition. I thought about the addict's strangled relationship to love and the truth. So I went to the dictionary, examined the word's etymology, and began to collect definitions. I saw that "habit" comes from the Latin *habere*, to have, to hold, to possess; ironically, it's the same root as to give, and connected to *habitus*, condition, demeanor, also a root of habitation, settlement, colony. Other meanings include clothing (a nun's habit, or a riding habit); one's bearing or manner of conducting oneself; one's mental makeup. One definition I stole wholesale: "a settled tendency acquired" or usual manner of behavior. Related to that is "a behavior pattern acquired by frequent repetition that shows itself in regularly or increased facility of performance," which leads to its newest (as of 1920) meaning, "an acquired mode of behavior that becomes involuntary or compulsive: addiction."

And so there were the makings of my poem. I would need to make a kind of argument to marshal all these meanings; there would be a turn, as love turned to addiction; and there would be a return to the enclosure of home. For all this, I would need the encircling arms of a sonnet. Here is the first version of the sonnet, written in April 2003 and now retitled "Habit."

> Habit lives at home, at habitation's door.
> Travel can't break it. She looked up and he was gone,
> the air still silk with his perfume; his voice a ribbon
> around her head. After all, she wanted more.
> To her, having (rooted in giving) meant taking.
> So first she took disguises: the prayerful nun,
> or that failing, she'd morph into the hunter
> who stalks a palliative that masks aching.
>
> Her settled tendency acquired, her fluid charm
> at work in service to her pain—how would we know?
> We saw it, but seeing doesn't always make it so
> despite those bruises in the crook of her arm.
> He would return and call, to our chagrin.
> We'd bar the door, but habit let him in.

Now that I had this Shakespearean sonnet ticking away on my desk, I could see that it still needed work. But revising a sonnet, or any fixed-form poem, is intimidating. Tinker with any of its clockwork parts and the whole thing can fall apart.

In general, I felt the structure of the argument in the octave and sestet was solid, as was the circular path from line 1 to line 14, leading from door back to door. I also wanted to preserve an ambiguity I saw in the poem about the nature of the addiction I was writing about, which had had its origins in my sister's early love affair with a manipulative drug-dealer boyfriend. The poem showed me (as is often the case) a truth, that the insanity of first love is similar to addiction.

So there would be some fine-tuning and clarification. The last four lines of the octave, for instance, were confusing. I was trying to pack in some information about the word-root *habere* with the idea of the addict's being a chronic liar who appropriates identities and alternative realities. One version went like this:

To have and to hold share their root with giving.
For her "to have" meant taking a disguise:
First the simple nun, her veil a net of lies;
Then, lady riding to hounds, fox unforgiving.

Still clunky. Heather McHugh, my MFA advisor, took a crack at it about two years into the process, slicing away verbiage (at the expense of my five- or six-stress lines) and making good use of the ellipsis in line 7. I liked the emerging internal and end-rhyming *ies* of the final version, the keening *ai-ai-ai* of lines 6 and 7.

The sestet was also troublesome, in an Al-Anon-ish way, as I grappled with what "we" knew, and did or didn't do. I had an image of the shape-shifting addict developing a habit, or "settled tendency acquired" in full view of those who love her, as if she, or we, were mesmerized, or charmed. I struggled over whether it was "facile" or "fluid" charm in line 9. I settled for the latter because of the fluidity of her transformation, and of the drug itself, from powder to liquid.

I also had an image of a kind of shoulder-shrugging "how would I know?" in-denial reaction to overt signs, those "pockmarks in the crook of her arm," which in some early versions were vaguely described as "bruises." Changing "would" to "could" in line 10 set a firmer limit to my sense of complicity as a co-dependent. On the formal front, in revising the third quatrain, I sacrificed the *effe* rhyme pattern that the Shakespearean sonnet calls for in favor of a nonregulation *efef* pattern. Another, final transformation, three years from the start.

Here is the poem as it appeared in *Iowa Review* 37/1, Spring 2007.

Habit

Habit lives at home, at habitation's door.

(Even travel can't break it.) When he was gone,
the air still silk with his perfume, his voice a ribbon
tangled in her head, she only wanted more.
Having (rooted in giving) meant taking,
and she took disguises: nun veiled in lies,
hunter in her guise…
even she forgot when she was faking.

By then her settled tendency acquired, her fluid charm
in service to her pain—how could we know?
There were those pockmarks in the crook of her arm,
but seeing doesn't always make it so.
He would return and call, to our chagrin.
We'd bar the door, but habit let him in.

Mary-Sherman Willis's poems and reviews have appeared or will appear in *The New Republic, The Plum Review, Archipelago, Shenandoah, Iowa Review, Hudson Review,* and *Poet Lore.* She teaches creative writing at George Washington University and lives in rural Virginia.

Leaving Eden

LUCY ANDERTON

First Draft

Leaving Eden

Like twins (and they were)
crawling through the gate,
the tender scents trailing
away, the mild fingers
of wind slipping down
their backs, tipping off
their skin, left curling
through the blossoms.

Into the spitting
sand. Battering
their cheeks.
The mask less
sun, rough
with its brush.
The water a mean
secret in the mordant
cuts of earth. Over their

shoulder
                    the garden,
gone.   The womb
closed up, as if tucked
under a wing. But it was
there, and inside,
the gentle beasts wept.

The first draft of the poem happened in one day, with one motion, as opposed to many of my poems that stutter-step their way into first form. And, stupidly, after some pinching and packing on that day, I thought it was done — something that is also unusual for me. Looking at it now, I cannot believe I thought this poem was finished, and I take it as a strong warning before I put my other poems to final page.

Narratively, the poem began as a brief, general portrait of the Eden myth, with no focus on either character — just a push toward capturing the loss of "home" and "safety." Technically, I am pretty conscious of line breaks as a poem is initially being written and rarely do the final line breaks of a poem look extremely different from those of the first draft, as actually happened in this poem. The interior and obvious rhymes also happen quite frequently in my work, perhaps because of my involvement in music, so this poem contained these initial interior rhymes from the first writing.

The language of Eden in the poem is, as I see it now, an attempt at capturing the lushness of the garden through sound, a lushness with which I unfortunately became enamored and pushed through their Expulsion in this first draft.

The second draft came a month later, and it was markedly mild, probably because I was lazily clutching to the hope that the poem was actually finished and just needed some tune-ups. My initial impulse was to re-steer the tone of the language. Seeing the early push toward lush language and recognizing how inappropriate this tone was for the moments after the Expulsion, I worked on scalping out a more violent, spare language for this center part of the poem. I also tried to "lush up" the first part with the words "magnolia," "ripe," and "silk." In my experience, it is difficult to do this tonally without coming across as flowery, and I am proud to parade my failure in this early part of the poem.

The most interesting change in this second draft is what happens with the narrative. The character of Adam emerges from the couple and suddenly they are pronouncedly separate with the "red red nest" between them. (I purposefully leave out many commas with repeated adjectives in my work as I enjoy the forward stomp of the uncaught-up list.) With the appearance of the nest and Adam's inability to bear children, I felt another narrative pushing to come through, and it was clear that the poem was nowhere near finished. I put it aside to simmer. I ate some chocolate.

Second Draft

Leaving Eden

Like twins (and they were)
crawling through the gate,
the ripe silk scents trailing
away, the magnolia fingers
of wind slipping down
their backs, tipping off
their skin, curling
back the reaching blossoms.

Into the spitting
sand. Battering
their cheeks.
The sun,
rough
with its brush.
The water, mean
with its tongue. Over their

shoulder
                                    the garden,
gone.   The womb
closed up, as if tucked
under a wing. But it was
there, between them, a red
red nest, and then was Adam
(always to be empty) mortal
King of Eden, where
the gentle beasts wept.

While I don't remember my exact response when I once again took up
the poem five months after the second draft, I can assume it was something like "Oh my God, how could I ever have written such a thing —
where is there something large and remote under which I can bury myself?" The "lush" language was gaudy and flowery. Eve was tucked away

out of sight. A fierce overhaul was necessary.

Narratively, Eve became the driving force as the poem became about their separation, their stepping out of the shade of initial blind love, and of Eve's knowledge gained through her ability to create humans. I stopped the dawdling of the first stanza and pushed the speed of the poem as the Expulsion became immediate, brief, and violent. I brought the two characters independently to view just as quickly, then turned the lens on Eve and her interior life as she walks the land outside the garden.

In this version of the poem, Eve became a woman defiant, taking on her punishment and embracing the reality in contrast with what she sees as Adam's idealistic and unattainable wish for Eden and Heaven. She is also pregnant, and through the "bite" she learned all that God had to teach her. She is triumphant in being filled with both child and knowledge. Technically, I pushed the language into a more brutal and stark arena. There are significantly more plosives and dentals that create tonally harsh sounds: "choked," "spat," "cracked," "hammered," "spitting," "tongue," "curses," "bone," "baking," "deep," "bite." I also shortened the length of the words. In the second draft, there are twenty-two two-syllable words, one three-syllable word, and one four-syllable word. In the third draft, there are only fifteen two-syllable words and none that exceeds two syllables. In my experience, the effect of using mainly monosyllabic words (Germanic in origin) is that I achieve a more clearly visual poetic image since the mind does not have to move out of the pictorial area of the brain into the more linear and intellectual area of the brain (all this said very scientifically, of course).

I also played around with the stanza making and line breaks, coming to no conclusion that I really liked. At this point, I decided to leave the poem alone for a bit, satisfied that it was close to conclusion. I took a bubble bath.

Third Draft

Leaving Eden

Like choked up apple they were
spat from the mouth
of the garden. He cracked
and hammered but she

was done
with the games, swung
into the spitting
sand, the thorny-head

sun, the dry tongue
of water—Yes

she thought, bring on
the shaking with curses,
the bone shelters,
the smell of baking
feet—Let him

leave, with his reach
for a bauble sunk
too deep. He will

always be empty—With that
bite I learned it all
from Him, she smiled

as her belly
grew larger.

In the final version, almost a year later, I once more stopped the stalling
and restarted the poem directly with the relationship between Adam and
Eve (after all, the title took care of the narrative placement of the poem).
Technically, I took up the task of physical shaping the poem, finding where
the lines broke well, and choosing the couplet form to reflect the tension between the characters (also, I like the way it looks).

In this version, not much changes narratively, except the key moment
at the end of the poem. First of all, any mention of God is out of the poem.
Further, it is not clear if Eve is pregnant or not, but she knows she can create humans and is using the word *seeds*, which points to her symbolically
as the earth. Moreover, she is now an Eve who not only embraces her reality and experiences her strength, but sees that Adam, in his reach for il-
lusion and inability to turn to face reality, is actually dangerous to "the

tree," which, one could argue, can be seen as the world and humanity. This poem knew of this danger in Adam sooner than I since earlier on danger was suggested in the first couplet where Adam "cracked and hammered." I often find that the poem is smarter than I am. The poem usually waits to reveal what it knows to me in its own time. The poem becomes something far outside me; in fact, I often feel that I am just its servant doing its crazy bidding.

When I look at it just now, I notice, and find it interesting that the poem is framed by Adam with the "He cracked and hammered" and "he will kill the tree." This can be perceived as a reflection of women's experience being framed in the reality of a "man's world." In any case, I far prefer this poem to the first version. The poem was shy, but finally forthcoming and took only half the time that many of my poems take to expose themselves.

Final Version

Leaving Eden

He cracked
and hammered but she

was done
with the games, swung

into the spitting
sand, the thorny-head

sun, the dry tongue
of water—Yes

she thought, bring on
the shaking with curses,

the bone shelters,
the smell of baking

feet—Let him
leave, with his reach

for a bauble sunk
too deep. In that bite

I learned it all. He will
remain

the empty one. I'll
swell with apple

seeds. And he
will kill the tree.

Lucy Anderton started writing in her middle 20s, after getting a degree in jazz composition from Berklee College of Music and holding jobs as a hip hop dancer in Brazil, gardener, waitress, Parisian runway model, janitor, and record sales clerk. Her work has appeared in *AGNI Online, The Iowa Review, American Letters & Commentary, Salt Hill J ournal,* among others. She held the Emerging Writer Teaching Position at Randolph-Macon Woman's College in 2005. She recently returned from Auvillar, France, where she was the writer in residence for the Virginia Center for the Creative Arts.

My Mother Keeps Dying in the Bed by My Cradle

HOLLY CLARK

First Draft

Asleep in fever's limbo,
I dream of women
chattering around my cradle,
my mother's milk sloshing
in my stomach, my skin
slick with sweat.
So many women's voices, their tongues
fluttering against the air,
as they fold my tiny gowns and tuck
my tiny booties in the wide bureau.

My aunt is dying, her ankles
twisted in the sheets, and she moans,
He hurt me; tell the young ones,
Stay away. The women lower me
into her arms, her damp face
cringing against the pain
that cinches her abdomen,
that cramps through her calves.

Her cracked lips brush my ear
as she whispers my grandfather's name.
The women smile, and I am grown,
marrow revolting in my bones,
my skeleton quivering, my stomach
heavy with my family's stones.
I am chasing him down second-floor hallways
in an empty elementary school,
angled shafts of light sprawling

from high-mounted windows, and I am chasing
his naked frame—illuminated, godlike—
as he steps steadily away from me,
effortlessly out-of-reach.

I dreamt this poem, but found that the emotional seed of the dream refused to take root in the "factual" circumstances of the dream itself. In other
words, the first draft announces itself as the recounting of a dream and recalls the images, dialogue, and characters just as I dreamt them; however,
by the final draft of the poem, new images arise, new utterances, and the
characters' relationships to one another are completely different: an aunt
becomes a mother, a grandfather, a father, and the speaker becomes, instead of a niece, the more intimate figure of a daughter. My instinct instructed me to use the guiding light of the emotional truth of the poem to
revise it, and, the trappings of factual truth fell away to reveal, in the end,
a far closer portrait of the dream's meaning and sinister mood than the
original more "truthful" draft could manage.

To construct mood-appropriate images, I did a series of freewrites using
the following words from the first draft as jumping-off points: "booties,"
"abdomen," "empty," and "school." I picked mostly concrete words like
"school," as opposed to abstract words like "pain" or "effortlessly," because, when I start with abstractions, my mind writes more abstractions,
but when I start with concrete words, my mind chooses concrete diction to
form sensory images that draw my reader into the narrative. Thus, I chose
the words that, to my mind, glowed with potential. All minds will find different "glowing" words because all of us have our own associations and
connotations we bring to our writing. This intuitive quick-snatching of
words from a draft, I find, often reveals my unconscious agenda for the direction of my revision process.

For this poem, my freewrites yielded images and metaphors for intro-
version, death, and memory, for example, "night's deaf black kettle," the
notion of a funeral pyre, "dark phone booths," "white echoes of late blossoms," and the notion of applause.

By the second draft, I had abandoned the original first two lines, which
label the poem a dream narrative. I struggled with the ethics of presenting
a dream as reality, thus allowing my reader to infer untrue autobiography
portraying my family in a terrible light. I believe poets should never feel
limited in what they are "allowed" to write, so, ultimately, I decided I

would trust my reader not to conflate the speaker and the poet and that my first duty is to the integrity of the poem's heart.

By the time I had added my new freewrite images, the poem felt surreal and powerfully dreamlike, and disclosing that "it was all a dream" broke that spell. I preferred my reader to enter the dream without warning because this disorientation loosens the reader's mind, lowering her resistance, thereby allowing her to navigate more fluidly the poem's emotional trajectory. I also cut all references to the flock of unnamed women in my dream, representing them instead in the figure of the grandmother. My revisions to this poem were mostly additions because the clarity of the narrative was muffled in the reticent language of the first draft. Usually my revisions involve more cuts than additions, since I try to monitor my poems for precise diction and purge any unnecessary words and syllables.

Second Draft

My Mother Keeps Dying in the Bed by My Cradle

Shhh, my grandmother smoothes
my mother's hair and slides
an ice cube over her swollen tongue.
My mother clasps me to her chest,
her face like changing
screens of sky, first, clear and still,
then, clouded with the pain
that cinches her abdomen,
that clamps her calves.
Keep him away from my baby.

His name breaks
against the shore of her lips
and laps against my ear, *Lawrence,*
Lawrence, Lawrence. Outside, snow
heaves its milky flood past the closed
window, everyone else already gone
from the house, and I can't forget
her simple sighs. I am knitting
alone in night's deaf black kettle.

When the marrow revolts
in my bones, when my spine quivers
under the weight of my family's stones,
I will hunt my father, whose feet like arsonists'
escaped to view this pyre.
I will find him
hiding in dark phone booths.
I will chase him
down second-floor hallways,
angled shafts of light sprawling
from the high-mounted windows,
and I will chase him through
the empty schoolyard,
through the white echoes
of late blossoms.
I will see him turning
—illuminated, godlike—
and listening.

Then, he will drop his hands
to his sides, done with winning,
and my mother's eyes, marbles, luminous
hovering planets, my mother's lips,
red and parted, will begin.
He will understand
how angry we are, how
sorry, and then we will applaud,
our palms like wooden blocks
echoing across the field.

In beginning the final draft, the issue of verb tense came to light. The consistent present tense throughout the second draft's first stanzas obscured the speaker's rise from babyhood in the first stanza to adulthood by the end of the second. To delineate the poem's timeline more clearly, I compressed the first and second stanzas into one past-tense stanza.

In the next stanza, which begins "outside, snow heaves" in the final draft, the poem shifts to present tense to indicate the time lapse between the memory of the dying mother and the grown speaker's vengeful stalking of the father. Then, the poem moves to future tense in the third and fourth stanzas. I switch back to present tense beginning with the fifth stanza and maintain present tense for the remainder of the poem.

In the final stanza of the second draft, the tone is hopeful and naïve as the speaker imagines the family applauding together. This tone seemed out of tune with the preceding tonal progression from melancholy, wistful remembrance to dogged, even vindictive pursuit. Furthermore, this family's history is too tumultuous and packed with resentments to realistically picture the family in any kind of unified action. I solved these issues by having the father applaud, which reads as false praise, sarcastic and cruel, a much more believable portrait of a father who physically abused his wife.

In addition, the fifth stanza's shift to present tense as the speaker continues to imagine the elusive chase demonstrates how fully immersed the speaker is in this nightmare imagining. She *is presently* living the nightmare in her head, which adds impact and resonance to the final applause of the father. It is very real to the speaker.

My best kept revision "secret" is the input of fellow writers both in and out of workshop settings and especially the opinion of my primary reader (and incidentally a wonderful writer), the man I am lucky to share my life with. Every page I mark with questions, concerns, and cuts makes its way to our kitchen table for a breakfast critique. Some poems seem endlessly open to revision, and each proposed change seems open to dispute. In such cases, I am grateful for French critic and poet Paul Valéry's reminder that waffling and frustration are unavoidable in the revision process: "A poem is never finished," he writes, "only abandoned."

Final Version

My Mother Keeps Dying in the Bed by My Cradle

I can't remember her breath on my cheek
or when it stopped,
but my memory has posed us,
huddled in the bed, *shhh*,
my grandmother plaiting my mother's hair
and gliding ice cubes over
her swollen tongue, my mother
clasping me to her chest.

Her face shifted like screens of sky,
clean and still, then, clouded
with the cinches of her abdomen,
my father's name breaking
against her lips, *Lawrence,*
and hissing in my ear, *Lawrence.*

Outside, snow heaves its milky flood
past the closed window,
and I am knitting
alone in night's deaf black kettle.
I am waiting.

When the marrow revolts
in my bones, when my spine quivers
under the weight of my family's stones,
I will hunt my father,
whose knuckles like pestles
ground down my mother,
whose arms like his father's
felled this forest, whose eyes
like arsonists' escaped
to view the pyre.

I will find him
hiding in dark phone booths.
I will chase him
down second-floor hallways,
angled shafts of light sprawling
from clerestory windows.
I will chase him through
empty schoolyards,
through the white echoes
of late blossoms.

He's turning. I see him turning
—illuminated, godlike—
to listen.

He drops his hands
to his sides, done with winning,
and my mother's eyes, hovering
planets, my mother's lips,
red and parted, begin.

He understands
how angry we are, how
sorry. The brittle wire of her voice
recedes among the rows of wheat
as my father's hands begin
their applause. Listen to my father,
his palms like wooden blocks
echoing across the field.

Holly Clark is an MFA candidate in poetry at Sarah Lawrence College. Her work has appeared in *Lumina* and *Conte: An Online Journal of Narrative Writing*. She reads regularly at such venues as Sarah Lawrence College's Slonim House, Cornelia Street Café, and the Ear Inn in New York City.

Shiver-Man

Judith H. Montgomery

"Shiver-Man" begins as a freewrite: I am haunted by a brief, flickering film of a British soldier, returned, shell-shocked, from World War I. The man, externally healed, struggles to rise from a bench and walk with a cane — but he cannot: he trembles violently, ceaselessly.

I trace "Shiver-Man's" evolution through numerous revisions. Keys to those revisions were (1) attention to the images, to make the experience present in the reader; (2) listening to the sounds and meter, to match them to the trembling of the solider; and (3) research and serendipitous discovery to open up the poem.

Original Freewrite

[Shiver]
1
The blade swung its green
axe, a shiver in rain,
on a level with my right
eye, the left blood-shut.

Later, a red drop crawled
and hung from the point,
last of the lieutenant
split above me on the birch.

The ground shivered my foot,
boot wrenched beneath the rock.
The next bomb. The next,
rained yellow sleet in the trench.

Shudder. The ground. Shudder,
The ice drop of night,
a weight on my neck. My body
cannot stop the shiver.

2

Later, the plus of the red
cross rides me from the front,
tires juddering on frozen ruts.
The pack on my eye peels off.

The hospital has propped me
straight on a bench, iron
wrought in curls of lily and rose
my fingers can trace while I wait.

They have buttoned me up
in new stiff brown, pinned
a shiny bit of gold to my chest.
My right hand clutches a stick.

In a moment, they will signal
the time, the rise. The camera
will swallow the light,
and print me as a shiver —

a man of 27, shuddering to his feet,
the arms shaking, the legs,
the hands, the neck a quiver,
a palsy, a walking shiver

as the body tries to shake off
what the brain has seen
where the brain has been
what the brain will not let go.

    I type up the freewrite and begin to revise by reading the poem out loud. For clarity, I add an epigraph, to place the reader in time and geography, guessing at an appropriate battle scene.

    I decide to try present tense, to plunge the reader into the experience. At the same time, I want the language to reflect a remote iciness. Chekhov says that if you want to move your reader, write more *coldly*. I try the word *medicos*: though anachronistic, it has the right "distancing" in its slangy reference. I scribble in "the film will jerk and shake" and "in the darkened screening room / exhibiting the symptoms," looking to focus on a distancing associated with scientific observers, with medical language, with making (documenting) and watching a film.

I add more details of physical injury (the bone in the thigh), but want the last scenes to emphasize that the trauma is to the psyche. I substitute "There are no visible wounds" for the mention of the "stick" but reintroduce the "cane" later. I imagine more details into the scene. The poem is getting longer.

Reading these changes aloud, I notice how the words that "feel" right to me have short, sharp "battle" sounds. I try *cataclysm* with its sharp *c*'s and *t*, instead of *boom* with its soft ending. The sound-center of the poem begins to move toward words with *t, b, k, p,* and, of course, *s* as part of the shiver in the man's body. Percussive sounds: like gunfire.

I tinker with the ending, which trails off. I try to increase its impact by shortening, by sharpening language and image to match the rest of the poem. I set the poem aside: too much work at once can be a bad idea.

Initial Revisions to Tense, Word Choice, and Detail

Shiver
              [Verdun? 191_]
1
The blade ~~swung~~ [swings] its green
[blade] ~~axe~~, a shiver in [the] rain [of ice] ,
~~on a~~ level with [the] ~~my~~ right [eye],
~~eye,~~ the left blood-shut. [. . .]

Later, a red drop crawl~~ed~~[s]
and ~~hung~~ [hangs] from the point,
last of the lieutenant
split above me on the [last] birch.

The ground shiver~~ed~~[s] my foot,
boot wrenched beneath the rock.
The next ~~bomb~~ [cataclysm]. The next,
rain~~ed~~[s] yellow sleet in the trench.

Shudder. The ground. Shudder,
the [night-]~~ice~~ drop of ~~night~~ [ice],
a weight [of tremble] on my neck. ~~My body~~
[My body] cannot stop the shiver.

2
~~Later,~~ The plus of the red [cross]
~~cross~~ rides me from the front,
tires juddering on frozen ruts.
The ~~pack on my eye peels off.~~
    [bone in my thigh splinters twice.]

[Now] the hospital has propped me
straight on a bench, iron
~~wrought~~ [curled] in [tendrils] ~~curls~~ of lily and rose
my fingers can trace while I wait.

They have buttoned me up
in new stiffbrown, pinned
a shiny bit of gold to my chest.
~~My right hand clutches a stick.~~
[There are no visible wounds.]

In a moment, they will signal
the time~~, the~~ [to] rise. The camera
will ~~swallow~~ [stutter] the light,
and ~~print me as a shiver~~ —
    [flicker me for the medicos]
[in the darkened screening room,
exhibiting the history of symptom:
the young man of a certain age
~~a man of 27,~~ shuddering to his feet,

the arms shaking, the legs,
the hands, ~~the neck a quiver,~~ rattling a cane,
[the neck a quiver,]
a palsy, a walking shiver

as the body tries to shake ~~off~~ [away]
what the brain has ~~seen~~ [received]
~~where the brain has been~~
~~what the brain~~ [and] will not let go.

I read the last draft aloud. My ear homes in on the sounds that caught me last time, and I generate a list of words that *jerk*: *tremble, quake, shiver, rattle, chatter, quaver, shake, falter, stagger, stumble.* I think about ways to use those words in the poem, substituting for "softer" words.

I also wonder whether I've made clear the different times and settings (battlefield, waiting for rescue, hospital, post-"recovery" and filming, the doctors' review). I divide the stanzas into sections, both to delineate scenes and to add to the fragmentation.

I read it again, trying to visualize the "story," which is taking shape literally as I write the poem. More detail, more impact: the "yellow sleet" (mustard gas, chemical warfare) was merely "raining in the trench" before; now it becomes "a yellow sleet that drowns my lungs": more direct, more personal and physically invasive. It is now "three days" before help arrives, and during this time there is icy rain, and a shivering, perhaps from cold, perhaps from the mental trauma of fear.

But something critical is missing: I can't "see" the stay in the field hospital. I write a new stanza to catch what his shocked brain might perceive: the iron white-enameled headboard (*arc*) of the bed, the feeling that everything is stuttering outside his body as well as within.

Next, I focus on his helplessness, both in context of his uncontrollable body and of those who have sent him into battle. I use "standard issue" brown instead of "new stiff brown," to underscore the sense that this soldier is merely another cog in the machine. I think of a puppet: his limbs shake as though someone else is (ineptly) controlling his body, perhaps the trauma, perhaps the generals, distant masters. In the *skewed* Morse code, the helplessness of the soldier and of the cane he cannot control, the cane "speaks" for the man.

I'm still not satisfied with the ending: it does not echo the other sharp sounds and images. I try changing it to *basin* and *lake* (the skull can be seen as hollow, as a container holding something).

Shiver

at the Marne, 1919

The grass swings its green
blade, a shiver in the rain of ice,
level with my right eye,
the left blood-shut . . .

A red drop shudders dawn,
hanging from the blade-point,
last of the lieutenant
split above me on the stump.
*

My boot still wrenched by rock.
Thunder shakes the blown trench.
The next cataclysm rains
a yellow sleet that drowns my lungs.

The third night, splintered ice
seeks out every rip. Skin sticks
to tattered khaki. Body shivers harder
than the smoke-jerked woods.
*

The plus of the red cross
rides me from the front, tires
juddering on frozen humps. Ruts.
Bodies. My fibula splinters twice . . .

A white arc of iron gleams
above red-wrinkled sheets
in the body-littered hospital. Still
the lamps jerk, silent by my bed.
*

Today the nurses prop me
straight on a bench. I can clutch
iron tendrils of ivy and rose.
There are no visible wounds.

They have buttoned me up
in standard-issue brown, pinned
a shiny bit of gold to my chest.
A cane quakes at my wrist.

*

In a moment, they will signal: my
time to rise. The movie camera will stutter
and catch me for the doctors
who will sit in the darkened room

and shake their heads at the mystery:
another young shiver-man
shuddering on healed feet.
Shadow-puppet arms shaking,

legs chattering their joints.
The cane banging helplessly
a skewed Morse code
as the body tries to shake itself

free of what has dripped and filled
the basin of the brain
that refuses to empty. That shivers
and shivers its terrible red lake.

Next revision: poet-friends in my critique group say "Make it even more splintered." I read the poem aloud, listening to sound and language. I move the third stanza up a notch, substituting "mortar tattoos," two words that feel like a drum beat or rain on a tin roof, more *tremble* and *rattle*:

Mortar tattoos
the blown-open trench.
The sky bursts yellow
sleet that drowns my lung.

Then I realize that it's the most dramatic of the initial stanzas, and the best wide-angle lens to set the scene. Wincing, I delete the so-so first stanza. I look at individual words and phrases to further that "drum-beat" feel underlying the poem. I work to cut every word and syllable to the bone, underscoring the sound of the poem read aloud. Instead of "body shivers harder / than the smoke-jerked woods," even better is "Torso jerks to rifle tempo," which can't be said aloud without the jerk of shots in the rhythm. Similarly, to echo the bumping of the Red Cross wagon across the battlefield, I substitute "ruts. / Bomb duds. Bodies."

This means I am sacrificing other lines, however. I ditch "My fibula splinters twice" because I think it distracts from the inner trauma. Because I've dropped the section dividers, I move the hospital line up in the sixth stanza so that the reader will know where the narrator is. And I continue to cut and focus wherever I can: it's now "the camera" instead of the "movie camera"; it's "a shudder on healed feet," not "shuddering on healed feet."

I'm still thinking about the end. I like the quatrain form that's felt right throughout, but now, with changes, I have a three-line last stanza. More important: I don't want to "sum up" what's happened in the poem already. I want to open it up somehow: reveal a new view, turn, expand the poem, not contract it.

Shiver-Man

shell-shock, 1919

Mortar tattoos
the blown-open trench.
The sky bursts yellow
sleet that drowns my lung.

Hanging from the blade-point,
a red drop shudders,
last of the lieutenant
split above me on the stump.

The third night stitches
each rip in freezing rain.
Skin sticks to tattered khaki.
Torso jerks in rifle-tempo.

The patched Red Cross wagon

bumps me from the front,
tires jittering at ruts.
Bomb duds. Bodies.

In the body-littered hospital,
a white enamel headboard
arcs above red-wrinkled sheets.
Lamps twitch silent by my bed.

Today the nurses prop me
straight on a bench. I can clutch
iron tendrils of ivy and rose.
There are no visible wounds.

They have buttoned me up
in standard-issue brown, pinned
a shiny bit of gold to my chest.
A cane quakes at my wrist.

In a moment, they will signal.
I will rise black-and-white
for the camera that stutters
to catch me for the doctors

who will sit in the dark,
shaking heads at the enigma:
another young shiver-man,
a shudder on healed feet.

Whose cane bangs helplessly
a skewed Morse code
as my body tries to shake itself
free of what has filled

the basin of the brain—
the dark lake
that refuses to empty.

I've been using "shell-shock" as the epigraph because I am afraid the reader will not "get it." But another poet suggests that this gives too much away at the outset. I ought to look for a quote on battle fatigue instead. I remove initial caps and almost all punctuation from the lines, to mirror the soldier's disoriented state. I get a new armload of books, settle in to learn more on WWI battles and shell shock.

Then, the unexpected gift: I read that Charlie Chaplin's films were tremendously popular during World War I: he is a come-up-from-under hero. One British soldier even stole a cardboard figure of Chaplin and took it over to the war front, as morale. Chaplin's famous stuttering walk links with the stuttering of the bodies of those with shell shock. With film. A camera.

This is it: but I need to shift and expand the poem — link Chaplin to the narrator. I make the narrator the soldier who took the cardboard figure to war: he will try to use it as shelter. I write an italicized interlude: the soldier, dazed in the hospital, relives a pre-war night when he took his girl to see a Chaplin film. "To Chaplin" becomes a verb describing his walk. I weave in other discoveries: soldiers without a gas mask were told that they could urinate on a piece of cloth and breathe through it to avoid the horrific lung-scarring effects of mustard gas. The yellow of the mustard gas echoed in the yellow of urine.

The last word, *empty* feels awkward; it ends on a weak stress. I substitute *discharge*. It's the right word: has two strong stresses, and "discharge" can be one's release from military service; a stream emerging from a lake or body of water; the release, often of contaminated material, from a wound.

Shiver-Man

He was an iconic figure . . . the great survivor. . . . some British Highland Light Infantryman stole a cardboard figure of Chaplin and brought it over to the western front.
— J. M. Winter, in *World War I: A History*

mortar tattoos
the blown-open trench
sky sleets yellow
rain to drown my lung

hung from the blade-point
a red drop shudders
last of the lieutenant
split above me on the stump

caved up under Chaplin
bent to save my bones
I piss on a rag
breathe stench not gas

third dawn stitches
shrapnel through a rib
torso jerks to rifle tempo
hail drums numb

ribs grate on the litter
away from muddy Somme
the red-cross wagon
bumbles over ruts

body-littered corridor
lamps still twitch
arteries artillery
blood-wrinkled night

I took Mary to the theatre
a soft star eve
watched the Little Tramp
bob and winkle on the screen

his smile lit her peach
face the reels flickered
perfume from her throat
his perfect strut

today the nurses prop me
straight on a bench
clutch iron ivy
watch wounds close

they button me up
in standard-issue brown
pin a gold bit to chest
cane at wrist

soon they will signal
me to stand for the lens
and Chaplin onto film
so the military doctors

who sit in the dark
bent shadow flick
can watch me walk
on white clinic walls

they beckon: I rise
puppet-arms chatter
knees hobble-jerk
the body tries to shake

free of what has filled
the dark brain lake
that refuses to discharge

One final major change remains. The poem is now much longer. And I am still bent on making it more "splintered," of having its form echo subject and sounds. I try melding four lines into two, but the splintering is dulled. Then I insert white space between the two elements joined in each line: this feels right. It is abrupt, fragmented, and yet balanced in ways that echo the earliest writing in English. I test each word on the tongue and ear, make a few more revisions. I am satisfied with the last couplet, which ends with a half-line: the suspended half-life of shell-shock continues for the man. The reader. I think: I am done.

"Shiver-Man" received the National Writers Union Prize, and the *Americas Review* Poetry Prize. It appears in *Red Jess* (Cherry Grove Collections, 2006), my first full-length book. The progress of the poems owes a debt to the attention of the workshop poet (Joseph Millar), and workshop participants, as well as to the keen comments of members of the Pearls critique group in Portland, Oregon.

Final Version

Shiver-Man

He was an iconic figure . . . the great survivor. . . . some British Highland Light Infantryman stole a cardboard figure of Chaplin and brought it over to the western front.
— J. M. Winter, in *World War I: A History*

mortar tattoos   the blown-open trench
sky sleets yellow   rain to drown my lung
hung from the blade-point   a red drop shudders
last of the lieutenant   split above me on the stump

caved up under Chaplin   bent to save my bones
I piss on a rag   breathe stench not gas

third dawn stitches   shrapnel through a rib
torso jerks to rifle tempo   hail drums numb

ribs grate on the litter   away from muddy Somme
the red-cross wagon   bumbles over ruts

body-littered corridor   lamps still twitch
arteries artillery   blood-wrinkled night

I took Mary to the theatre   a soft star eve
watched the Little Tramp   bob and winkle on the screen

his smile lit her peach   face the reels flickered
perfume from her throat   his perfect strut

today the nurses prop me   straight on a bench
clutch iron ivy   watch wounds close

they button me up   in standard-issue brown
pin a gold bit to chest   cane at wrist
soon they will signal   me to stand for the lens
and Chaplin onto film   so the military doctors

349

who sit in the dark   bent shadow flick
can watch me walk   on white clinic walls

they beckon: I rise   puppet-arms chatter
knees hobble-jerk   the body tries to shake

free of what has filled   the dark brain lake
that refuses to discharge

Judith H. Montgomery's poems appear in *The Southern Review, The Belling-ham Review, Gulf Coast,* and *Northwest Review,* among other journals, as well as in several anthologies. She's been awarded residencies from Soapstone and Caldera; and prizes from the National Writers Union, *Americas Review,* and *Red Rock Review.* Her chapbook, *Passion,* received the 2000 Oregon Book Award for poetry. Her first full-length collection, *Red Jess,* appeared in February 2006. Recently a recipient of a 2005 Individual Artist Fellowship from the Oregon Arts Commission and a 2006 Literary Fellowship, she has just completed a year as poet in residence at Central Oregon Community College.

It Was Snowing and
It Was Going to Snow

JENIFER BROWNE LAWRENCE

The first draft of the poem was written longhand, in a spiral notebook. In the transfer to the computer, some minor editing took place, mostly in the structuring of stanzas. Here it is, rough and not knowing where it is headed:

Snow Elegy

While you played in the deep packed snow of the yard,
a cat crossed the road.
Padded feet maneuvered the icy ruts.
A blue and white station wagon swerved to miss him,
plowed you under instead.

It was the first Christmas since we moved
from Santa Cruz to Valdez,
the first snowy winter of our lives.
In a white helicopter, you went,
taking our mother with you.

The neighbor stayed, kissed us goodnight.
She smelled like daddy always did after dinner.
We took down the tree,
nobody to tell us
which box each ornament came from.

Twice each day we walked past the discolored ice—
to catch the school bus, to come home.
The darkening red, hot when it splashed,
must have seeped all the way to the asphalt,
all the way to the hibernating iris in the yard.

Snowfalls came and went,
and with each melting the stain showed itself.

351

You returned wide-eyed and unstained,
re-learned the names of your siblings,
the cupboard where we kept the toys.

You were younger, different,
all the knowing gone out of you.
Frightened, we tried to pour it back in.
We bought you a cat of your own,
sleek as your cropped hair.

The doctors recommended tactile stimulation,
but we were all afraid to hold you.
A family of strangers,
we gradually returned to knowing.

While I liked the assonance and alliteration that came in this first version (played / packed / plowed, Cruz / Christmas, winter / white), the poem is heavy with adjectives and drama, and tells the reader what to feel in the closing stanzas. I needed to look into what the "project" of the poem was, to let the poem generate images, instead of making them explicit. Simple, vivid imagery works to engage me in a poem, and allows me to enter the world of the speaker. This draft does not accomplish that necessary work.

I removed some of the descriptors ("blue and white station wagon" in the first stanza; "twice each day" in the fourth; "wide-eyed" in the fifth). I revised some of the language in the last stanza, and deleted the telling of emotion in the penultimate stanza ("Frightened, we tried to pour it back in"), and the too-tidy summary of the closing lines ("A family of strangers, / we gradually returned to knowing"). I tried to keep the musicality of the lines, listening for assonance, consonance, and rhythms to preserve or enhance (played / yard / road / plowed, maneuvered / swerved, Cruz / Valdez) and repetitions ("to catch the school bus, to come home"; "all the way to the asphalt / all the way to the hibernating iris").

At this point, I set the poem aside in the manila folder I use to "ripen" work in progress. After several months, I returned to the poem. Here's the next version:

Prelude to an Elegy

While you played in the deep packed snow of the yard,
a cat crossed the road.
Padded feet maneuvered the icy ruts.
A station wagon swerved to miss it,
plowed you under instead.

It was the first Christmas since we moved
from Santa Cruz to Valdez,
the first snowy winter of our lives.
In a white helicopter, you went,
taking our mother with you.

The neighbor stayed, kissed us goodnight.
She smelled like Daddy always did after supper.
We took down the tree,
nobody to tell us
which box each ornament came from.

Every day we walked past the discolored ice—
to catch the school bus, to come home.
The darkening red, hot when it splashed,
must have seeped all the way to the asphalt,
all the way to the hibernating iris in the yard.

Snowfalls came and went,
and with each melting the stain showed itself.
You returned unstained, relearned
the names of your siblings,
the cupboard where we kept the toys.

You were younger, different, all the knowing
gone out of you. We bought you a cat
of your own, sleek as your new-grown hair.
Doctors said frequent touch would be of use,
and we were all afraid to hold you.

Well, this version is an improvement, but I still felt it was ineffective, and overly full of adjectives. I'd found a casual structure in the five-line stanzas. Each stanza is end-stopped here, and that had the undesirable effect of stopping the flow of the poem. The poem was not compelling enough to satisfy me as the writer or the reader of the poem.

Another year went by in which I occasionally pulled out the poem and tinkered with it, but it wasn't until I was reading Wallace Stevens in bed, late at night, and came upon "Thirteen Ways of Looking at a Blackbird" (for at least the thirteenth time) that a conscious direction came to me. I keep a manila folder of work in progress with me at all times (you never know when something wonderful might happen), and reached for the poem, penciling along its margin the line from Steven's poem "It was snowing and it was going to snow." This, I felt, was what the poem was trying to tell me. This event was a precursor to how my sister's life was going to turn out. It was snowing, and it was going to snow. I decided that was the perfect title (and credited the line to Wallace Stevens upon publication of the poem). The piece is part of a collection of poems about my sister's childhood (she died in a second, similar accident five years after the event depicted in this poem). I slept on it, and in the morning woke with the revisions forming in my head. Here's the nearly finished draft:

It Was Snowing and It Was Going to Snow

Maybe we were making angels
in the yard. A stationwagon swerved,
plowed you under, the neighbor's cat
crossed the road. A white helicopter
took you. It was the first
Christmas since we moved

from Santa Cruz to Valdez.
The neighbor stayed, kissed us
goodnight, her breath like Daddy's
after supper. We took down the tree,
no one to tell us which box
each ornament came from.

We walked around the ice
to catch the school bus,

to come home. The stain
seeped all the way to asphalt,
all the way to hibernating
iris in the yard. Each snowfall

brought the plow, its blade
uncovered your blood. You relearned
our names, the cupboard where we kept
the toys. You were younger, different.
We bought you a cat of your own,
black as your new-grown hair.

The poem has a richer music to it in the long assonance in the opening
line (maybe/making/angels), and the image is more vivid — making snow
angels rather than the generic "playing" in the previous drafts. The images
jump quickly from one to the next, similar to how scenes flash across your
vision during a traumatic event. I enjambed some of the stanzas, and that,
I think, helps the reader move through the various images more easily,
drawing the eye down the page. The repetition is subdued but still present,
as is the alliteration in select scenes (stain seeped; blade, blood, cupboard).
I tried to keep as much consonance as possible, especially the repetitive *d*
sounds, which are reminiscent of the sound of the impact itself.

I thought about line breaks during the editing process, and aimed for
lines that would stand on their own, and line breaks that might allow more
than one meaning to enter the reader's awareness: "uncovered your blood.
You relearned."

I chose to end the poem with it opening up to possibilities — "We
bought you a cat of your own, / black as your new-grown hair" — rather
than closing it up with a statement about the family's feelings as in previous versions. I think this allows the reader a certain freedom to invent the
subject's life for himself or herself. I spent a little over three years on this
piece. Some things cannot be hurried. I try to allow each poem to proceed
at its own pace. Here's the finished poem, at long last:

It Was Snowing and It Was Going to Snow

Maybe we were making angels
in the yard. A stationwagon swerved,

plowed you under. The neighbor's cat
crossed the road. A white helicopter
took you. It was the first
Christmas since we moved

from Santa Cruz to Valdez.
The neighbor stayed, kissed us
goodnight, her breath like Daddy's
after supper. We took down the tree,
no one to tell us which box
each ornament came from.

We walked around the ice
to catch the school bus,
to come home. The stain
seeped all the way to asphalt,
all the way to hibernating
iris in the yard. Each snowfall

brought the plow, its blade
uncovering your blood. You relearned
our names, the cupboard where we kept
the toys. You were younger, different.
We bought you a cat of your own,
black as your new-grown hair.

Jenifer Browne Lawrence was born in California in 1958. Raised in Alaska, she currently lives near Seattle, Washington. She was a 2006 Washington State Artist Trust grant recipient, received the Potomac Review's Annual Poetry Award, and was a finalist for the 2005 James Hearst Poetry Prize. Her work has received a Pushcart nomination and is published in various journals and anthologies, including the *North American Review, The Comstock Review,* and *Potomac Review.* Blue Begonia Press published her poetry collection, *One Hundred Steps from Shore,* in 2006.

Jack in Love

LAURA CHERRY

I write a handful of lines when I have a few minutes at work: I have had lunch with my friend Jack. He has "met someone" and, while unable to talk about it, is also unable to talk about much else. It's almost antithetical to my experience of Jack, normally a charmingly irascible lunch companion. Something snags my attention — the contrast between Jack's usual sarcastic patter and this new, confusing radiance — and I scrawl it down before losing it altogether, a quick constellation of notes. I enter the subject through the side door, describing a photograph that is unrelated to Jack's current adventure. The poem has no title, just a dedication to provide context, and it stops short when I come to the end of my first set of thoughts.

_____, for Jack in Love

The picture of you and Donna hangs over my desk:
her long gloves and short dress, your white jacket and lopsided grin.
You sign it "007": undercover, lovelorn, ashamed and ecstatic
to feel nineteen, all your tough-guy humor gone goofy and slack.
This time at our monthly lunch you eat almost nothing, drink
two Italian beers, try to keep eye contact as if listening,
but you're outta here, in that chemical swirl of fighting
to land the struggling fish, years of practice knotting your arm.
At first you won't even tell me her name.

The poem saw months of changes; here, I include just three key moments in its drafting. In the second version printed here, I'm still free-associating, brainstorming, not trying to shape things, figuring out what this poem has to say and how to get there. I've given the poem a title based on that original dedication, and there's a new epigraph, some lines I loved and associated with the "beginnings" in this poem. I've moved a stronger line up front, to open with Jack and his altered state — now seen as "adrenalin fog" rather than "chemical swirl," which sounds nauseating (not my intent here). I've had some salted focaccia and it was delicious; I like it as a not-too-sweet image of beauty. Adding it, I riff on infatuation, its unknown future, its simultaneous highs and lows, its distance from everyone who is not the object of desire. I've brought in a cartographer with surreal tools and finally located some humor, the "tragic loss / of good conversation." Oh, I'm feeling neglected! That's a revelation, part of the heat of this poem for me. I play it up, Jack's courtliness and the "retro" prom picture also standing in for his age, a way to avoid saying, "You're 52 and acting as if you're 19!"

For Jack in Love

> Is it the right beginning? We march into it;
> it is open all around like a meadow;
> we come naked, sweet as tea, secular, joyless, intent.
>   Jon Anderson, "It's the Beginning; So Much for Sentiment"

All your tough-guy humor gone goofy and slack.
this time at our monthly lunch you eat nothing,
drink two Italian beers, try hard to maintain eye contact
and ask appropriate questions. But you're outta here,
in that adrenalin fog of fighting to land the fish,
years of practice knotting your arm.
At first you won't tell me her name, then you can't stop,
and the word "beautiful" falls endlessly into the conversation,
thick as salt on bread. You wrote an opening sentence
last week that could take you anywhere, have
a business presentation due in twenty-four hours,
hundreds of days and weeks ahead of you to chart
this familiar terrain, spelling it all out with colored chalks,
with fire-ants, with hypodermics. It's a tragic loss
of good conversation. Gallant as ever,
you pay with plastic and offer your arm as we leave.
Your prom picture, so retro it's hip, hangs over my desk:
her long gloves and short dress, your white jacket and lopsided smile.
You sign it "007": undercover, lovelorn, chagrined.

I give in. In the final draft, it's "you're / fifty-something and feeling nineteen." A little bald truth is helpful here after all.

By this point, I've found my strategy, creating a hybrid something like Jack himself, a mix of Hemingway and James Bond (though the "007" reference is now merely implied). That is, some of the moves are toward a tough leanness (the sparer title, the "loser acquaintance," the staccato "you... you... you"), and some are smooth, manicured, almost pretty ("as if spilling flowers all over me"). I've removed the epigraph, realizing that what I wanted was its juxtaposition of disparate elements; Anderson's catalogue echoes in my own, in the middle of the poem and particularly in its final line. The fish and the knotted arm now also seem beside the point.

I've set the poem into quatrains, stanzas long enough to feel solid rather than delicate, but still provide some air, more complex opportunities for pauses and pivots than the single unbroken block of text, and a more elegant look on the page.

I've lost the "opening sentence" line — if Jack is the only one in a glorious haze, *I* get to be the only writer. That's my revenge — as is the quick image of him as a corporate hack effusing over his "business presentation." I've added more tools to the cartographer's kit, a list that could go on endlessly if I let it. "Ambrosial air" becomes "leather-coat atmosphere," much better suited to the poem's hyper-masculine presentation of Jack, and hinting at a sexual muskiness as well. The prom picture, it's now clear to me, was a false start. It muddies my relationship with Jack (why is it over my desk? is he my nephew?), and it's not useful as a detail. Instead, I exhume a few details from earlier drafts: the name, the arm (without knots), and the fog, into which Jack disappears à la Bogart in *Casablanca*. My unspecified longing becomes the focus of the final stanza. I mean also to bury a hint, a fantasy, that *I'm* the object of interest after all ("I know her name") — just before Jack goes up in smoke.

Commemorative plate, artifact, souvenir — only a few years later, this poem now celebrates things that are gone: the unnamed relationship imploded, the business presentation shredded and forgotten, Jack killed by a car that intersected with his cycling commute. I've since gathered in a room with his beautiful mourning-swathed exes, toasting to his life, agreed by all to be "larger than life," as if anything could be. Unexpectedly, "Jack in Love" reads to me now as both elegy and memento mori, a stark reminder of the loser acquaintance picking his nose in the next room.

Jack in Love

All your tough-guy humor gone goofy and slack,
this time at our monthly lunch you eat nothing,
drink two Italian beers, try hard to maintain eye contact
and ask appropriate questions. But you're

fifty-something and feeling nineteen. You've
written off death like a loser acquaintance.
You won't tell me her name, but the word "beautiful"
falls endlessly, thick as salt on bread.

You mention your business presentation
as if spilling flowers all over me. You reach
for the butter knife to chart this familiar terrain,
mapping it out with colored chalks, with fire-ants,

with hypodermics and lilacs and smoke.
It's a tragic loss of good conversation. Gallant as ever,
you pay with plastic, offer me your arm as we leave.
I breathe your leather-coat atmosphere,

keep from resting my cheek on your shoulder.
I know her name. I see it on your arm
and in the fog. You tilt your hat and disappear:
undercover, anachronistic, chagrined.

Laura Cherry's chapbook, *What We Planted*, was awarded the 2002
Philbrick Poetry Award by the Providence Athenaeum. Her work has been
published in journals, including *Asphodel, Argestes, Forklift: Ohio, Agenda,*
and *The Vocabula Review*. It has also appeared in the anthologies *Present
Tense: Writing and Art by Young Women* (Calyx Press), *Vocabula Bound 1* (Vocabula Books) and *Letters to the World* (Red Hen Press). She received an
MFA from Warren Wilson College. She lives and works near Boston.

In the First Place

BRIAN TAYLOR

The first symptom of a poem coming on is often the intuition that experiences different in time and place are somehow related and that there is significance in their connection. The gestation may take years, may take hours, but for me it usually takes a month or two. So it was with "Atlantis," a poem that is still in its infancy.

In July 2005, I was in France sharing rental properties with my brother and his family, whom I rarely see because they live in England. The first triggering experience occurred after the five of us had finished our dinner on the porch of a country house in the Aveyron. We were miles from anywhere, and I noticed that when no one was speaking not a sound could be heard. I told everyone to be quiet and to listen. I doubt my young nieces had ever listened to silence before — not the faintest hum of a car or airconditioner, no splutter of plumbing, no bird call or insect buzz, not the least breeze in the fig-tree leaves or meadow grasses. For me at least, the moment was to be treasured, recorded. Like Hamlet, I reached for my mental scratch pad: "Meet it is I set it down."

For the second experience, I was alone. To accommodate four more members of my British family we had moved to a house not far from the town of Uzès, on the edge of the Côtes du Rhône. At dawn on the last morning of our stay, with a feeling that this might well be my last morning ever in France, I went out to the swimming pool with towel and goggles, my bare feet crushing the tiny white snail shells that in their thousands mingled with the pine needles. As I swam a few lengths, the dark-tiled pool became an undersea ruin — Atlantis perhaps. When I climbed out of the water, the sun was up and the roosters in neighboring farms were making a lively din.

So, in the liminal moments of a sunset and a sunrise, I — a city person — had been singularly aware of both silence and sound. I thought there might be a poem in all this, but it's never enough just to make a poem out of personal magic moments. It was not until September that I began to write. By chance, I watched a television program about hydrothermal vents, which proposed the notion that the earliest organisms on the planet might have originated where volcanic activity creates hot water springs at the bottom of the ocean. I was back in the dark swimming pool. This was my cue. This is what I wrote:

Atlantis: The Last Morning

In the orchard snail shells
explode under my feet. Then silence.
Day is reaching through the cypress hedges
as I stand at the edge of the swimming pool,
the water a slab of black aspic my dive will slice.

But I pause as one always pauses
poised on a brink, and there is no sound.
Listen, I want to say, except saying it will spoil it.
Listen. What fills your ears is silence,
silence as dense as the dark water.

And I shut my eyes against the slow
orange-green event of the sky and I wait
the better to hear from a distant pasture
the single knock of a cowbell, a drop of water
the thin cry of an owl,
a crescent moon of sorrow.

So I cut into the water
and go down
down into a different silence
of dark tiles, of fish scales,
flecks of rust and gold and of the rusty slime
of algae, of substances that live without oxygen
and that feed on the heat of the earth's iron core.

My legs kick and my arms pull on so many tons
of water

And then I am out of it, naked, shivering,
feeling now the air move. No one in the house is awake.

Then a cock calls and another and another and another.
The world speaks to itself in raucous dialogue.

I would call this the first saved draft. Very rarely do I handwrite drafts, so whatever word-processed version I save will have undergone dozens of minor revisions, generally of word choice, syntax, and line breaks but also — through cutting and pasting — of content organization.

The second saved draft mainly involved breaking the poem into ten three-line stanzas. The great majority of my poems in recent years have been cast in this form; the choice — admittedly somewhat arbitrary — gives to the poem a tidied-up appearance. This is free verse, but the lines generally are a loose tetrameter; very few of the lines are end-stopped, and I test line-breaks and enjambment by reading with no change of inflection at the end of a line but with a pause that can be the lightest hiatus or longer for dramatic emphasis upon a stressed syllable. When I read aloud, I am, of course, following the sentence structure, but — if they do nothing else — the line breaks of verse slow one down and guide one to articulate every phrase. Always, as I revise, I am performing the poem in my mind's ear.

> In the orchard | empty snail shells
> explode under my feet. | | Then silence. | |

In this second draft, few changes were made to the content; the only things I added were "a slowly dropping mist of silt" after the "dark tiles" (a visual image evoked more by the submarine world than by the memory of the pool) and two and a half lines following "the earth's iron core":

> I am billions of years below all wars, below
> the first ships and the ark with its freight
> of chromosomes...

I must have wanted to reinforce the notion of the dissemination of life since the beginning of time. In the last few years, several of my poems have alluded to the story of Noah along with the story of Adam's naming the animals in Eden. I was probably thinking, too, of the not exactly encouraging notion that life has one purpose and one purpose only — to replicate itself. Its connotations of heaviness and of impersonal commerce made *freight* seem a choice more appropriate than *cargo* or *load*; also, I didn't want another *o* sound in this context.

In the third saved draft, I reverted to loose strophes and got rid of some images I had thought true to my initial impulse. Much as I liked them for

363

their own sake, I saved for another poem the orchard with its mysterious empty snail shells, and I threw out the two rhetorical sentences beginning with "Listen" and the distracting metaphor of the water's being a "slab of black aspic." The metaphor might have accurately described the appearance of the pool, but the poem has nothing to do with gastronomy.

Having no problem in transferring images from the recollections of the evening to those of the morning, I now had this as a second strophe:

> The better to listen
>> I shut my eyes against the orange-green
>> event of the sky. Listen:
>> the distant knock
>> of a cowbell, the moon-pale
>> cry of an owl.

I liked the generalized term *event* to refer to the dawn, *dawn* itself carrying too much poetic baggage, but in the fourth saved draft, I deleted these lines. Perhaps the experience of total silence (here expressed through two barely detectable sounds) belonged in a different poem. Though I had started to write with this memory uppermost in my mind, I realized it had little or nothing to do with the origin of life. What I wanted was to conflate my own emergence from the pool/ocean with the sunrise and the noisy chorus of roosters, the embodiment of hopeful testosterone.

Subsequent revisions dealt mainly with layout. Finding that I had settled on twenty-five lines and not wanting to use five-line stanzas, I tried a version in which two-line stanzas alternated with three-line stanzas. Then, I went back to writing strophes of four, three, or two stresses per line. Eventually, I set out the poem in alternating longer and shorter lines arranged in two strophes, the first longer than the second (a vestige of the Petrarchan sonnet form?). This has a "natural" feel for me, and as for the reading, I am guided by alliteration and assonance and by an abundance of spondees — "dry grass," "dive slices," "first ships," "light flecks," "arms pull," "cock crows" — that provide a rhythmic undercurrent, albeit a syncopated one.

The end of the poem, which brings in the idea of nature speaking, remained pretty much unchanged in all versions. I recorded these:

The world speaks/talks/squawks to itself in raucous dialogue.

The living world
communes with itself in raucous dialogue.

The living world
communes with itself
in persistent raucous dialogue.

The following draft of the poem, dating from mid-December, proved not to be final. I had become too used to the title, but I wasn't sure whether it should now be titled "Visiting Atlantis" or "Return from Atlantis." Part of the problem was that, for the sake of file management, all drafts had been saved with the original title.

I began to think the alliteration in the second sentence draws too much attention to itself, and I also saw that, in reading "The phosphor of fish / lights flecks of rust," someone might fail to read *lights* as a verb. I know how to read it, but proper revision should prevent any reader from stumbling. Probably, I should ask someone else to read the piece, cold. Here, then, is what may be the tenth or eleventh draft:

Atlantis

As daybreak smolders in the dry grass
under the cypress hedge
I pause at the edge of the pool,
as one always pauses
poised on a brink. My dive slices
the surface of the water's
black slab, and down I go, down
into a different silence
of dark tiles and a slowly-dropping
mist of silt. I am billions
of years below the first ships, below
the ark with its freight
of chromosomes.

This is where the living world began.

The phosphor of fish
lights flecks of rust and the rusty slime
that feeds on the heat
of the earth's iron core. My arms pull
on a billion tons of water,
and here I am shivering in sunlight
and a cock crows and
another and another—the living world
communing with itself in raucous dialogue.

I liked this, but was this poem "finished"? Surely, there was much more to be done. What if I were to use the present tense solely to describe the hydrothermal vent, still pumping away at the bottom of the Atlantic? And what if I cast this story in the past tense more appropriate for narrative memoir — notwithstanding the current "intimate" practice of telling all anecdotes in the present tense ("Guy goes into a bar ...")? Why should I be shy of identifying the ark as Noah's? Someone hearing the poem at a reading might not catch the mention of the ark, and in revision one must always empathize with the numbed listener who doesn't have the text to look at. (How I wish more poets would bear this in mind!) And what, by the way, were fish doing in the place where life begins? And why was I so embarrassed by passages dense with assonance? After all, I grew up on Alfred Lord Tennyson, Edith Sitwell, Dylan Thomas. Finally, why was the poem titled "Atlantis"? There is nothing left in the poem to suggest the concept of a lost civilization.

I responded to these notions, and, finding that the midpoint of the new version falls after the word *chromosomes*, I thought I might try stanzas again, this time quatrains that bear some visual relationship with the ballad form. Should I then try to alternate tetrameter lines with trimeter? No, this does not want to be an Emily Dickinson poem. I have already written (and published) poems that allude to the ballad while still being governed by the rhythmical priorities of free verse. They seem to work when I read them aloud.

So this, for now, is where I leave the poem. However, I decided that I should look again at Adrienne Rich's "Diving into the Wreck," a poem I haven't read for years. Yes, it is justly admired: someone called it one of the great poems of the twentieth century. Should I be dismayed, discouraged? Of course not.

In the First Place

Daybreak held a match to the dry grass
under the cypress hedge,
and I paused at the edge of the pool,
as one always pauses

poised on a brink. My dive split
the surface of the water's
black slab, and down I went, down
into the submerged grotto

of dark tiles. I was billions of years
below the first ships,
below Noah's ark with its freight
of chromosomes, groping

down to where the world was first alive.
And there, in a persistent
drizzle of rusty flecks and misty silt,
the slime was still feeding

on the heat that seethes from the earth's
iron heart. My arms tugged
down a billion tons of water, and there
I was, shivering in sunlight.

And a cock crew and another and
another—the brilliant
and living world communing with itself
in raucous laughter.

Brian Taylor has lived in St. Louis since 1968, prior to which he lived in Belgium, in France, and in Britain, of which he is still a citizen. After a long career as a high school English teacher, he now teaches writing and literature in University College at Washington University. He has also taught poetry writing at the University of Missouri–St. Louis and at St. Louis Community College–Meramec. Almost a hundred of his poems have been published on both sides of the Atlantic, most recently in *Prairie Schooner* and *Natural Bridge* as well as in two anthologies, *Vocabula Bound i* and *Margie: The Review of American Poetry.* He was a featured poet in *The Missouri Review,* and his work also appears in *Seeking Saint Louis: Voices from a River City, 1670–2000,* published by the Missouri Historical Society. A prize winner himself, he has served as a judge in poetry contests. He was awarded the Cholmondeley Award for Poets by the British Society of Authors in 1985, the year London Magazine Editions published his collection *Transit.*